W9-DGC-260

SHIPPING ONLY

A Being More Intense

"Salt Point Bay," from Daniel Defoe's *The Four Years Voyages of Capt. George Roberts*, 1726.

A Being More Intense

A Study of the Prose Works of
Bunyan, Swift, and Defoe

Paula R. Backscheider

AMS PRESS
New York

Library of Congress Cataloging in Publication Data

Backscheider, Paula.
  A being more intense.

  (AMS studies in the eighteenth century; no. 7)
  Bibliography: p.
  Includes index.
    1. English fiction—18th century—History and
criticism.   2. Bunyan, John, 1628-1688—Criticism and
interpretation.   3. Swift, Jonathan, 1667-1745—Criticism
and interpretation.   4. DeFoe, Daniel, 1661?-1731—
Criticism and interpretation.   I. Title.   II. Series.
PR851.B3   1984   823'.5'09   83-45274
ISBN 0-404-61473-6

AMS Studies in the Eighteenth Century: No. 7
ISSN: 0196-6561

Other titles in this series:

MANUFACTURED IN THE UNITED STATES OF AMERICA

For Nick

'Tis to create, and in creating live
A being more intense, that we endow
With form our fancy, gaining as we give
The life we image.
—GEORGE NOEL GORDON, LORD BYRON

Honest John was the first that I know of who mix'd Narration and Dialogue, a Method of Writing very engaging to the Reader, who in the most interesting parts finds himself as it were brought into the Company and present at the Discourse.
—BENJAMIN FRANKLIN

CONTENTS

ACKNOWLEDGMENTS

IT is my pleasure to offer the thanks I owe friends, colleagues, and students for their encouragement and help. My dissertation director, Jacob H. Adler, and my Purdue teachers, Alan McKenzie and Hugo Reichard, encouraged my interest in Defoe, set high standards of scholarship before me, and never wavered in their faith in my ability. Paul Alkon, Paul Korshin, Edward Rosenheim, Jr., Calhoun Winton, and the late Hopewell Selby read portions of the manuscript carefully. J. Paul Hunter and Maximillian Novak suffered through drafts and generously discussed books, ideas, and rhetorical strategies with me. My colleagues, particularly Lewis White Beck, George Ford, and J. W. Johnson; my special friends from the 1975 Clark Library Seminar, Felicity Nussbaum and David Tarbet; and numerous students have shared my enthusiasm, served as critics, and enriched my insight. Some of these people will surely disagree with my conclusions, and I take full responsibility for this book.

I am indebted to UCLA and the University of Rochester for Mellon Fellowships and to the Clark Library and American Philosophical Society for their support of my work. I remember with special pleasure and gratitude the Dennis Hunter family who gave me a beautful and friendly place in which to live and work in Los Angeles where I completed the final draft.

This book is dedicated to my husband; he and my children, Andrea and Nick, contribute immeasurably to my happiness and willingly make the sacrifices that give me the freedom to write.

Rochester, New York
1981

INTRODUCTION

SINCE the late nineteen fifties, criticism of the eighteenth-century novel has flourished and matured, and a dozen important books have provided historical, generic, rhetorical, and critical material which allows us to work with increasing certainty and sophistication.[1] A great deal remains to be done; none of us, I believe, is yet satisfied with our understanding of the development of the form we call "novel." We cannot explain without some uneasiness the historical and cultural forces which spawned the modern novel. We cannot explain the remarkable variety of the "new" form. How could Defoe, Richardson, Fielding, Sterne, and Smollett write such different "novels" in a form so young? How could they include elements of the modern anti-novel before the shape of the genre was determined?[2] What made them group their efforts and identify themselves as engaged in a similar enterprise? What made them precociously, technically self-conscious? We do know, however, that John Bunyan, Jonathan Swift, and Daniel Defoe contributed in ways that can probably never be fully assessed and can hardly be exaggerated to the birth and shaping of the novel.

We also feel that "novels" have a few indisputable characteristics; they are prose fictions, they have characters and incidents of a somewhat "familiar Nature," readers have come to expect and demand resolutions, and most of their langauge is what Ian Watt calls "referential." Although 1977 saw distinguished critics holding a symposium titled "Character as a Lost Cause,"[3] *character* has always been and will probably always be the nerve center, the core, of the novel. Bunyan, Swift, and Defoe drew together in technically new ways the various aspects of their characters' persons. In particular, they displayed them in their societies, and, in so doing, created characters which were more gripping, more familiar, more real than any created in English literature before. These characters were social beings, people somehow both made in the image of their

society and yet unlike any other member of that society, the same person
in different places possessed with an inner life. The psychological depth
of their personalities makes these characters more intense and more
intensely affecting beings, and the absorption of their society gives them
wider significance. For the first time, character, story, and meaning were
so mingled that character became setting and event.

My study begins an examination of Bunyan's, Swift's, and Defoe's
treatment of character. An exploration rather than a thesis, *A Being More
Intense* examines the societies which these writers designed and analyzes
the implications of the relationships between society and the individual.
We find two extremes in the societies described in these prose works.
One is English society as contemporary Englishmen knew it. When
Defoe writes about Moll and Jack in England, when Bunyan describes
his early ministry, and when Swift writes political essays, English law
and English moral codes operate, and, with allowance for a bit of personal
bias, the obvious purpose of the work and a touch of poetic license, we
know we are close to the ordinary world of experience. At other times,
these writers create societies which are highly imaginative and quite
different from England around 1700. Bunyan's Beulah Land, some of
Defoe's pirate colonies, and Swift's Laputa share some of the characteristics of England, but they are obviously fanciful creations. Most of the
societies in these works fall somewhere between a realistic rendering of
England and a fantasy world, and their location on the continuum guides
the reader to insights about the writer's opinions concerning society and
the individual's place in it.

A society can be defined as consisting of members who stand in definite
status and role relationships to one another, as functioning coherently,
and adhering to a set of values which regulate the behavior of the
individual members. Every society has distinguishing features and adheres to principles of group dynamics. In other words, it has an identity
and a mode of existence which sets it apart from its content. Although
a society may be studied as an organic unit, and these writers create
communities which conform to the definition, Bunyan, Swift, and Defoe
are primarily concerned with a central character in the society; to a large
extent, the society exists to exhibit his personality, to allow him to seek
his own destiny or discover his limits, or to dramatize theme.

These writers give form to extraordinarily vivid and sometimes bizarre images of reality. Some of their characters are unashamedly

allegorical, grotesque, or unrealistic. Some of their societies differ in conspicuous ways from the ordinary world, and my study will concentrate on those that do. Such societies allow the writer to put his projects and theories into operation without the hindrance of normal, everyday laws and customs. He can delineate practices, suggest their influence on individuals, and imply criticism of his own society. He can present human beings in a less complex, less rigidly conventional world and thereby explore human motives from fresh perspectives and examine usually forbidden areas of life. He can ease the reader into accepting motivations that they would ordinarily be loath to accept and into evaluating them more freely and openly. Because these societies removed from the ordinary world parallel the larger world of the work, their explications illuminate the same concerns and themes as does exegesis of the larger societies, and, because of the smallness of size and simplicity of organization, these "particular" societies are often especially revealing.

The consideration of these three writers together allows a fuller understanding of the context of the development of the novel and a more complete description of the early writers' contributions to the diverse paths taken by the early novelists than a study of just one writer could. Defoe and Swift knew and praised Bunyan's work, and scholars have often paired Defoe and Swift.[4] Yet few men occupying the same approximate historical space appear to have as little in common as these three. All of them shared the world transformed by the Cromwell years, the Battle of Sedgemoor, the Act of Settlement, the wars with France, the Royal Society, and the infancy of modern materialism.

Bunyan, a Particular Open-communion Baptist, spent twelve years in prison and emerged a cautious man who distrusted government and equated kings with tyrants. Defoe, a Presbyterian, angered Dissenters all his life and went to the pillory and Newgate for insisting he had described the opinions of High-Churchmen in *The Shortest Way with Dissenters,* but he never seriously considered conforming. Swift, an ordained Anglican, had the reputation of being profane, "the man who introduced swearing into the English language," but had family prayers and the love of his parishioners. All three experienced England's turbulent domestic politics; they could recall heady days of influence and favor and troubling times of restrictions and prejudice. Bunyan managed to avoid legal problems after 1672; Defoe worked for the government for most of his mature life but was never free from the fear of prosecution, and even Swift, the man who once walked freely around Windsor, on occasion had a price on his head. Bunyan responded to the inhospitable political climate with veiled remarks, apparently innocuous religious tracts, and tactful silence; Defoe reminded the public of his popular Dissenting pieces (*The True-born Englishman*), became more allegorical (*The Consolidator* and *The Dyet of Poland*), worked for Harley in 1704–1705, and tacked with the wind in 1714; Swift reacted to the death of Queen Anne with four years of reflection and retirement.

All three engaged in pamphlet warfare: Bunyan against the Baptists, Anglicans, Quakers, and other sects; Defoe against those who disagreed with his political, religious, and economic opinions; and Swift against the enemies of his Tory friends' policies and peace plans as well as those who would aggravate the Irish situation. Bunyan argued technical, Calvinist theological points, Defoe mingled politics and religion to dispute occasional conformity, the balance of power, and poor laws, while Swift saw religion and constitution equally inseparable but insisted upon the supremacy and necessity of the Church of England. Effective as some of these works were, they are seldom read today and their targets, Fowler and Danvers, Maynwaring and Hare, Haversham and Leslie, are forgotten. Even their educations, moral and traditional as they were, set them irreconcilably apart. Bunyan learned arithmetic and reading and knew the Bible, Foxe, and Dent in detail. Defoe benefited from a fine education at Newington Green Academy and read histories, travel books, periodicals, everything voraciously. Swift, bred in the same Irish school that produced Congreve and Berkeley, educated traditionally for the ministry at Trinity College, Dublin, and matured under the influence of Temple, knew not only the classics but also contemporary intellectual points of view.

Each had serious literary ambitions as he labored over his early poetry and wrote apologia for his *Pilgrim's Progress, Tale of a Tub,* or *Robinson Crusoe.* Yet Bunyan's models were guidebooks, tracts, spiritual autobiographies, romances, and sermons while Defoe had all of these and histories, memoirs, Dryden and Marvell. Swift added the influences of Horace, Lucian, classical models and rhetorical arts, and more poets from the mainstream of English literature. Bunyan wanted to explain religious truth better than anyone had done, Swift wanted to produce enduring art for Prince Posterity, and Defoe insisted that his satiric muse was aroused in times of need and wrote thousands of words to shape the novel and journalism forever. Bunyan admired Quarles and Baxter, Swift the precision and clarity of Pope, and Defoe Dryden and the innovations of Dunton and the Spectator. All make penetrating remarks about their styles. All wrote hundreds and hundreds of pages: Bunyan to pave a road to Heaven, Defoe as part of his role as public servant and responsible human being, and Swift as a fulfillment of his ambition to have reputation and influence. Only Defoe, however, boasted confidently that he would never go hungry so long as he could write.

Other apparent similarities dissolve under analysis. Bunyan's evangelical charge included Cambridge, Hertford, Buckingham, and London, yet the mythic Jerusalem blotted out contemporary London for him. His references to the city are usually typological or metaphoric. London glimmered and tantalized Swift and made Dublin tawdry and dull, and London was Defoe's métier, like the briar patch for Brer Rabbit to him, and he called it "the crossroads of opinion" and "The Mart of Europe, and Magazine of the whole World." What did Bunyan have to do with Newton and Boyle and Graunt? Defoe admired scientific advances and, like an engineer, turned them to speculative uses—his works are full of images of wheels, gears, and machines, of references to the circulatory system, and to navigation aids. For Swift the new science was part of a world of ideas to be mastered and evaluated intellectually and ethically and to be discussed dispassionately. Bunyan's mind strains toward Heaven and Truth; Defoe's intelligence thrusts, speculates, spins out schemes and strategies, and Swift's evaluates, analyzes, and pronounces judgment.

Bunyan's *Life and Death of Mr. Badman,* Defoe's *The Complete English Tradesman,* and even Swift's Drapier papers and *Journal to Stella* have dozens of anecdotes about shopkeepers and their customers, but again the perspectives are different. For Bunyan, although a man's work is temporary, yet it is an inseparable part of eternity, a vocation of which he must "walk worthy." Although Defoe recognizes this point of view, he sees such scenes in the context of trade, credit (economic and moral), and the social fabric of changing England. Swift thinks in terms of the consumer pricing books and chocolate, going to market to buy bread, selling his goods and feeding his family, worrying about the quality of wine, and converting his work into coins. Bunyan lived amid the rural tradesmen and farmers, the sober, hardworking, pious men of English folklore. He signed petitions with other sectarians and talked with housewives, carters, and other itinerants. Swift was the respected guest and intimate of the literary *beau monde,* conserved his coal, wrote letters to Stella and his friends before he got up in the morning, and lived largely in quiet order. He was acutely aware of the Irish as diminished men; he describes them as stooped, diseased, frail, begging, and yet he dispassionately adds details of their delusion and corruption. Defoe, in contrast, seems immersed in the hurry and variety of London, beseiged by creditors, carping hacks, and the needs of his wife and six children. He knew, visited, and exchanged information and anecdotes with Dissenting clergymen, printers, booksellers, political hacks, tradesmen, and merchants all over England and Scotland. Bunyan's friends were all around him, Defoe left dry, businesslike correspondence suggesting a life of hard and secretive work, while Swift left a record of intimate and engrossing friendships sustained for years through adversity and separation, expressing profound ideas and deep sympathy.

We can take even more of their differences for granted, but they lived in the same world, eternal and temporal, nevertheless, and their shared cultural and psychological concerns dwarf their differences when we examine them as creative, literary artists. We have hardly begun to explore their shared opinions, their treatment of similar themes, and their numerous, shared rhetorical strategies. The average reader would surely ascribe the following passage to John Bunyan:

> It is a long time since my Lord Understanding, Mr. Judgments, Mr. Charity, my self, and others of our Friends, did solicite that you would be pleased to discard Mr. Malice, Mr. Spite, Mr. Jealousy, Mr. Headstrong, Mr. Discontent, Mr. Uncharitable, Mr. Reproach, Mr. Calumny, and all others of their Kidney; but it has been our misfortunes and yours too, that hitherto they are still entertained by your Highness and their Advice preferred to ours.

The author, however, is Daniel Defoe; it is part of the beginning of *A Letter from Mr. Reason to the High and Mighty Prince the Mob* [1706]. Swift once observed that the loss of a big fish which he thought safely hooked was "a type of all my future disappointments." Except for the attitude, the words could be by any of the three. In another place, Swift wrote, "I have been better entertained, and more informed by a Chapter in the *Pilgrim's Progress,* than by a long Discourse upon the *Will* and the *Intellect,* and *simple* or *complex Ideas.*"[5] Defoe quotes and paraphrases Bunyan in *Review* #128 (6 December 1707): "And HE DREAMED, and it seemed unto him as if it were but he awoke and behold it was a DREAM." Defoe catches the significance of "as if it were" and plays upon the intensity of kinds of experiences and problematic aspects of perception. Swift and Defoe were contemporaries, but they carried Bunyan's world and art in their consciousnesses. With them we have the added interest of their often simultaneous reactions to events and ideas, and we also have the tensions inherited from Bunyan's moral universe.

Much of the discussion in my study considers narrative, or even what might be called fictional strategies, yet I do not want to imply that I am defining "novel" or labeling these works as "novels." Everyone acknowledges the ways that *Pilgrim's Progress, Gulliver's Travels,* and *Robinson Crusoe* approximate novel,[6] yet nothing Bunyan, Swift, or Defoe wrote is sufficiently extended narration with the unity of action, analysis of character, and resolution of complication which we associate with the genre we have learned to call "novel" since the mid-eighteenth century. Narrative literature orders experiences, examines a culture, illuminates the meaning of social actions, structures aspects of the world, and moves men into a verbally created universe. In order to accomplish these things, it uses characters, dialogue, event, and symbol in many of the ways that novels do. A great deal of the power and fascination of the works of these three writers comes from the ways they combine the perceptions and forms of pre-Restoration western culture with those of the new era scientific, economic, and secular modes of perception. In integrating the forces in tension in their time, they naturally move toward the methods and insights of the novel, and their influence on the birth and development of the form is rightly a subject for continuing inquiry.

More or less concerned with secular life in a moral universe, these writers exploited the techniques of spiritual autobiography, sermons, occasional meditations, epic, history, periodical essays, travel and picaresque literature, satire, and romance, but their transformation of allegory into a modern mode of expression is especially creative. All of them could draw upon a common pool of metaphors and symbols, and all of them believe in a literature which revealed a truth beyond that of the visible, empirical world. Whether they allied themselves with the creators of exempla, parable, or satire, they acknowledged a symbolic form of expression and, therefore, developed works with allegorical elements, sets of symbols which carried special meaning. Their allegories, however, differ from earlier ones in significant ways. The symbols often exist as physical objects, as familiar *things* which give new verisimilitude to the works. The landscapes, the selection of objects catalogued and described, even the number and importance of these objects add a dimension to their narrative value and function. Furthermore, the symbolic and allegorical elements insist upon the reality of the double threat and promise of the external world and of the character's internal state. The relationship between the two becomes more problematic and more dynamic, and a shift inward begins. What happens within a character begins to be at least as important as what happens to him. The threats to that unique core which is the individual, in fact, the conception of such a core, absorb the writers, and the possibility of the loss of soul in new ways through the dehumanizing possibilities of the market or scientific mentality occur alongside the metaphysical themes. This internalization of theme coupled with the recognition of external and internal experience affects dialogue, as dialogue becomes a way to externalize inner conflict. Conversation, then, becomes not only the vehicle for the presentation of ideas, but also a means of character revelation.[7]

Philosophy, economic changes, and the new science threatened the hard-earned certainties of the seventeenth century, and the externalization of a character's inner conflict provides the ideal setting for the presentation of the uncertainty and anxiety felt by thinking men. These writers recognized and explored contemporary epistemological uncertainties and their consequences. First, their symbols and metaphors often stand apart from those of their characters, and signs and types become treacherous guides for the protagonists. Ignorance's heart, Crusoe's sprouting seeds, and Partridge's prophecies mislead. Are there really "signs"? If so, what are "signs" and how can they be recognized? Are signs evidence? What is evidence? Is the evidence being interpreted aright? Suddenly understanding, even perception, ceases to be reliable.

Second, the interpretation of events, even the nature of experience, becomes problematic. The question of what we can know raises greater anxieties in a moral age than in a materialistic one. If we cannot know, how can we know how to behave? How can we recognize calling? How can we recognize salvation? If we blot out story and setting, Bunyan's dreamer, Swift's Gulliver, and Defoe's Jack occupy the same anxious space; the tone they give the works is the same. Swift's Examiner, his Drapier, and the projector of *A Modest Proposal* could exist only in a world of uncertain ethical structure. That they pose a universal, eternal, rational standard only serves to underscore the moral craziness and confusion of their time. Swift's "Sermon on the Trinity" describes the problem, "Reason itself is true and just, but the Reason of every particular Man is weak and wavering, perpetually swayed and turned by his Interests, his Passions, and his Vices."[8] Jack, Moll, and Roxana find themselves in situations in which they cannot avoid violating some code of ethics; the laws of England, of God, or of survival must be set aside. Christian and Crusoe weigh every event, every sight, as a potential sign from God. Jack laments, "Man is a short-sighted creature." Doubt is the fabric of the great protagonists' lives.

Third, because of the anxiety over evidence and knowledge, the characters change their minds; reason is uncertain, moral imperatives are cloudy, and revelation unreliable. Yet the individual is responsible for his behavior and, ultimately, his salvation. The milieu for these protagonists is relentlessly moral. The pilgrim must be steadfast, the citizen must be responsible, and the orphan may not remain victim or predator. ". . . of what use is freedom of thought, if it will not produce freedom of action, which is the sole end, how remote soever in appearance of all objections against Christianity?" Swift wrote. With the perception and meaning of the external world in doubt, the protagonist is thrown back on himself, his inner core, that being which has a consistency and existence in every situation. This realization arouses yet another anxiety. What is this core? Is it truly immutable? permanent? Gulliver goes to his mirror at the end and asks a question more agonizing than "What is man?" He asks, "Who am I?" Bunyan, Swift, and Defoe often explore this ambiguous dilemma in antithetical ways, but the problem and its consequences are the same. In *The Holy War*, Mansoul is a single character with a relationship to Diabolus and Shaddai, yet Mansoul is made up of individual characters capable of fighting. While the rhetoric is awkward, the conception is gripping. Mansoul has a center, yet Mansoul incorporates a very modern image of the difficulty of the integrity of self. The shifting environments of Swift's narrator in *The Tale of a Tub* and Gulliver on the island allow the same kind of dramatization between the possibilities for disguise and change simultaneous with the existence of a core that Mansoul's schemers and doubters within the city do. The narrator can become a scribbler or a critic, Gulliver can learn languages and trotting, but many such manifestations merely testify to the complexity of character; they do not compromise its integrity. Crusoe, Moll,

Jack, and Roxana are static characters in many ways, yet they shift societies, try on identities, change clothes, and lose themselves in the London or Paris streets. Their single-mindedness and *characters* hold all of the experiments, flights, and changes in orbit. They are both personalities and consciousnesses. The social selves exist within the individual beings. Although many characters in the works of these writers are allegorical, agents of ideas, or even verbal constructs, many others point to the directions that character creation would take and all together create the tone of searching and anxiety so common to the novel. For them, complexity, adaptation, and disguise are threat and possibility just as they are for Huck Finn and Augie March.

Concomitant with the idea of the ambiguity of experience and inherent in many of the traditional literary forms comes the freedom to violate the Aristotelian conception of probability in order to create truth about the individual and his relationship to society. Bunyan, Defoe, and Swift break down their readers' convictions about experience in order to precipitate new conceptions. On the one hand, they want to bring their readers to new perceptions about the world, and their transformations often serve didactic purposes. On the other hand, they intend to suggest the reality of singular visions and reinforce the uncertainty of perception and interpretation. By describing the societies which these writers create, defining their laws and mores, and examining the characters who inhabit them, I propose an heuristic instrument and a perspective rather than an argument. This study applies the method to the prose works, with particular emphasis on *Pilgrim's Progress* (1678), *The Holy War* (1682), *Pilgrim's Progress, The Second Part* (1684), *A Tale of a Tub* (1704), the *Examiner* papers and *The Conduct of the Allies* (1710–1712), *Gulliver's Travels* (1726), *Robinson Crusoe* (1719), *Moll Flanders* (1722), *Colonel Jack* (1722), *The Fortunate Mistress* (1724), and *A General History of the Pirates* (1724).

The early chapters attempt to define and describe the societies which the authors have created, paying special attention to the ways in which the particular societal organizations reflect the individual writer's beliefs about human nature and the social polity. The remaining chapters explore the individual's roles in such alternative environments, examining the interaction between self and society, as the authors move ever inward: Bunyan's Christian is revealed as a familiar western hero figure; Defoe's protagonists are torn between feelings of alienation and centrality; Swift's concern is seen to be the nature of individual moral responsibility. The use of dream, satire, and personal perspective become the tools which free the authors from many of the traditional constraints imposed by the reader's demand for probability in the depiction of these alternate worlds and their inhabitants. Finally, we see the characters' conflicting feelings of control and helplessness, limitation and fulfillment, as Bunyan, Defoe, and Swift move toward a new understanding of that property of mind which finds meaning and pattern in life.

CHAPTER I

INITIATION AND INTEGRATION

JOHN BUNYAN, Jonathan Swift, and Daniel Defoe—the great prose writers, the popular prose writers, before Richardson—all wrote in ways which associate them with the seventeenth century, and all insisted upon a demanding, even rather old-fashioned, morality. Yet many of their techniques are clearly "fictional" and their subject, man as individual radically, perhaps ineluctably, shaped by society, allies them with the "modern world." Their acute recognition of the dynamic relationship between society and whatever it is that makes a person a unique being who retains his same character in varying situations enriches their works immeasurably. As the writers provide conflict, explore the nature of man, describe social institutions, posit cause-effect relationships in countless ways, their perception of the isolated, lonely man unremittingly touched by society and its institutions protects their work from losing its immediacy.

To a great extent the movement in many of the works of Bunyan, Swift, and Defoe is the protagonists' movement from one society to another. In a sense, that is what all life is—the reader moves from home to job to party, society changing with each move; behavior, assumptions, and values shift in varying degrees for each. Each move requires a transition period, a time when the person is between societies and a time when he gradually becomes fully integrated in the society. For example, an individual can never join a conversation and instantly become a full participant. The transition from a familiar society to an unfamiliar one naturally takes longer and may be more traumatic; moving to a new city or section of the country suggests the greater adjustment involved. The speed and ease—in fact, the possibility of adjustment—depends both on the individual and the society which he needs to enter.

A character's initiation into a society reveals much about the author's perception of the world, his opinions about human nature, and his understanding of human needs, desires and personality, as well as the institutions that have developed to deal with men and women as social animals. Episodes in which the individual must adjust to a new society tell us a great deal about character and theme. The speed and ability with which a character can become a part of a new group reveal the writer's perception of the nature of the internal and external influences operating on men and women.

I

Bunyan's works include both imaginative and highly realistic societies. Each of his societies, whether symbolic or familiar, has a distinctive character, and that character is either God's image or the devil's. Bunyan's characters, each of whom was chosen to become part of this world or to renounce the world and seek Heaven, find the world divided into the societies of the blessed, by their nature alien to the worldly, and the societies of the damned, by nature enemies of the elect. All of Bunyan's works represent life in these terms. In *The Strait Gate* (1676), for example, two groups, "the world" and "we" have opposing relationships with the pilgrim. "The world" tries to bar him from heaven with "mocks, flouts, taunts, threatenings, jails, gibbets, halters, burnings, and a thousand deaths" while the "good" labor with prayers, tears, gentleness, love and sound doctrine.[1] The pilgrim must be wary and, therefore, lives in a nearly perpetual state of anxiety. The blessed give the pilgrim respite, and he is usually their apprentice. The damned try to seduce or persecute him. He is often threatened and alone, and, ironically, those periods of communion with other pilgrims work to exaggerate his alienation from "the world."

Bunyan's three great protagonists, Christian, Christiana, and Mr. Badman, are variations on this theme of man's relationship to the world. Bunyan uses the characters as didactic instruments by establishing patterns of experience, portraying their acquisition of knowledge, and illuminating the implications of choice. Within mythic narratives, his characters illustrate various responses to encounters which are simultaneously symbolic and referential to contemporary experiences.

Christian represents the most isolated man. *Pilgrim's Progress* begins with the dramatic scene of Christian standing, back to his home, crying, "What shall I do?" This scene serves Bunyan's dual purpose masterfully.

First, it establishes Christian as "a man" whose psychological state is immediately familiar to us. Second, it shows Christian stripped from the comfortable state of the insensible, blind sinner described in detail in *The Life and Death of Mr. Badman,* and yet incapable of imagining or joining the state of the saved. In this opening scene, with the desperate question, Bunyan isolates "the man" psychologically, socially, and physically from all other men in his town as effectively as Defoe will Crusoe.

Christian's journey marks his gradual initiation into the society of the saved, first on earth, then, symbolically, in heaven. He must learn the rules and responsibilities through experiences with successively more beatific groups. Several days after his initial questions, he finally asks, "What shall I do to be saved?" By this time, his wife and neighbors have treated him rudely, called him mad, and demonstrated that he is no more solitary on his walks that he is in his home. Because he is one of the elect, Evangelist directs him to the wicket gate. Christian, however, is still so insensate that he will follow Mr. Worldly Wiseman's advice as readily as Evangelist's. His progress from Interpreter to the Shining Ones to Palace Beautiful to the Shepherds to the Celestial City parallels his developing Christian identity. At first, he fears each new encounter and listens dumbly; eventually he comes to recognize fellow believers and participate and finally to interpret for others.

A crucial step in his initiation is learning to interpret and apply the lessons offered him. Interpreter shows Christian a series of tableaux, explains five,[2] and then leads Christian toward independence. Christian understands the sixth tableau, a man hacking his way into a castle through an armed rabble, because it so nearly duplicates his own situation.[3] Christian needs to question the subject of tableau seven, the man in the cage, until he is stuck with horror and exclaims, "God help me ... shun the cause of this man's misery." After the eighth, Christian recognizes that the visions have been designed to put him in "hope and fear." He is more conscious of the difficulties and perils of his undertaking, of the wretchedness of the damned, and of the value of his journey. Shortly after this the burden falls off his back and the Shining Ones mark him as God's. The first ministers to the spirit by granting him peace.[4] The second changes his rags for a robe symbolizing his changed status, marking him as consecrated to the service of God. The third unites the first two, designating him as one of the elect. The three represent the way the Trinity aids the Christian, healing, providing a model of effort and service, and inspiring and encouraging.

Christian is now ready to participate in a society of the blessed. Palace Beautiful, where the conversation analyzes and interprets experiences, is another part of Christian's education as the inhabitants question Christian about his life and journey in ways that lead him to understand events and his relationship to God in more profound ways. The virgins show him artifacts from Christian history and the Delectable Mountains, and he begins to see himself as part of a great tradition. His knowledge is tested immediately in the next incident when he fights Apollyon. For the first time, he feels that God and other believers are with him in spirit even if he cannot see them.[5] He is now part of a community of believers, initiated into the mysteries and responsibilities of the group.

The change in Christian becomes apparent in the gradual sharpening of his perception and understanding. With Faithful, Christian is the guide. He says that Talkative "will beguile with this tongue of his twenty of them that know him not." Talkative is one of the hypocritical proteans who "is for any company and for any talk."[6] With a familiar simile, "His house is as empty of religion as the white of an egg is of savour," Christian convinces Faithful. Christian becomes Faithful's instructor, and Evangelist congratulates him. Although Christian's trials have not ended, he is never deluded or ignorant again.

Christian's relationships with the worldly also serve as a barometer to measure his progress. He makes his townsmen angry, and they are the first to persecute him. He can, however, feel temporarily comfortable with Obstinate, Mr. Worldly Wiseman, Timorous, and Mistrust. As he progresses, he becomes wary, perceives the temptations of others and suffers more from the evil.

The worldly men fall into two categories: those who would mislead and corrupt him by appearing helpful and those who would frighten and kill him. Together they form the army of rabble through which the Christian must fight his way to reach God. These groups dramatize the total conflict between the forces of good and evil: the good always in the service of God, the evil associated with the devil. The greatest snares for Christian may be fear and sloth. The violent arouse his fear, and the cunning lure him astray. Fear leads to despair, and sloth rules out watchfulness. Christian's weakness lies within and can be preyed upon by the enemies of salvation. Like Swift, Bunyan sees envy in man motivating destruction. Whether it be tearing a coat or destroying peace of mind, the evil man tries to lower others to his level of misery.

In the last part of Christian's trip, the cunning no longer deceive him. The violence toward him, however, increases. He witnesses the martyrdom of his friend Faithful in Vanity Fair and is nearly beaten to death by Giant Despair. Part II of *Pilgrim's Progress* refers to him in the same ways that the book describes other historic figures in Christian literature. The hostility and warfare between Christian and the damned underscore the significance of the conflict for men's souls as Bunyan saw it.

The Life and Death of Mr. Badman is far less dramatic than *Pilgrim's Progress*. It fails to establish a fictional world, but Mr. Badman's life, the interposed lively and concise sermons, and the joke Mr. Wiseman plays on Attentive maintain interest. Mr. Wiseman begins the tale by whetting Attentive's curiosity about Badman's death. Attentive stands for the ordinary man, a character Bunyan can create perceptively, bitingly, and surprisingly quickly. Attentive clearly believes that the bad die agonizing deaths and waits with increasing impatience for the horrifying details. Mr. Wiseman keeps the tale going, asking with mock solicitude if Attentive is tired, until he suddenly reveals that Mr. Badman, like many evil men, died a quiet death.

Christian has been periodically badgered by evil men, Badman is disturbed by good men. His parents, the first man to whom he is apprenticed, and his first wife cause him some measure of discomfort. He ridicules them, steals from them, and abuses them, but they never quite allow him peace of mind. Besides the many examples of the incompatibility of the two groups, Bunyan quotes Scripture to underscore his point: "An unjust man *is* an abomination to the just; and *he that is* upright in the way *is* an abomination to the wicked."[7] Even on his death bed, he greets the good with boredom and rudeness.

In the company of sinners, however, Mr. Badman displays a different personality. As Bunyan says, he is a bird of their feather. Whether he is joining his fellow apprentices in cheating the master, drinking with lewd men and women in taverns, or joking with his rowdy friends in his home, Mr. Badman displays a realistic personality. He can join their company easily but can never really merge with groups of good people. The good and the bad compete. Each wants followers; the Badman children, apprentices, even adults can occasionally be won from one society to another. The evil try to cheat or corrupt the good and the good try to defend their purity and, at times, their possessions. Each feels contempt for the other, and their feelings of superiority further polarize the groups.

Rather than being traumatic, the evil man's movement from one society to the next is relatively easy. He *is* of the world and any group shares his characteristics. As predator instead of pilgrim, he is in his own milieu. Christian enters each group alert and ready to flee. Mr. Badman has little to fear but tedious reproofs from Christians since they will not corrupt, cheat, or physically assault him. Christian and Badman travel through the same world, but because of their differences in election and personality, those societies into which one is accepted, the other rejects.

Part II, of *Pilgrim's Progress* duplicates the path and initiation process of Part I, but it presents an alternative salvation experience. Christian represents the person who is saved by a fairly dramatic conversion, and Christiana symbolizes the person born into the church and supported through her life by a community of believers. Christian (and the patriarchs, disciples, and early Christian martyrs) have left her landmarks and a road well marked with cautionary signs. She recalls Christian's discomfort, her unsympathetic treatment of him, learns from his example, and resolves to undertake the journey. His guidance has made her decision easier and, once begun, her dedication to the quest is as constant as his.

Her story duplicates Christian's, but she is accompanied from the beginning by Great-heart, Mercy, and her children who offer companionship and comfort. Although each resting place prepares her for heavenly society and she begins to assume increasing responsibility for guidance and interpretation, her visits are leisurely and social instead of marked by tense seeking. Christian is a pioneer who alternately glories in and fears the difficulties of the quest; Christiana rejoices and is confidant in the reward of struggle. By the time Bunyan wrote Part II, persecution of nonconformists had temporarily abated, and he had had far more experience with people reared in the Church from childhood whose decisions to undertake the Christian way had a sense of inevitability and early commitment. Without destroying the adventure, the vicissitudes, and metaphoric steps, Bunyan creates a different experience based upon the personality of the protagonist and a changed perception of the degree of threat in the temporal world.

As Christian and Christiana travel, Bunyan translates their brief good experiences and their longings into a vivid conception of heaven. Heaven becomes a feeling, a tangible community as opposed to a visual representation. Most writers shared Bunyan's techniques of defining what Heaven was not and of referring to brief feelings and familiar longings of the type Augustine describes in the lines, "*Inquietum est cor nostrum, donec requiescat in te.*" Defoe writes on the possibilities of understanding Heaven in his *The Character of the Late Dr. Annesley* (1697):

> No pen *can write,* or Thought *can comprehend,*
> But he who at that happy Place arrives;
> For Heaven is only known by negatives.
>
> . . .
>
> The bright transforming Rays of *Heavenly Light,*
> Their *Likeness with* their *Light* communicate,
> The Spirit exalt, and all its Frame dilate;
> Infusing with the bright Similitude
> *An inexpressible* Beatitude!

and in *A Hymn to Peace* (1706):

> For PEACE within is Heaven Anticipate,
> And does Similitude to Heaven Create;
> 'Twill open that Bless'd PEACE at once, and show
> That Presence there, whose Glory makes it so. . . .

The episodes with the virgins and the shepherds in *Pilgrim's Progress* approximate the communion in heaven, but the sense of time (more pressing in Part I than in Part II) and the sense of incompletion, of longing, are equally real. Bunyan's picture of heavenly society is highly traditional, replete with the landscapes, colors, and comforts expected of Heaven. Bunyan tends to place these descriptions at the beginning of his books as images of the rewards of the journey designed to lure men forward. The comforts of heaven will be duplicated in part in the communities of the blessed encountered on the journey, thereby reminding the reader of the consummation of the quest. The comforts of heaven are of five sorts: physical ease (shining garments, good food), security (no tears, no malice), spiritual joy (sights of saints, martyrs, and angels, songs of praise), tangible rewards (a crown, a gold necklace, a harp), and companionship with God and good people. The Christian experiences each of the comforts on his journey but never all of them simultaneously. The pleasure of companionship and of transcending worldly considerations to contemplate God and his mysteries will finally be joined with the assurance of salvation and the admission to God's company. Each succeeding group reinforces the peace of heavenly society while at the same time intensifying the sense of incomplete joy. Therefore, while the pilgrims can move into some societies with pleasure, they are never satisfied and always in temporary groups.

Bunyan, like most people in his time, believed that love and gratitude brought more people to sincere faith than fear. He does, however, remind his readers of the reality of Hell. Again, his portrait is highly traditional. Descriptions of heaven strive to recreate a mental experience; hell, the price of the triumph of the body and its passions, is described as physical pain intensified by the passions of envy, anger, despair, and regret.[8] The traditional components of hell—suffering fire, torture, and fiends—never become a sustained picture but appear in explicitly rendered incidents. For example, in the epistle to the reader prefacing *The Life and Death of Mr. Badman*, Bunyan asks if a magistrate were appointed to pluck a portion of flesh with burning pincers as punishment for every offense, would the person continue to lie, drink, and swear? At another point, a man narrates his dream of a voice saying

> "Gather together the tares, the chaff, and stubble, and cast them into the burning lake. " And with that the bottomless pit opened, just whereabout I stood; out of the mouth of which there came, in an abundant manner, smoke and coals of fire, with hideous noises.[9]

The sense of the immediate, "just whereabout I stood," and the constant reminder of the sinner's perpetual peril lie at the core of the impact of the book. Physical sensation, however, is not the worst part of hell. Man's reason plays a special part. Reason continually reminds the sufferer that his state is eternal, that he has lost not only ease but heaven, and that he suffers for sin, for nothing worth his suffering. Hell is the lonely confrontation between the sinner and his own heart.

II

The experiences of heaven and hell in Bunyan's works illustrate one of the most basic perceptions that writers attempt to recreate. The awareness of the external and the influence of the mind shift so that first one, then the other predominates. Although the pilgrim can be simultaneously aware of his solitary decision and his tranquil pleasure in the company of the blessed, and the damned can feel physical torture at the same moment he is engaged in self-recrimination, either thought or experience will be uppermost in consciousness, and the interactions of external and internal cause the balance to shift with varying intensity and frequency. Defoe, like Bunyan, creates the tangible distinction between self and other even as he reproduces the tense awareness of both. Like Bunyan, Defoe often uses the journey as controlling metaphor.[10] In addition to its associations with quest and progress toward understanding, the journey provides a natural framework in which the protagonist encounters a variety of groups. The ways the characters perceive and react to these groups, their treatment by them, and their subsequent absorption or escape provide additional ways to explore character and personality in the world as the author perceives it. Defoe introduces his characters into new communities in some of the ways that Bunyan does: through accidents, as punishments meted out by societies, and from the character's own desire for safety, advancement, or even adventure. The frequency of the ways characters change societies and the characters' reactions to their initiation into the groups expand our understanding of Defoe's conception of the ways society affects the individual.

Defoe often introduces his characters into new societies abruptly. Natural disasters such as shipwrecks or plagues account for the most shocking initiations into societies. Such events strip away conventional patterns, and change the way life is lived even as the community's rules must be created anew. When cast precipitously into new situations, Defoe's characters feel disoriented, strange, and anxious.[11] They are subject to sudden excesses of emotion and rapid vacillations between extremes of moods which Defoe feels may endanger health or sanity. Robinson Crusoe, for example, is transported with ecstasy on his deliverance. He likens his feelings to those of a man pardoned even as the hangman steps away from putting the halter around his neck, and remarks rather pointedly that it is no wonder that the messenger brings a surgeon to let blood. Moments later, Crusoe recognizes his is a "dreadful deliverance," and he begins to enumerate his needs and suffer "terrible agonies of mind."[12]

Defoe, in contrast to Bunyan, insists that the mind usually submits to the body and to events. He describes his characters' feelings with a catalogue of gestures as well as with a recital of their words and thoughts. In joy Crusoe walks, lifting his arms and his "whole being" making a "thousand indescribable gestures and motions." Emotions too violent for articulation are expressed by compulsive and extraordinary movements. "Lifting . . . my whole being" fuses the mental feeling with the kinesthetic sensation, giving an apt description of Crusoe's thankful joy in being alive. In grief, Crusoe "runs about like a mad man." In walking, he savors his life; in running, he fears that there is no escape.

In *Farther Adventures,* when Crusoe is afraid he will be mistaken for a pirate and tortured by the Dutch until his men confess to the falsehood, he dreams and breaks his knuckles against the cabin wall. When he thinks of this while awake, his "blood would boil, his eyes sparkle, as if engaged." Physical release again accompanies violent feeling. In describing the dangers of the joy felt by a shipload of survivors from a burned ship,[13] Crusoe finds symptoms of illness (vomiting, swooning) as well as those of happiness (dancing). The scene recalls his deliverance from drowning and the way the mind of even a resolute person cannot contain violent emotion without release.[14] Emotion, then, is felt and expressed in much the same way in all people, Defoe says. The differences between men lie in their awareness of their immediate duty and of their future course. Their perspective is always larger than that of the person who loses himself entirely in the experience.

Defoe wants to represent the realities of an individual's sense of what he could become and of his immediate situation; he is as concerned with presenting those aspects of personality which make possible the realization of this potential and those which hinder it, as he is with describing an exciting series of events. The Defoe hero, always a character consciously engaged in improving himself and his position, has the ability to master himself, to see the broader context, and to improvise.[15] Crusoe is typical. He stares at hardship, death, grief, financial disaster, squares his shoulders and says, "There is a little relief in that," and begins to repair or even to carve out his fortunes. Crusoe finds water and a safe tree and sleeps "as comfortably as, I believe, few could have done in my condition." The next morning he begins to unload and dismantle the ship until he salvages every usable part from rice to tools to ink. Every admirable Defoe character shares this quality. The younger priest who has been saved in *Farther Adventures,* for example, is cited as an example of the "well-governed" mind; he prostrates himself in thanks to God, speaks calmly and seriously and, then, like a good shepherd, begins to work to compose the other survivors.

Having regained self-control, Defoe's characters begin to take inventory and make a place for themselves. The priest resumes his position as pastor and soon delights Crusoe with his conversation about religion. The two agree on rules for discourse, a gentlemen's agreement which opens the way for dispute-free, civilized dialogue, thereby assuring the priest of Crusoe's esteem and a position on the ship. The priest also makes a place for himself in the island society, and he is rewarded by not being needed there. By his action he proves that he is too useful to be left in isolated exile on the island, and a commendable but lower class woman replaces him as missionary to Crusoe's colony.

Crusoe is the most famous example of Defoe's characters' self-mastery and resourcefulness. As soon as Crusoe awakens, he seems to have put consternation and despair behind him, and he examines the situation dispassionately. Later we find that he has fought a constant battle against desolation and despondency. When he gives "some little account of" himself he lists "a dismal prospect":

> ... I had great reason to consider it as a determination of heaven that in this desolate place, and in this desolate manner, I should end my life. The tears would run plentifully down my face when I made these reflections, and sometimes I would expostulate with myself, why providence should thus compleatly ruine its creatures, and render them so absolutely miserable, so without help abandon'd, so entirely depress'd, that it could hardly be rational to be thankful for such a life.[16]

He calls this account a "prospect," bringing to mind the unobstructed, extensive views as well as a mental looking forward. This account he gives years later when time has softened his recollections, yet he still rises to dramatic rhetoric and remembers weeping and blaming God; in the journal begun a few days after his landing on the island, he tells us he named the place "Island of Despair" and spent the first day "afflicting myself at the dismal circumstances I was brought to." His "Island of Despair" may have inherited its name from Christian's dungeon kept by Giant Despair. Both sites combine physical imprisonment with the threat of mental breakdown. Christian and Crusoe add to the misery of the situation, and they struggle against their despair as much as their environment. Because each recognizes the double threat, he values endurance more. However, Christian and Hopeful supply for each other what must come from within Crusoe. Revealingly, Crusoe's next days' journal entries are catalogues of tasks carried out, of a rigid schedule of a man working to forget, creating a purpose and order where he fears there is none and on which he fears to reflect. He tells us he has omitted "many dull things" which we can only infer are hideous "shocking, private, and indecorous things" and for two years he fights lapsing into madness.[17] He turns to God, to extra fortifications, and to ironic reflections. After wanting company so desperately, he finds the footprints of a cannibal.[18] Struggling with himself, he builds a raft and strips the ship, he reconnoiters the island and notes resources and edibles; he begins to build a house, storage room, an ironically named "summer home," and he endures for twenty-eight years. The repetition built into the narrative shows him working steadily and silently even as he suffers intensely within. The journal entries underscore his courage.

Another character who discovers himself in a situation as disasterous and perilous as Crusoe's is a "Mulatto" captured in Magadoxa in *The General History of the Pirates*. The Magadoxans hate white people so much that they seize them, rip the flesh, and consider the chunks prizes to be exclaimed over or as tasty morsels to be savored. The Mulatto hears that this has happened to his shipmates and spends a most miserable night. Perhaps because the account is purported to be from the journals of Captain Beavis and the Mulatto, whom the reader can assume did not take notes in the first days of captivity, or because *The General History* is a different kind of book, the account of the Mulatto's suffering is much sketchier than that of Crusoe's.[19] In any case, the Mulatto's suffering is acute. He finds out what has happened to his white comrades and is thrown "into the utmost consternation and fear, as imagining himself to be near suffering and cruel death." He too, is subject to dangerous vacillations of emotion. At one instant he thinks he will not die because he is mulatto and because the natives have killed all of the others. The next moment he trembles with fear and looks "upon himself to be a dead man" because he has given the white men a good character. From what we know about emotion in *Robinson Crusoe* and what we know about Defoe's opinion of fear, we can surmise the Mulatto's agony of mind to be similar to Crusoe's or even greater since it is implied he could not have slept in any circumstances:

> Betwixt these doubts and fears he passed the night, in a place all covered with nastiness, where there was not the least conveniency for easing nature, and where, had his mind been at rest, it would have been hard for him to have slept.[20]

The next morning, he weighs the odds, his spirits rise, and he begins to take care of his most immediate needs: he makes friends with the jailer, gets food and water, sweeps the nasty cell with a "tosee," and begins to ingratiate himself with the king. He duplicates in compressed form the Crusoe pattern of adaptation and moves rapidly from trauma to emotional release through physical action to inventorying to modifying what he can as he adapts to what is immutable.

A second group of Defoe's characters are put into small, isolated societies as punishment. Although some of these transgressors expect to be caught and punished, their reaction to their new society may be as traumatic as those thrown into such a society by unexpected natural accidents. After all, imprisonment or transportation, like shipwreck, forces the character to assert himself in resisting the depression and experiences occasioned by his new situation. An exception to the catalogue of Defoe characters who are nearly overcome by their changed surroundings is Captain Singleton who is set ashore for his part in an abortive mutiny on an island quite like Crusoe's. He, like Crusoe, manages to salvage weapons, extra clothes, food, books, and tools before the ship finally leaves him. The failure to react to the dangers of this new community reflects critically on Singleton; he himself remarks that he was "either so young or so stupid" that he was little affected by being put ashore on such a dangerous island. At this point in the narrative, he prefers to hunt alone rather than participate in camp councils. He will, however, learn to rely on others and to value companionship; his initiation into the community of men occurs even as Defoe works out the now familiar initiation pattern.

Singleton speaks out and assumes leadership because he finds his companions "void of" "Presence of Mind." Participating, then, for him is not psychological membership or responsibility in the group but another part of the process of taking inventory and adapting. A sailor erects a sign reading, "Point Desperation. Jesus Have Mercy," but Singleton and a few others "set to work immediately to build us some huts. . . ." No Defoe hero abandons hope or wastes much time giving way to passions; they voice the code of heroic endurance that delineates the Defoe adventurers from ordinary men: few regrets, no "if only's," just preparation to take advantage of some opportunity. When no opportunity comes, they make one. Singleton learns to value the skills of some of the men in the group, particularly those of the surgeon, the gunner, and the cutler who can make birds, dogs, hooks and rings to trade with the natives. Men, however, are like resources or tools until he meets the Quaker William Walters who gradually draws him toward human compassion, reflective thought, and finally religion and marriage. The pattern of movement from self-control to adaptation to security and pleasure in society made familiar in *Robinson Crusoe* takes on a different emphasis when acted out by Singleton, the man who can say to Walters, "Why, Man, I am at Home [on ship], here is my Habitation, I never had any other in my Life time . . . I have no where to go."

An incident in *Moll Flanders* presents an illuminating contrast to the usual pattern acted out by characters initiated suddenly into new societies. Moll's reaction to Newgate is particularly revealing when contrasted to that of another thief, John Sheppard.[21] For once helpless and without resources, Moll "degenerates into stone," turns "first Stupid and Senseless, then Brutish and thoughtless, and at last raving Mad as any of them."[22] All through her career as a thief, Newgate has shadowed her; she has been continually conscious of it, and her fear of it has added tension to the book.[23] She sees her escapes with the loot as escapes from Newgate, and she feels she is outwitting Newgate rather than the owner of the goods. The organization of the narrative itself suggests that Moll feels Newgate is in her blood, is a threatening and important, even an inevitable, part of her history. Newgate looks like Hell to Moll; it even sounds and smells like Hell to her and, in the later passages, it deadens her senses. As her horror lessens, she notices the similarity to an emblem of hell. Emblem books made complicated philosophical, metaphysical, or theological concepts visual; by using the symbols and elaborate pictures from medieval illustrations to dramatize and heighten the importance of the subject, the ideas became associated with concrete representations. From making this connection, Moll's mind goes on to picture Newgate as the literal gate to Hell for her. Hell itself is horrifying, but in many ways objective and remote to Moll at this moment. However, seeing Newgate as an emblem adds immediacy and participation; because an emblem is explanatory, it translates into terms that threaten and involve rather than merely horrify. Moll logically translates Newgate into the gate to Hell in two ways: momentarily, she will be embroiled in it and feeling its torments; second, should she be hanged as she expects to be, Newgate will be the gate to the biblical Hell. The emblem metaphor serves much as real emblems do: it condenses and explains the purely verbal.

John Sheppard, in contrast, sees none of these aspects of the prison. Manacled, chained to the floor and locked in the Castle in Newgate, Sheppard says, "I was still far from despairing." He sees each succeeding horror as a test of his ingenuity and skill. His mental state and Moll's are polar opposites: he remains very much in command of himself and feels in control of his situation while Moll loses her identity and becomes a "Newgate bird." He jokes and stares back at the curious, but Moll is humiliated by them. As the "habit and custom of good breeding and manners" slip away so does her self-respect. Just as Crusoe turned to God, so does Moll; both also show the same signs of an unsound mind: psychosomatic illness, physical weakness, indecisiveness, strange dreams, uncharacteristic dependence on others. Throughout her career, Moll has been convinced of her superiority; Newgate ends her self-deception, and her collapse is inevitable.[24] This incident is unique in Defoe's fiction; here alone the central character fails to adapt. Rather than taking inventory of resources as Sheppard does, Moll catalogues horrors. Rather than maintaining self-control, she "degenerates into stone." Rather than modifying the society, she is modified and becomes "as easy with the place, as if indeed I had been born there." In her confused state of mind she lapses into a common figure of speech, unaware of the irony that she was born there. Once reprieved, however, she returns to her characteristic resiliency and to the usual pattern of coping found in Defoe protagonists. In contrast to Jemmy who takes several months longer than she to recover from the shock of his imprisonment and never achieves her optimism, Moll begins at once to chisel out a comfortable new life for herself.

Less abrupt but often with as unpredictable results are the changes which the characters themselves initiate. At times, they seek more security or more respect; they want to reform in order to escape one situation and create a place for themselves in a new society; some even want adventure. Roxana's structure depends on such moves. Although necessity plays a large part in her first moves, Roxana seeks to better herself, to profit financially and socially. Later she moves from place to place in the vain hope of building a new life in which she can respect herself. As long as she is a whore in her own mind and the eyes of the world, neither her children nor decent people will respect her. Since her self-respect is based on what others think of her, she cannot tolerate her situation in Kensington.[25] Amy locates the Quakeress, and Roxana begins the short interlude which is the happiest time of her life.[26]

Captain Misson builds Libertalia in *The General History* for many of the same reasons Roxana moves in with the Quakeress. After years of peril, both are ready for more security and a life more in harmony with their consciences and ideas of respectability. He tells his men that at last they will have "some place to call their own and a receptacle when age or wounds had rendered them incapable of hardship, where they might enjoy the fruits of their labor, and go to their graves in peace. . . ." [27] Roxana's final days and Defoe's own troubled old age add eloquence to this plea.[28]

Many of Defoe's characters move into isolated societies seeking either adventure or financial betterment. Robinson Crusoe's trip to the Orient and across Asia and northern Europe in *Farther Adventures* is an excellent example. Until his wife dies, Crusoe suppresses his wanderlust, cultivates a farm, and enjoys his family and retired life. His wife's death "drove him, by its consequences into a deep relapse into the wandering disposition." His grief is deep; he describes himself as "unhinged," "desolate and dislocated in the world by the loss of her." Just as he resists telling us many "dull things" about his feelings on the island, so he says, "It is not my business here to write an elegy upon my wife." He suggests his grief, he tells us enough of his reaction to imply what a great blow her death was, and then modestly turns to what he says we are interested in: his adventures. Defoe uses eloquent metaphors instead of actions to describe Crusoe's grief: "the stay of all my affairs, the centre of all my enterprises, the engine that, by her prudence, reduced me to that happy compass I was in" (earlier described as "a kind of heavenly life"). His despairing eye sees a world

> busy round me, one Part laboring for Bread, and the other Part squandering in vile Excesses or empty Pleasures, equally miserable, because the End they proposed still fled from them; for the Man of Pleasure every day surfeited of his Vice, and heaped up Work for Sorrow and Repentance; and the Men of Labour spent their Strength in daily Strugglings for Bread to maintain the vital Strength they labour'd with, so living in a daily Circulation of Sorrow, living but to work, and working but to live, as if daily Bread were the only End of wearisome Life, and a wearisome Life the only Occasion of daily Bread.[29]

This is the vision of a man bewildered by tragedy and tired of life, but he plans a new place for himself and begins traveling again.

Other characters such as those in *The General History* go to sea and turn

pirate in search of adventure. In *Memoirs of a Cavalier,* a nameless younger
man gets permission to leave an arranged marriage and travel for a while.
He goes to France, Switzerland, and begins to observe the Army for
amusement. In the same spirit of adventure and curiosity, he fights all
over Europe and then on the side of King Charles I. Colonel Jack a
puzzling combination of insight and intelligence and insatiable insecurity, dissatisfaction, and greed, runs illegal goods to Cuba. He, the pirates,
Moll, Roxana, the Cavalier, and Singleton can adapt and blend into a
wide variety of societies.

Defoe's novels contain dozens of small societies quite different from
ordinary eighteenth-century English life. They incorporate special situations and hazards which test the protagonists and develop Defoe's themes.
Whether the character is the victim of an accident, the captive of legal
machinery, or the seeker of security, gain, or self-respect, his experiences
in these authorially created-special societies demonstrate Defoe's ideas of
human nature, social institutions, and their interaction. For example,
regardless of the motivation for the character's being in a society, he
tends to follow a pattern of behavior: he reacts violently and emotionally
to his predicament, he takes stock of the resources available to him in
his situation, and he begins to carve a place for himself in the particular
society. After his psychological orientation, he also follows a fairly
consistent pattern in organizing his society. The development of the new
society, created to meet his needs yet never free from the limitations of
man's nature, also follows a fairly consistent pattern.

III

Although Swift's characters are usually the perceiving intelligence just
as Bunyan's and Defoe's are, they are significantly different because they
are satiric. The satiric character exists to experience and reveal, the
fictional one to experience and react. We can talk about Bunyan's characters in relation to Defoe's because Bunyan drew so heavily upon spiritual
autobiography (a source the writers shared) and upon dream allegory
which locates narrative in the consciousness of the central character. Yet
Bunyan's characters and Swift's represent something more abstract than
the individuals Moll, Roxana, and Singleton because their characters
appear in settings designed to reach beyond the particular experience of
the character in a time and place largely bounded by that character's

consciousness. If Defoe and Bunyan share an attention to the thoughts and internal experience of the protagonist, Defoe and Swift share the fear that external forces, what they (but probably not Bunyan) would join us in calling "society," can overwhelm the inner man, and Swift and Bunyan share the desire to transform the world through fictions so that the transformation reveals neglected truths about the familiar world. Swift and Bunyan often create stories which must be read on two levels (allegory and satire); Swift and Defoe often invent fictions which present characters as minute points in time which can show the influence of the intersections of biography and history within a society. Where Defoe and Bunyan describe conscious resistance, Swift chooses satire to demonstrate how the individual can represent society.

Swift's characters tend to gravitate toward a group in which they will be as comfortable as Badman is in a tavern:

> For, there is a peculiar *String* in the Harmony of Human Understanding, which in several individuals is exactly of the same Tuning. This, if you can dexterously screw up to its right Key, and then strike gently upon it; Whenever you have the Good Fortune to light among those of the same Pitch, they will be a secret necessary Sympathy, strike exactly at the same time.[30]

> so there are naturall absurdityes from which the wisest Sages are not exempt, which proceed less from the nature of the Clymate than that of their government.[31]

Gulliver, like Robinson Crusoe, believes he has always been an uneasy member of English society. He confesses "having been condemned by Nature and Fortune to an active and restless Life." Swift sets Gulliver in three differing relationships to the societies which he encounters: as a member of the English society, as a captive of alien societies, and as an observer of societies. In all three situations, Gulliver examines, judges, and experiments with belonging.[32] Each of Gulliver's experiences at sea confirms his discomfort. His entries into the four island societies are motivated first by a shipwreck, next by the understandable desertion of his shipmates, then by pirates, and finally by a mutiny.[33] The progression from accident to the "natural" weakness of man to villainy contributes to Gulliver's increasingly negative description of the motives and actions of his countrymen while reminding the reader of Gulliver's place in a familiar world. By the time he describes his adventures to the Houyhn-hnm, he sees poverty and crime, perjury, rape, and murder as predictable motives for the conduct of men in any society. He can refer in a casual way to vices and follies "which Nature hath entitled" men to and, even as he does so, the reader can see Gulliver as the emblem for this society, Swift's archetypal Englishman.

Gulliver's initiation into each island society indicates the thematic pattern Swift has designed to illustrate Gulliver's increasingly sophisticated human needs. In Lilliput, his needs are almost entirely physical: sleep, the sun out of his eyes, food, drink, freedom to urinate. Even his demands for liberty are mostly physical. He is a docile captive, content to amuse the Lilliputians, eager to be recognized as useful and well behaved. He learns their language and reassures them.

In Brobdingnag, his anxieties reflect the size reversal. He exists in a state of awareness of physical fragility. He can never forget that he could fall, be dropped, stepped upon, or squeezed to death. Immediately respected for his size in Lilliput, he struggles ludicrously to gain respect in Brobdingnag.[34] His initiation here is not merely a matter of accommodation, of learning to see himself as "Man Mountain" restrained by the mutual respect and social contract between man and government. The giants remind him of his status each time he is displayed or laughed at. His efforts to gain acceptance remind the reader of Swift's shrewd observations about society's values and criteria for status. Gulliver displays good breeding whenever he can (he takes off his hat and bows, pays his respects to assembled crowds of gawkers in taverns, demonstrates fencing, and toasts the Queen); he tries to display physical prowess (with flies, rats, and a frog); and he insists on demonstrating knowledge (of government, war, and music).

The islands of Part III reinforce Gulliver's sense of exclusion and shift the emphasis to human needs other than the physical. Gulliver talks only with women, tradesmen, and servants in Laputa, makes a fool of himself over the Struldbruggs, and leaves posing as Dutch. Again his self-respect comes under attack. The Houyhnhnm society combines the threats of the earlier islands. The horses are larger and stronger than Gulliver. They show contempt for his body, his country, and achievements. He worries about food, shelter, clothing, security, and respect. In addition, their society, more than either Lilliput or Brobdingnag, holds opinions and espouses values foreign to his own. He is constantly threatened with identification with a group he abhors. The Brobdingnag king had been appalled and amused at Gulliver's description of Englishmen; the

Houyhnhnms, however, judge him even more harshly, and assign him to a group not according to size or appearance, but by a moral standard as well.

In each country, Gulliver is able to learn the language and the customs of the people and adapt. Each part finds him a more adept and more willing student. He can detach himself from the Lilliputians' demands and judge them beneath his dignity. In Brobdingnag, he is unable to give up the attempt to impose his opinion of himself on the giants. He can still separate reasonable from unreasonable opinions. After all, the Brobdingnagian king is both morally superior and naive. In spite of the king's discourse, Gulliver is perceptive enough to discover a history of internal strife and to remark on the shared illusions of England and Brobdingnag. Gulliver adjusts to his rescue more slowly. Yet he laughs at the size of things and fears stepping on others, signs that he has identified with the only clearly superior characteristic of the Brobdingnagians and that he now sees through their eyes.

Gulliver shifts with each new society in Part III. He explains the movement of the flying island in the Laputan's words and complains of neglect, becomes a projector in Lagado, and believes the spirits of Alexander and Hannibal, accepts the Luggnaggian king's poisonings as lenient, and easily imagines a life for himself as a Struldbrugg. This adventure, the most bizarre and disrupted of the group, prepares Gulliver and the reader for creatures in non-human shapes and for the translation of unfamiliar systems into full-fledged philosophies.

In Houyhnhnmland, Gulliver regards the horses first as unusually intelligent, then as magicians. Although he follows the usual initiatory steps into the society (anxiety, conciliatory gestures, adaptation to available shelter and food, learning the language, recognition of status), he has been on the island for weeks before he equates the Yahoos with men. At this point, however, he insists upon basic differences and imagines his position when he returns to England,

> . . . and that upon my Arrival hither, I was as much astonished to see the Houyhnhnms act the rational Beings, as he or his Friends could be in finding some Marks of Reason in a Creature he was pleased to call a Yahoo; to which I owned my Resemblance in every Part, but could not account for their degenerate and brutal Nature. I said farther, That if good Fortune ever restored me to my native Country, to relate my Travels hither, as I resolved to do: every Body would believe that I *said the Thing which was not:* that I invented the Story out of my own Head:

And with all possible Respect to Himself, his Family, and Friends ... our Countrymen would hardly think it probable, that a *Houyhnhnm* should be the presiding Creature of a Nation, and a Yahoo the Brute.[35]

Here Gulliver admits his resemblance "in every part" to the Yahoos but distinguishes their natures. By the end of the passage he substitutes "Yahoo" for "man" for the first time. Clearly Gulliver hopes to go home and accurately describes his countrymen's future reaction to his tale.[36]

Gulliver's account of his countrymen's behavior is thoroughly Hobbesian.[37] He assigns money the role of universal motive and describes human nature perpetually in a state of "Profusion" or "Avarice." Finally the Houyhnhnms become false gods.[38] They appear without flaw to him[39] and his grateful attention to their conversation, usually on familiar sermon topics (benevolence, order and economy, virture), leads Gulliver to conclude that the horses understand mankind better than he and confirms his low opinion of his species. He reacts with humility and a sense of unworthiness. He had rather, he insists, listen to the Houyhnhnms than dictate to Senates. "Natural Awe" grows upon him "and was mingled with a respectful Love and Gratitude, that they would condescend to distinguish me from the rest of my Species."[40]

When Gulliver is banished, he despairs. He expresses the necessary effect in Biblical terms:

... how could I think with Temper, of passing my Days among *Yahoos,* and relapsing into my old Corruptions, for want of Examples to lead and keep me within the Paths of Virtue.[41]

Gradually, he realizes he can be a disciple. He can preach the Word to his countrymen. He promises the Houyhnhnms that he will be useful to men, praise the horses, and espouse the imitation of their virtues to men. This, he feels, will "preserve a wretched Being." He, like Robinson Crusoe, imposes order and meaning on his life when he is nearest despair. The Christian's need to separate himself from sinful men yet perform works of charity and spread the Gospel works itself out ironically in Gulliver's sickness. He comes back and sets up idols in the shape of gods, believes he must go to considerable lengths to remain uncontaminated, and even writes a gospel.[42]

He has experienced a conversion,[43] a recognition of his sin and a longing for his gods, and now tries to share his vision. The essential features of a gospel are that it is a direct revelation from the gods, that it is indisputably true, and that it is of major importance in the lives and social institutions of man. Gulliver claims all of this for his book. He recounts the teachings and interpretations learned directly from his "master." He insists repeatedly that he has never deviated from the truth. His goal, to make the company of Yahoos not insupportable, is less grandiose than the scheme he lays on his Cousin Sympson, to reform his countrymen.[44] The specific nature of the list of reforms Gulliver desires, however, contrasts with the publisher's letter. Sympson has changed the book to accommodate England's political situation and readers' tastes; Gulliver has never wanted to entertain others.

The Houyhnhnms offer a false religion for men. The basic premise of their lives, expressed in the phrase "the Thing which was not," coined with Gulliver's introduction into their society, rules out the heart of the Christian faith, "the assurance of things hoped for, the conviction of things not seen."[45] They have no words for such concepts as power, law, and punishment, and reject the study of literature, history, and higher mathematics. Reason alone offers an incomplete faith, providing only for the existence and nature of God, natural law, and the immortality of the soul.[46] Gulliver becomes the nominal Christian of the *Argument against Abolishing Christianity* all over again. Swift explains, "It is an old and true distinction, that things may be above our reason, without being contrary to it." [47] The Houyhnhnms lack the characteristics which distinguish good men from Christians. Their lack of need for history exemplifies the static state in which they live.[48] They become the measure of their own potential and stature. Gulliver, then, has his final meeting with a non-human group whom he cannot imitate because he lacks the power to free himself from a human restriction. The Houyhnhnms are the most morally superior group he meets; therefore, it is appropriate that Gulliver transforms them into a religion.

This transformation, however, is a hideous perversion. Gulliver creates a proud and cynical calling out of his refusal to belong to any society of humans or humanoids. He accepts no guilt, feels no need to repent, and denies the most basic religious definitions of the human condition. Even as he creates a religion to "save" men, he isolates himself irredeemably from them. Here Swift brings together a lifetime of dissatisfaction with the directions of religious thought and practice and makes them flesh in Gulliver. The implications of accepting the teachings of the Socinians, Deists, and Free-Thinkers shape the character of Gulliver and the apocalyptic satirical figure he is. Before us stands a religion based on distrust and hatred of men, smug self-righteousness, assumed omniscience, and denial of responsibility.

Swift, like Defoe, relies upon small societies throughout his works. Even in his political pamphlets, he creates particular groups which move to their own mores and interpret their actions and the world in nonstandard ways. For example, Swift treats the Whig ministry as an aberrant, deplorable society. One by one, men become members for self-interest. Godolphin, for instance, refuses his position until he is offered more power. Unlike other ministries, they feel no loyalty to the monarch, treat Anne with disrespect, and do not have the Church and constitution as foremost considerations. Swift carefully distinguishes between apparently similar historical situations motivated by English values and immediate necessity and the actions of the Godolphin ministry. The *Examiner* papers depict a progressively isolated group: First, they are Englishmen with patriotic motives, then part of a party formed out of the fringes of other parties and groups, and finally individuals held together by shared guilt and fear.

The Irish tracts draw much of their power from Swift's creation of Ireland as a small society. His created societies function as parables, making worlds recognizable as like our own, yet moving visibly from what Golding called "the darkness of the human heart." A truth somehow more accurate than social realism emerges. In *A Modest Proposal,* the narrator is symbol, spokesman, and fusion of a number of complex groups. Perversely, he *is* the reasonable and humane man. Before the Modest Proposer understood the nature of the world, he made suggestions long recognized as representing Swift's best ideas.[49] Now his plan represents what is possible given the nature of the English, the Irish, and the politico-economic projectors who determine British policy. Like the worst of the projectors in the Grand Academy of Lagado, he now tries to exploit the worst elements of human nature for good ends. His moral insensitivity and shortsightedness are but reflections of the groups he addresses. The English, as surely as if they approved the plan, are "eating" the Irish nation. The Irish, as surely as if they were raising infants as a cash crop, are participating in the immorality. The economic politicians are similarly working within perimeters dictated by limited perceptions of the situation and severely restricted conceptions of implications and ramifications. Swift, well aware of the suffering, the weaknesses of decision making and present policies, and the moral ideal familiar to all Western thought, manages to create a projector of his own society and yet makes us aware of the moral failings and narrow possibilities of men working within contemporary British sensibilities. The image of the ideal looms behind the compromising individual.[50]

Likewise in the Drapier papers, Swift creates a world both particular and fictional. Only in a fantasy kingdom could men consider approving Wood's coins and other men consider submitting to using them. In such a world, wagon loads of coins might be necessary to pay rent or buy supplies; the Houses of Parliament, the Privy-Council, the greatest number of Corporations, the Lord-Mayor and Aldermen of Dublin and Grand-Juries might be "Papists"; 50,000 might be employed to make the Irish swallow the coins. Swift moves adeptly between the imaginary consequences and the rights of the people and the actions he would like them to take. In the letter to the shopkeepers, he describes how buying and selling will be carried out, traces the effects on shopkeepers, small tavern owners, and beggars, and finishes with a concrete list of the people's legal rights. Wood and the Irish people are caught up in a fiction which is absurd when placed inside the frame of English history, constitution, and powers of coercion.[51] By reminding the Irish that they cannot be forced to submit and by belittling Wood, Swift substitutes his wider understanding for their passive submissiveness. "A People long used to Hardships, lose by Degrees the very Notions of *Liberty;* they look upon themselves as Creatures at Mercy; and all Impositions laid on them by a stronger Hand, are, in the Phrase of the *Report, legal,* and *obligatory.*"[52] In the person of the petty shopkeeper, he transfers the conflict from a grand and threatening scale (England vs. Ireland) to an amusing one (hardwareman vs. drapier).

For Defoe, Swift, and Bunyan, the movement from one society to another represents the spirit of the quest as well as psychological need, embodies late seventeenth- and early eighteenth-century optimism, and parallels the rapidly changing society. While Bunyan's thematic emphasis on "what shall a man do to be saved" places him in the older literary traditions, his characters, his realistic scenes and idiomatic language, and his instructions for tradesmen testify to the influence of the cultural, economic, and philosophical forces so dominant in Swift's and Defoe's work. When characters undertake a pilgrimage, they must encounter a series of societies which alternately try their constancy and initiate them. Just as Christian must study Interpreter's tableaux, fight Apollyon, and escape the dungeon of Giant Despair, so must Defoe's and Swift's protagonists reckon with society's categories based not only on birth and even clothing, but also with events such as shipwrecks and political upheaval. In becoming what they want to be, they "try the fit" of various groups, and the experience of their integration interprets their social and moral position for the reader.

For Swift, the restless nature of man sends him out to create bizarre corruptions of rational groups. His societies are as imaginary and as symbolic as Bunyan's and are rich in parable, but draw from other myths and other literary traditions. Defoe, writing in a genre which had already come to insist upon its truth,[53] created societies to answer the psychological needs of his characters just at the Aeolists answer Jack's and the Houyhnhnms Gulliver's. For all three writers, these fictive societies provide a means of studying man as a social being, as a being searching for a place in society, as a creature of eternity, and as a being quite possibly possessing a unique personality. This being is caught by the forces of community, God, and self as he or she struggles to realize a personality integrating and harmonizing them. Such new, created societies provide the testing grounds for theories of influence on the individual.

CHAPTER II

ORGANIZATION AND GOVERNMENT

BY creating insulated societies, Bunyan, Swift, and Defoe participate in the growing interest in forms of government and the nature of leaders. Beginning with the Cromwell years, English literary men joined philosophers, politicians, clergymen, historians, and pamphleteers in the scrutiny of government and leadership. Dryden's *Absalom and Achitophel* ends with a prescription for a good king. Nahum Tate's *History of King Lear* repeatedly mentions Lear's responsibility and relationship to his subjects. Panegyrics had the double purpose of praising and presenting an ideal for those in power. Marvell, Milton, Rowe, Otway, Behn—all of the best writers of the time wrote about politics, power, and leadership. Bunyan, Swift, and Defoe saw the power of government and church over the individual, and all wrote about this force in imaginative ways. Furthermore, all had considerable experience with English politics which led them to speculate and criticize with special insight and personal involvement.

Between the birth of Bunyan and the death of Swift, Englishmen did not merely experience a series of monarchs with contrasting personalities and attitudes toward their prerogatives. Rather, they experienced regicide, republic, restoration, abdication, an Act of Settlement, a Queen without an heir, periodic Jacobite invasions and rumors of invasions, and rapidly shifting attitudes toward the divine right of kings, passive obedience, religious tolerance, and Parliamentary power. Defoe probably speaks for his contemporaries when he writes in *The Validity of the Renunciations of Former Powers, Enquired Into:*

> But Time has taught us to see, that neither the Opinion of Princes, or Parliaments, are so infallible, as not to be Subject to the Mutations and Alterations, which the Accidents of Government, and the Revolutions of Nations bring upon them; and that which may to Day be esteemed dangerous and impracticable, to Morrow becomes not only safe but necessary; so that it ceases to be an Argument against

a Thing to say, that such was the Opinion of such or such, at such or such a Time; for as Circumstances alter, the Judgments of Men will and ought to be altered.[1]

Defoe is speaking specifically of the "balance of power" and the accession to the Spanish throne by the Duke of Anjou, for the deaths of Joseph and several members of the French royal family had changed the situation drastically. Defoe in this pamphlet, as he does habitually, sees the situation in the context of history and draws experience from similar events in the past. For this reason, the phrase, "But Time has taught us to see" must be interpreted broadly.

Time had shaped Bunyan, Swift, and Defoe to examine decisions, statesmen, policies, and even the administration of policies in far more critical ways than their predecessors. Responsibility, choice, and result became increasingly problematic. All three men held fairly consistent opinions about the most effective and beneficial forms of government, about the nature of man, and, more particularly, about man's need for government. These opinions influence the portrayal of and speculations about society, its leaders, and governments, but they do not provide dogma or solutions. Again and again, these writers describe the formation of a society and the customs which hold it together. They create one fiction after another to explore the behavior and implications of kinds of leaders and forms of government. In so doing, they portray the created society in ordinary situations as well as in incidents designed to comment upon contemporary policies and practices such as those associated with the legal system, war, colonization, and slavery.

I

Both Swift and Defoe believed that government was a necessary condition. Like Defoe, Swift analyzed political situations and tried periodically to influence statesmen and even Parliament. His writings about government include general, theoretical passages influenced by his conception of the nature of man, speculative and creative passages on leaders, and similar passages on the governed and the impact of government upon them. Although these three topics are inseparable in some ways, Swift's treatment of them differs and the degree of moral anguish rises when Swift portrays the ruler's subjects.

In many ways the least traditional and most metaphorical of the writers in treating government, Swift integrates opinion and fable subtly. For example, his small societies demonstrate class stratification and the necessity for government. Perhaps the most consistent idea in *Gulliver's Travels* is the ordering of the classes. The Lilliputians are divided into nobility, gentry, businessmen, "the meaner sort," and cottagers and laborers. Each class is educated differently, and women are divided into parallel classes. In Brobdingnag, Swift treats lower-class life more fully. The attitudes and occupations of the farmer and his wife can be compared to those of the King and Queen, and Gulliver's airings introduce him to other groups. The islands of Book III are similarly divided, and Gulliver is especially insulted to be left to women, tradesmen, flappers, and pages in Laputa. Houyhnhnm classes are marked by education, ability, duties, and color. The chances of shifting classes are remote.

Because citizens continue to jockey for power, wealth, and advantage, they require government. Every island except Houyhnhnmland keeps a standing army.[2] Fear of faction and internal strife greatly outweighs the threat of foreign invasion. Even the Houyhnhnms find laws and punishments necessary and must vigilantly control and govern the Yahoos. Governments impose order and reason. Gulliver's narrative and the contrast to the Houyhnhnms make the point. The master muses that nature and reason should be enough of a guide for men; the horses govern themselves, after all. Gulliver argues that law is a science governed by internal rules, but his description of lawyers, judges, and Parliament convince the Houyhnhnms that reason does not govern men's laws.

Swift believed that men required restraint and that the Church and state should work in tandem to control men's uncivil propensities.[3] In *A Discourse of the Contests and Dissentions in Athens and Rome,* Swift describes the sheeplike characteristics of ordinary men. These people can be led by others to forsake their own reason and become "as Wind is through an Organ." They become opinionless followers; they regurgitate "digested" ideas and assume a rude self-confidence based on their faith in the opinions of their leader. Swift's description of this common follower anticipates the picture of the Yahoos' selection of a leader:

> . . . it is hard to recollect one Folly, Infirmity, or Vice, to which a single Man is subjected, and from which a Body of Commons either collective or represented can be wholly exempt. For, besides that they are composed of Men with all their Infirmities about them; they have also the ill Fortune to be generally led and influenced by the very worst among themselves. . . .[4]

Once this unstable group attains a little power, it can never be satisfied. ". . . when a Lover becomes satisfied by small Compliances, without further Pursuits; then expect to find popular Assemblies content with small Concessions," Swift cautions[5], and goes on to describe the mischief caused by the balance of power shifting into the hands of the common people. Swift's conception of this behavior and its dangers undergirds many of his explanations of undesirable political events. Groups, often joined by little more than common interests, spring up in the *Examiner* and endanger Church and state.[6] The argument of "A Sermon upon the Martyrdom of King Charles I" blames, among other factors, the shift of power into the hands of the people and the House of Commons for the Puritan triumph.[7]

Because the common man is such a potential threat and the aristocracy unreliable, the character of the leader (the third element holding power in a mixed government)[8] assumes crucial importance. After Polybius, mixed governments were seen as a balance of political powers rather than of social classes, and it was a commonplace that they had a strong tendency to degenerate. The pessimism of ". . . the Example alone of a vicious Prince, will in Time corrupt an Age; but the Example of a good one will not be sufficient to reform it without further Endeavours" [9] underlies the descriptions of governments and statesmen. Like most men of his time, Swift believed change occurred primarily because of the actions of great men.[10] Over and over Swift complains that "the Source of most Mistakes and Miscarriages, in Matters debated by publick Assemblies, ariseth from the Influence of private Persons upon great Numbers. . . ." [11] The ripple effect of the vibrating string in *A Tale* and "a Whore can govern the Back-Stairs" in *Gulliver's Travels* convey this puzzling fact. Once a leader appears, men scamper after him. Marlborough, Godolphin, and Wharton become an evil somehow greater than their human qualities because of the power the mob assigns them, and the burden becomes heavier for the good leader. Any leader stamps his image on his society and the common people are a flawed surface. The good man must, therefore, exert himself to control his subjects. "Princes must therefore supply this Defect [the tendency to corruption] by a vigorous Exercise of that Authority, which the Law hath left them, by making it every Man's Interest and Honour to cultivate Religion and Virtue. . . ." [12] The leader, then, can err by neglecting to exert all the authority "Law" gives him as Charles I did, by lacking the stature to inspire the respect necessary to a leader, or by providing a bad example for his people.[13]

Although these opinions are consistent, Swift continues to puzzle over the way leaders arise and spread their influence. The metaphors of winds, vibrating strings, and climbing describe symptom, not source, and testify to his fascination with the process. Given his artistic aims, the frequency with which he describes the ways the process infects and riddles a society might be predictable, but the imagination and energy present in the creation of threat goes beyond art to an analysis of human nature's relationship to society.

Many of Swift's opinions about and practical experiences in politics become imaginative fables in *Gulliver's Travels*. The *Travels* has nearly a dozen model governments, varying from tyrannical monarchies to oligarchies to the Houyhnhnms' representative Grand Assembly. These governments vary according to the nature of the leader, the statesmen surrounding him, and the duties of each, and each government assumes something of the personality of its leader. Because most of the monarchs are petty, power-hungry opportunists, their courts are insecure and strife-ridden. Self-interest frequently motivates the courtiers' behavior, and they are willing to praise the king for the quality he is most deficient in. The Lilliputian king provides the most obvious example. He enjoys praise and legislates it, and his followers are eager to supply what nature has deprived him of. The conventional opening of the treaty between Gulliver and the king praises those qualities most obviously absent: "Delight and Terror of the Universe," "Taller than the Sons of Men; whose Feet press down to the Center, and whose Head strikes against the Sun. . . ." The more presumptuous the ruler, the more absurd the formulaic praise. The Luggnaggian king insists upon being greeted with the blessing made ironic by our knowledge of the Struldbruggs, "May your celestial Majesty outlive the Sun, eleven Moons and an half."

The criticism of leaders in Book IV is especially vituperative. Queen Anne is passed over as a "female man," but the chief minister is a monster. The description of Yahoo leaders sounds the themes begun in Lilliput:

1. Leaders are singular, somehow unnatural.
2. Favorites are sycophants.
3. Favorites enjoy a short tenure.

4. Leaders are chosen neither for ability nor integrity.

Gulliver observes that these maxims place men and Yahoos below the "common Hound, who hath Judgment enough to distinguish and follow the Cry of the *ablest Dog in the Pack,* without being ever mistaken." One of the most dangerous desires of would-be governors is their rapacious seeking of converts. Jack, the Aeolists, even the Houyhnhnms enjoy imitation. Swift often associates subduing others to individual "visions" or madness, but goes on to extol the joys of credulity.[14] Such submission to another's ideas not only frees the person from responsibility but allows the imagination to substitute more pleasant things for reality. That this state is one of "being a Fool among Knaves" defines Swift's attitude. His ambivalence toward the Irish indicates his attempts to define the extent of culpability.[15]

Swift lived in the time when England and her continental neighbors were forming colonies, and he had examples of new governments being established before him. His objections to religious, philosophical, and military imperialism are well known, and English colonial policies gave him fruitful ground for satire. He and Defoe both saw the base motives and dubious conduct even as they heard the patriotic justifications. Gulliver, for example, considers that it might have been his duty to claim the islands for Britain. He quickly explains how the first three are undesirable, but he rationalizes the neglect of Houyhnhnmland. First, they would fight tenaciously and effectively. Here Swift repeats his belief that loyalty makes the best fighters. He goes on to explain his ethical objections to colonization:

> . . . they give the Country a new Name, they take formal Possession of it for the King, they set up a rotten Plank or a Stone for a Memorial, they murder two or three Dozen of the Natives, bring away a Couple more by Force for a Sample, return home, and get their Pardon. Here commences a new Dominion acquired with a Title by *Divine Right.* Ships are sent with the first Opportunity. . . a free Licence given to all Acts of Inhumanity and Lust; the Earth reeking with the Blood of its Inhabitants: And this execrable Crew of Butchers employed in so pious an Expedition, is a modern Colony sent to convert and civilize an idolatrous and barbarous People.[16]

The contrast between the friendly and generous natives and the "civilized" colonists emphasizes the irony of their claims. Defoe's *General*

History of the Pirates has a remarkably similar passage in the life of Bellamy. Here a stroller urges Bellamy and Williams to land and found a new kingdom "which in time might subject the world, and extend its conquests beyond those of the Roman Empire." He is qualified, he argues to be Secretary of State for he has been a servitor at Oxford and has "ambition, avarice and learning enough." This satire of the English governing class was commonplace. The plans for success include keeping the people in abject poverty, annexing Indians and discontented people from neighboring colonies, and maintaining a state of war. After all, the stroller argues,

> Rome, the Mistress of the world, was founded by a couple of sheep-stealers, and peopled by run-away slaves and insolvent debtors; how much more advantageously might you two undertake the erecting of a new monarchy, whose subjects are no strangers to the art of war. . . . raise every useful man to some dignity in the state, and share the prisoners (I mean those who won't swear allegiance) as so many slaves unworthy of liberty among your great men; build more vessels, keep them constantly on the cruise, and force all the prisoners either by fair or foul to acknowledge your sovereignty. It was thus the greatest empires of the world were founded. Superior force was always acknowledged a just title. . . . I leave it to the mature deliberation of your great wisdom, whether it is not more eligible to found here an empire, and make war by a lawful authority derived from your royal selves, than lie under the opprobrious appelations of robbers, thieves, profligate rogues and pirates. . . . But, when you have once declared yourselves lawful monarch, and that you have strength to defend your title, all of the universities of the world will declare you have a right *jure divino,* and the kings and princes of the earth will send their ambassadors to court your alliance.[17]

The formation of nations is the result of contracts aimed at security and power. Policies of interest, intimidation, and continual watchfulness assure the endurance of the colony. Eventually power gives respectability and society constructs arguments and names for the rights that governments have seized.

The qualifications of rulers are viciously satirized in the stroller's speech. This son of a miller has "learning enough" plus avarice and ambition enough to be Secretary of State. Being "servitor" at Oxford—a servant, perhaps a waiter—is good enough apprenticeship. In *The Secret History of the October Club,* Defoe had criticized in much the same way the meager education of the men who filled the Houses. As the stroller explains how wisely he will govern, the exploitation which was the foundation of empire building stands out. Since 1710, Defoe had complained about the English taxation system and policies and warned England against imposing too many taxes, and when the stroller promises to demonstrate his patriotism by "squeezing your subjects," he uses phrases common in such pamphlets as *The True State of the Case between the Government and the Creditors* and *Peace, or Poverty*. By raising useful men rather than honorable or capable men to high positions in the state and keeping great numbers as slaves, the stroller can raise this new nation in the same way that all "the great empires of the world were founded." Defoe's final stroke comes in the contrasting pictures painted of the world's opinion. Should such an empire be founded, composed of pirates, based on war and slavery and imperialism, sustained by heavy taxes, corrupt leaders, and continual intimidation of other countries, "all the universities of the world will declare you have a right *jure divino,* and the kings and princes of the earth will send their ambassadors to court your alliance." Both Swift and Defoe mock the contrast between the methods of colonization and the phrase, *"jure divino."* Both comment on the fact that such pirates are beyond the law; Swift's are pardoned, and Defoe's two captains promise to pass an act of indemnity after fleecing their subjects.

Swift's strongest reservations seem to apply to leaders who do not inherit their thrones. He believes that orderly administration and exercise of power is best served by an hereditary monarchy[18] and portrays ambition as a form of madness. In *A Tale of a Tub,* the narrator speculates about the kind of man who "did ever conceive it in his Power, to reduce the Notions of all Mankind, exactly to the same Length, and Breadth, and Heighth of his own."[19] In *Gulliver's Travels,* avarice replaces singularity as prime motive. In both cases, the leader's personality and actions affect all of the people.

Gulliver's justification of his failure to claim Houyhnhnmland for England sets up a contrast between the colonies established and administered by "pirates" and the "wisdom, care and justice" of England in establishing her colonies. Gulliver nominates the English as a model, lists the obligations of a country to its colonies, and allows the reader to study the ideal institution. First, Gulliver insists that the mother country should make liberal endowments for religion and learning. In fact, American colonial governors' commissions and instructions made them responsible for overseeing the religious and moral life of the colony.

Their specific duties included making sure the Book of Common Prayer was read every Sunday and and encouraging assemblies to build schools. The "liberal endowments" Gulliver mentions were lacking, however; in practice, governors had neither the power nor the resources to lead movements for moral reform. Although England made some efforts to assure that the governors would have some independent funds, the greatest single problem for many governors was the lack of control of the budget.[20]

Second, Gulliver recommended a strict regard for justice. As concerned as the Board of Trade was, the actual administration of justice in the colonies was often a scandal. Few lawyers lived in the colonies and the appointed judges were often nearly illiterate. *The Present State of Justice in the American Plantations* describes courts so inept that English merchants preferred to lose trade rather than appeal to them. Irregular schedules, delays, and biased juries seem to have been the rule rather than the exception.[21]

Third, Gulliver noted the importance of sober settlers, carefully selected pastors, and virtuous governors. England, of course, did very little to select settlers except during the years when they sent criminals in large numbers. Many of the early settlers wanted a new life, and Defoe's *Colonel Jack* decribes a representative assortment of early settlers. The pastors were often poor men who could not make a good living in England although there were notable exceptions. Some men motivated by missionary zeal had real ability and others appointed by the Bishop of London exhibited unusual administrative ability. James Blair, for example, served the colonies for more than fifty years and founded the College of William and Mary; Thomas Bray brought the Society for the Propagation of Christian Knowledge, the Society for the Propagation of the Gospel in Foreign Parts, and Dr. Bray's Associates to America and helped establish the Anglican influence. Dissenters, whether in England or America, were considered potential rebels by many Englishmen, yet they were encouraged to emigrate.[22]

The virtue and ability of the governors varied considerably. Nomination of governors was the privilege of the Secretary of State for the Southern Department and required political connections and enough money (usually at least £300) to pay the fees of the various offices through which the commission had to pass. Governors usually came from three sources: some were men long familiar with colonial problems whose appointment was in fact a promotion and recognition of service; some were former military men whose appointment was a reward; the majority, however, were Englishmen with political influence, many of whom hoped to profit from their office. While many governors worked tirelessly and effectively, cases in which the governor never came to America are not uncommon.[23]

As is often true in *Gulliver's Travels,* Swift describes the concept rather than the reality when he has Gulliver offer England as a model for colonization.[24] The design of England's colonial policy, like the early Lilliput, provides a model; the administration of the policy, however, frustrates even well-intentioned men, and the result is far from ideal. The heavy irony of "governors, who have no other views than the happiness of the people over whom they preside" concludes with the reminder that the three motives for colonization (zeal, valor, and interest)[25] are often obscured by excuses such as the colonists' wanting to join the Empire. Both Defoe and Swift cast the English as pirates and make their point by setting their stories in a fiction where avarice is readily admitted and *jure divino* a joke. That Swift makes few distinctions between Yahoos, natives, the Irish, and English settlers and that Defoe treats natives and shipwrecks as potential subjects emphasize the abuses. The leaders, like the masses they govern, share common characteristics. Ironically, the mutineers and the Houyhnhnms set Gulliver afloat, and both the cannibals and the English mutineers bring men to Crusoe's island in order to kill them. These juxtapositions make power and abuse of power synonyms and break down the barriers between civilized men and natural men.

II

Swift's writings reflect his experiences with leaders and governments specifically. His treatment of the causes of war and leaders' motives provides a good example. In *A Tale of a Tub* wars are caused by madness; revolutions and vapors rise in mad individuals:

> For, if we take a Survey of the greatest Actions that have been performed in the World, under the influence of Single Men; which are, The Establishment of New Empires by Conquest; The Advance and Progress of New Schemes in Philosophy; and the contriving as well as the propagating of New Religions: We shall find the Authors of them all, to have been Persons whose natural Reason hath admitted great Revolutions from their Dyet, their Education. . . .[26]

Swift then argues that an anal fistual explains Louis XIV's behavior and reduces Henry IV's restlessness to a frustrated sex drive, comparing him to the disappointed Bully who breaks the whore's window.

These mad men, who alarm the world and scurry about taking and losing towns, beating and being beaten, will become the subjects of systematic scrutiny in *The Conduct of the Allies*. Swift will go beyond individuals' motives (mostly mistaken or settled by circumstances) to the ministry's, factions', and England's in *The Conduct*. The movement in *A Tale* is rapid and the assertion outrageous. The credibility of the audacious statement depends upon the reader's agreement that only a singular vision excites a plan to upset peace and order in the world. Even the tone of *A Tale*, with its seeming playfulness, underlines the absurdity of the examples and the purported motives for waging war. The narrator is enjoying his diminution of motive to the madness of a single vaporous individual. The highly figurative style of *A Tale* uses fairy-tale phraseology and syntax ("A certain Great Prince raised a mighty Army, filled his Coffers with infinite Treasures, provided an invincible Fleet. . ."). The effect is to emphasize that the real world would not harbor such behavior. Even at this early date, Swift sees that such action requires things no nation has: infinite Treasure and an invincible Fleet, the stuff of fantasy. *The Tale* had begun with *"Once upon a Time,"* and Swift never completely abandons the satiric fiction aimed at exposing the delusions of men.

Each of the three excerpts on war begins with an investigation into the causes of war. The tone in each is restrained, rational, and temperately paced. The world of *A Tale* is cleverly depicted, however. It presents three pictures (one theoretical, two dramatic) of a swelling reduced by bursting. This comic and shaming ridicule of the ambitious prince suits the piece. Such a prince, swollen and bloated with his own ambition, bursts when his poison is too great to be contained. These kings, however, exist in an abstract world. Although the misery they cause is mentioned, the description is clever rather than detailed: "fright Children from their Bread and Butter; burn, lay waste, plunder, dragoon, massacre Subject and Stranger, Friend and Foe, Male and Female." The frenetic pace as well as references to "bread and butter" lessen the impact. The kings explode and disappear as Swift moves to the next form of madness.

In *The Conduct of the Allies,* the persona is a reasonable man. He sets the basic premises by which he will judge English actions and from which he will derive the proper course for England in the opening lines:

The Motives that may engage a wise Prince or State in a War, I take to be one or more of these: Either to check the overgrown Power of some ambitious Neighbor; to recover what hath been unjustly taken from Them; to revenge some Injury they have received; (which all Political Casuists allow); to assist some Ally in a just Quarrel; or lastly, to defend Themselves when They are invaded.[27]

England's motives for war are absurd when compared to the ideal, and Swift is equally audacious in stating them bluntly. He clothes the discussion, however, in formal logic. "These are the premises," he says, "upon which reasonable men act." "If this were not the motive, then surely this equally despicable one was." After enumerating the causes of war, *The Conduct* relentlessly totals up evidence, discriminates among England's motives for war and among those who argue that they believe these motives.

The content Swift chooses contributes to the change in tone between *A Tale* and *The Conduct*. In *The Conduct,* he has begun to analyze the participants in political maneuvers and identify the abuses. Where he saw madness and singularity in *A Tale,* he now sees interest and inhumanity and conniving. *The Conduct* breaks relentless summation with devastating analogies:

England's motives for making war	"make France acknowledge the late King, and to recover Hudson's Bay"
English reactions to victory	impoverished people light fires to celebrate the conquering of a new town for the Dutch to garrison
The spoils of war	rags hanging in Westminster Hall
The Queen's favorite warm cottage	"It is better to dwell in a corner of a housetop than with a brawling Woman in a wide House"
Financing the war	"maintaining a War by annually Pawning its self"
The victories of ten campaigns	"we are expiring with all sorts of good Symptoms"

The world of *The Conduct of the Allies* is a journalist's world, represented in selected portraits. For example, we see England waging a war
"where the Enemy was best able to hold us at Bay," on land. Swift points
out that England has almost nothing to gain from conquest on the
continent and would have been more effective and profited more from
exploiting their supremacy at sea. The picture of England taking a town
a year for the Dutch at a cost of six million concludes with the mock
lamentation: "It was the Kingdom's Misfortune, that the Sea was not the
Duke of Marlborough's element."

These pictures move from the reasonable causes of war to England's
motives, to the Godolphin ministry, to Marlborough, to the Allies. The
series of portraits catches individuals in poses representative of their
characters and motives. The Allies, for example, perpetually take advantage of England's good-natured, honorable Queen and blind willingness
to prosecute the war. They renege on their agreements and treat the
Queen with contempt. King Charles, for instance, refuses to pay his share
for winter maintainance, and when told the Army would starve, replies,
"Let them starve!"

The story which *The Conduct* tells does not end. The aim was to do
what propaganda is meant to do—to influence opinion—presumably to
a good or "believed in" end. Swift was employed to manipulate, and
history records his success. He watched in joy as his pamphlet was quoted
in Parliament during the debates,[28] peace became policy, and "by a false
and ungrateful reading of the past, helped to secure a satisfactory liquida-
tion of the future."[29]

A major difference exists between *A Tale* and *The Conduct*. In *A Tale,*
Swift was a clever young man. He stood at a distance and later could
remark nostalgically how brilliant he had been when he wrote it. But
when he was writing effective propaganda with the help of the men who
ruled England, Swift the man was a participant in war in a way he could
not be in *A Tale*. Whatever the consequences, and here the consequences
were real, he shared the credit and the guilt. When the Harley-
Bolingbroke ministry split apart and their hopes were in shambles
and Swift exiled to Ireland, he remembered his involvement with pride
and agony. War seen by Swift the journalist had a power beyond his
control. He could not conclude it. That he had been a participant helped
pave the way for the dramatic changes in the description of war in
Gulliver's Travels.

Each book of *Gulliver's Travels* includes a section on war. Significantly in each case, the greatest threat comes from internal factions. The Big-Endian exiles are largely responsible for the Lilliput-Blefescu War; the Brobdingnagian king finds recent English history to be "the very worst Effects that Avarice, Faction, Hypocrisy, Perfidiousness, Cruelty, Rage, Madness, Hatred, Envy, Lust, Malice, and Ambition could produce." Almost all of these qualities are more threatening when found within a nation than in its allies or enemies. Swift had assigned motives of avarice, faction, hypocrisy, perfidiousness, malice, and ambition to the principal actors in *The Conduct of the Allies*. The Laputans use their floating island to crush rebellion, mutiny, faction, and refusals to pay tribute. Nothing except the interest and distrust of his ministers keeps the king from trying to conquer the earth. Finally, the Houyhnhnms fear a Yahoo uprising. The very nature of the ordinary citizen is discontent and unrest.

Books II and IV of the *Travels* include Gulliver's descriptions of recent English history. His Houyhnhnm master asks him specifically to list the causes of war. Gulliver names the ambition of princes, the corruption of ministers, and differences of opinion, explaining that there are no "wars so furious and bloody, or of so long Continuance, as those occasioned by Difference of Opinion, especially if it be in things indifferent."

The figurative style of *A Tale* gives way to the totaling up of evidence in *The Conduct* and that in turn into the painful *reductio ad absurdum* of Gulliver's explanation to his Houyhnhnm master. The comic and shaming ridicule of the discomfited prince is far from the outraged moral intensity of Gulliver's definition of a soldier ("a Yahoo hired to kill in cold Blood as many of his own Species, who have never offended him as possibly he can"), his graphic description of war ("dying Groans, Limbs flying in the Air: Smoak, Noise, Confusion, trampling to Death under Horses' feet"), and the devastating judgments on men of the Houyhnhnm master and the Brobdingnag king. By the time Swift wrote *Gulliver's Travels,* he understood that the rules of war are thoroughly dishonorable. Gulliver, unlike the wit of *A Tale* or the rationalist of *The Conduct,* spells everything out. Chapter V of Book IV moves from Gulliver's explanation of the causes of war to his enumeration of the rules of war to the vivid description of fighting and plundering. In the first part, he reduces differences of opinion to "whether Flesh be Bread." The second depends primarily on irony, and particularly upon the discrepancy between the meaning of the word and the way the word is used:

> "It is justifiable" to enter the town of an Ally if his territory would give the country a better shape. It is a very "kingly, honourable, and frequent Practice" to kill and banish his recent ally and keep the territory they jointly conquered.

The last part uses far less figurative language, but by cataloging all of the effects of war builds to the final exaggeration:

> I had seen them blow up a Hundred Enemies at once in a Siege, and as many in a Ship; and beheld the dead Bodies drop down in Pieces from the Clouds, to the great Diversion of all the Spectators.[30]

In exaggerating the reaction of the spectators and making the result of the explosion visual, he completes the movement of the section from diminution to exaggeration and condemns Gulliver.

Mankind is petty, vicious, conniving, and cruel, not mad and not primarily deluded. Evil is not couched in fistulas or a group of ministers clinging to power but in the very reason which should light man's way to salvation. In *Gulliver's Travels,* Swift wrote,

> Plots are usually the workmanship of those Persons who desire to raise their own Characters of profound Politicians; to restore new Vigour to a crazy Administration; to stifle or divert general Discontents, to fill their Coffers with Forfeitures and raise or sink the opinion of public credit as either shall best answer their private advantage.[31]

Whatever good might be intended by those who want to restore a "crazy Administration" or "stifle Discontents" is swallowed up in "answer their private advantage." Within the nature of man, evil breeds. The Houyhnhnm speaks for Swift when he muses that the corruption of reason might be worse than brutality itself. Appropriately, Gulliver's reason is corrupted.

As narrator, Gulliver is a flexible, powerful satiric instrument and evidence of Swift's command of a variety of strategies developed in earlier writings. Charles Beaumont argues that the "degree of irony is directly proportionate to the rhetorical distance set up between the reader and the thing satirized. Swift's working through a separate character creates a greater distance" than other satiric modes.[32] For instance, the unparalleled force of *The Modest Proposal* has long been acknowledged to come from the gradual discovery of the nature of the narrator and his moral depravity compared with his stance. The way Swift has the narrator diverge completely from Swift's attitudes, illustrate and allegorize England and Ireland's behavior, and yet speak with Swift's intense pain at the situation is nearly equalled in the war passages in *Gulliver's Travels*. Here Gulliver is insensitive and blind to the implications of his words. His corruption by his nationality, by his very patriotism, appalls. He chooses England's power in order to impress and exposes an abuse of reason frightening in its wide-ranging indictment: Gulliver is corrupted into believing in and bragging about making war; war becomes the chief glory of the English nation in a time when its scientific and literary achievements were unsurpassed; the English government had spent its economic, mental, and physical resources on making war; war sets man as a species apart from all other creatures. Gulliver functions as straight man, as clear glass for all to see war as it is, and as victim of the mentality of his nation. The plain citizen of *The Conduct* who is no longer deluded and who argues passionately for his country's return to reason has become the plain citizen indistinguishable from the values and wrongs of his country. Gulliver in Book I has left Lilliput in disgust over the king's ambition. He has chuckled over the Laputans being outsmarted by the Lindalinians. In Book IV, he is, in Swift's plan, the human race's epitome.

In the first three books, Gulliver has close contact with the monarch of the islands and in the fourth, the ear of a member of the governing class. He describes England or compares England to each of the islands, but he must modify his accounts in each place for two reasons: to be understood and to be respected. In each place, Gulliver tries to present the English as clever, and his changes reflect distinctive characteristics of the island society and of England, but his descriptions also affect the reader's perception of the island societies and of England. In Lilliput, English ingenuity entertains. The immediate effect is to enhance and sharpen the conception of Lilliput, and the long-term result is to contribute to a composite picture of England. In Brobdingnag, Gulliver tries to present the Augustan ideal of "arts and arms." In order to impress his larger-than-life host, Gulliver exaggerates almost every aspect of English life. His pompous, overly optimistic words make him vulnerable to the king's questioning while they simultaneously reflect the grandeur of the Augustan dream and expose its weaknesses.

Gulliver's Boast	Exposing Evidence
Extraordinary Care always taken of their Education in Arts and Arms, to qualify them for being Counsellors to the King and Kingdom	The King asks what Methods were used to cultivate these Minds
Venerable Sages and Interpreters of the Law, presided, for determining the disputed Rights and Properties of Men, as well as for the Punishment of Vice, and Protection of Innocence	Gulliver can explain this better because he was nearly ruined in a Chancery suit
Prudent management of the Treasury	Taxes of 5 or 6 Millions a year

In Houyhnhnmland, Gulliver has a stake in showing his superiority to the Yahoos; therefore, he tries to impose his idea of Houyhnhnm values on his interpretation of his countrymen.[33] Constrained by the limitations of the Houyhnhnm vocabulary and the simplicity of their society, Gulliver resorts to simplified examples which make the English appear more callous and morally impervious. "If my Neighbour hath a mind to my cow . . ." is but one example.

Here as in Brobdingnag, Gulliver needs to exaggerate in order to swell England to the size of his auditors. The Houyhnhnms are not only physically larger but morally superior. Gulliver tries to make Englishmen, too, larger than life, and Swift has prepared a means of measuring as clever as the dwarf in Brobdingnag. The horses have no word for "lie," the "thing which was not." The eighteenth-century reader would remember Lycurgus, the Spartan ruler who would not make a law against parricide because he would not allow the possibility that any of his citizens were so evil as to commit such a crime. Defoe, in *The Validity of the Renunciations of Former Powers* (a tract Swift must have read when it was published in 1712) asserts that Lycurgus' action "put a greater Brand of Infamy upon the Crime than he could possibly have done, by making the severest Law against it imaginable."[34] Gulliver ironically must demonstrate English superiority by putting a "favorable coloring" on his narrative.[35] Not only does he falsify in this way, but he discovers lies to be integral to occupation after occupation. Men are bred up to lie, to make law confute truth, to tutor others in lying. By judging and describing men as he believes the Houyhnhnms would, he loses perspective and misrepresents England. He hopes to show that he comes from a society superior to the Yahoos and that he himself is superior to mankind. He becomes, then, the epitome of what his narrative builds up to condemning: the self-serving court hanger-on who perjures himself for favor. Appropriately, he assigns himself membership in his species and, incidentally, makes a mockery of Lycurgus' optimism.

III

Swift was especially caustic when he observed how groups created leaders and initiated rules. One way of looking at *A Tale of a Tub* is as the document of a society with its own heroes and rulers, ironically exposing its faults while purporting to parade its strengths. Swift criticizes the modern's society (fashionable London) by isolating facets of it and presenting them as separate and independent subcultures in contrast to and against the background of rational existence. Distinguished by Swift's clear disapproval and the society's difference from sensible times, one fashionable society after another is dissected and ruthlessly satirized. For example, fashionable men write out of contempt for learning. They ignore the tradition of high demands on writers described by Horace and by Englishmen such as Jonson, and write when they are unfit for company or pressed for pennies. Other fashionable men buy and quote these books. The *Tale*'s bookseller, we recall, intends to whisper that the book was written by D'Urfey or Congreve or whoever has just had a successful play. The modern writer buys these books and often composes by pasting sentences from them into his own paragraphs.

Swift is illustrating every abuse about which he says the learned complain and, at the same time, exposing and satirizing what should be reformed. He intentionally avoids conventional organization, plot, and theme; although there are recurring ideas and even characters, the point is that the writer can fill pages and pages without resorting to content as usually defined. The modern book encompasses fable, digressions, puffy introductions, prefaces, and dedications, self-praise,

unacknowledged quotations, italicized words, and false claims. The metaphor of horse running away with rider fits the author as well as mankind
in general. "I have thought fit," the author explains, "to make *Invention*
the *Master,* and give *Method* and *Reason,* the Office of its Lacquays." With
invention as the highest value, the modern feels comfortable with his
lack of method. He can pat himself on the back for the ways he expands
his book, "a Circumstance by no means to be neglected by a skillful
Writer," and he can compose when he has nothing better to do on rainy
days and sleepy Sundays, during drunken vigils, and when afflicted by
headaches or debts.[36] His product, then, is ideally suited to his temperament and his time. The modern writer has energy without direction and
confidence without talent.

The demand for fashion leads to the corruption of religion. Peter, Jack,
and Martin ruin their coats in order to avoid ridicule. They must learn
to conform:

> On their first Appearance, our three Adventurers met with a very bad Reception;
> and soon with great Sagacity guessing out the Reason, they quickly began to
> improve in the good Qualities of the Town: They Writ, and Raillyed, and
> Rhymed, and Sung, and Said, and said Nothing; They Drank, and Fought, and
> Whor'd, and Slept, and Swore, and took Snuff. . . .[37]

The penalties for ignoring fashion include embarrassing mistakes and
humiliations. They are mistaken for vulgar people and denied everything from ale to female company. Later Lord Munodi in Book III of
Gulliver's Travels will lament the same forces which dictate a choice
between conformity and persecution as an eccentric.

The modern revels in his mastery of the rules, in his success, and in
his freedom from the onerous demands of earlier moral and cultural
codes. The joy he feels in his mastery of the subgenre, "preface," is a good
example. Fielding, obviously a close reader of the *Tale,* recognized the
anatomy of the prefatorical style.[38] Using words and phrases from hundreds
of empty prefaces, the writer asks for support, praises the addressee for
predictable virtues, apologizes for writing at all, describes fears and
hopes, and hints that there are profound ideas hidden in the work. The
use of capitalized abstractions, italics, and convoluted sentences is
especially important. The preface writer must accomplish several apparently exclusive tasks: on the one hand, he must, according to convention,
insist that he writes at the urging of great men and because of the

applause of "the world"; on the other hand, he asserts his hopes and fears and insists upon the recent birth of his creation. At one point, he insists he is the universe's secretary,[39] yet he must plead his unworthiness while praising himself.

Swift's dedication to Lord Somers is one of the first playful contrasts to the modern method exhibited in the *Tale*. While apparently practicing the craft of the modern, he actually does something quite original as he fulfills the traditional purposes of dedications. The dedication begins with a mock, modest comparison to the Author's dedication which turns the satire against modern writers, booksellers, and conventional prefaces. By relying on the techniques of his early panegyrics and his later poems to Stella, Swift uses and comments upon the conventions of praise and, thereby, asserts the superiority of his subject. The much-named virtues are empty from overuse and taken for granted by those who know Somers, he says; therefore, nothing can be gained by using them. Swift can, however, praise Somers's patience (and, thereby, his modesty) in listening to so many formulaic dedications. That Somers's enemies, other eager patrons, and readers of the dedication recognize him as the epitome of the composite preface written by hacks becomes a biting indictment of a subgenre and a genuine tribute to Somers. Swift manages to expose and invert the conventions in order to praise.

The address to the critics also follows conventions while exposing them. The empty allusions which imply learning rather than demonstrating it, the arrogant tone of confidence, and the transparently hypocritical deference label the writer as a "modern." Swift again explains the rules of a group in order to show their deviation from sense. The modern classifies critics so astutely that he describes the true function of a good critic and censures modern practice. The first type, the critic who identifies and praises excellence, and the second, the critic who is a scholar intent upon preserving ancient learning, have disappeared. Modern critics, descended from the critics of Horace and Homer, exist to point out faults, not excellence. These critics are like rats, wasps, and dogs. The maxims for critics emphasize their lack of reflection, their foolish inconsistency, their sycophancy, and their lack of vision. His conclusion, written in a tone of glib goodwill, suggests membership in their ranks.

Swift treats other groups in *A Tale of a Tub* and his other works similarly. For example, lawyers in *Gulliver's Travels* are distinguishable from other groups by their code of behavior: "I said there was a Society of Men among us, bred up from their Youth in the Art of proving by Words multiplied for the Purpose that *White* is *Black,* and *Black* is *White,* according as they are paid."

Using Locke's example of the drastic misuse of language, Swift begins with the primary characteristic for members of the society, refusal to tell the truth. This society adheres to rigid rules: preferring falsehood, following precedent, attending to circumstances rather than the case, and submitting to power. In the brief description of lawyers in Chapter V of Book IV, Swift catalogues the abuses which still thwart justice in every civilized nation. In arguing to win, lawyers disregard truth, and since truth and probability may appear quite different, the liar has the advantage. Like the moderns, the lawyers have invented their own language which "no other Mortal can understand, and wherein all their Laws are written." This language makes them essential to anyone with legal problems and allows them to disguise truth even further. They, like the moderns, relish their language, and it is one of the badges of membership.

The good societies in *Gulliver's Travels* do not present an ideal but rather show satiric contrasts to these small groups which have established their own customs and leaders. Brobdingnag, as we recall, has diseases, beggars, beheadings, and a history of civil wars. When Swift does want to remind his readers of the norm, he does so in straightforward prose:

> In the School of political Projectors I was but ill entertained. . . . These unhappy People were proposing Schemes for persuading Monarchs to chuse Favourites upon the Score of their Wisdom, Capacity and Virtue; of teaching Ministers to consult the publick Good; of rewarding Merit, great Abilities, and eminent Services; of instructing Princes to know their true Interest, by placing it on the same Foundation with that of their People: of chusing for Employments Persons qualified to exercise them; with many other wild impossible Chimaeras, that never entered before into the Heart of Man to conceive. . . .[40]

This passage, reminiscent of the "let no man talk to me of other Expedients" section of *A Modest Proposal,* lists the ideal means of governing.

IV

Defoe analyzed, wrote about, and even influenced government throughout most of his adult life. His opposition to Sir Humphrey Mackworth's

Workhouse Bill has been judged "totally successful," [41] his work for the Scottish Union, the Harley ministry, and as an ameliorating voice for Mist's *Weekly Journal* are but a few examples of his effectiveness. When he laid aside his expository tools for his fictional ones, he could be very creative indeed. The 1705 *Consolidator*'s Lunarians satirize party controversies as delightfully as Swift's Big-Endians, and *Reasons against the Succession of the House of Hanover* (1713) begins with an idiomatic speaker lamenting the "pother" over Anne's successor when she may "linger out Twenty or Thirty Years, and not be a Huge Old Wife neither." Many of Defoe's "projects" such as those for settling the Palatine refugees and the poor have dramatizations in his novels. And his concern to present the benefits of various forms of government as well as the difficulties of attaining personal autonomy in a society of institutions hostile to change finds expression through narratives about government and leaders as they appear in *Robinson Crusoe, Captain Singleton, Journal of the Plague Year,* and *The General History of the Pirates.* Underlying his fictional creations of society and their governments is his belief in man's need for government and order coupled with the conviction that a single, strong, exemplary ruler is most efficacious.

As Maxmillian E. Novak has demonstrated, Defoe consistently described ungoverned man as brutal, subject to his passion and his fears.[42] Ascribing to the principle that

> Society to Regulation tends,
> As naturally as Means pursue their Ends;
> The Wit of Man could never yet invent
> A Way of Life without a Government[43]

throughout his works, Defoe argues that government is necessary for men to live securely and happily. In fact, government is synonymous with society and order for Defoe. Without it, the individual is miserable and nothing is accomplished.

So great is Robinson Crusoe's need for a society that he fashions one out of his dog, parrot, cats, and goats.[44] He becomes part of a system which he has modified and adapted to while remaining distinct from the environment itself, and his thoughts and behavior have made the island a society even before Friday arrives. Rather than creating a society after Friday and the others come, he fits them into the society he has already conceived and created. He embodies Locke's theory that man's need for

order will drive him to set up rules which will imitate natural and moral
law in a way that gives man security and a sense of harmony with his
surroundings. As Novak has pointed out in *Defoe and the Nature of Man*,
Defoe incorporates the philosophical contexts of his time throughout
Robinson Crusoe.

Crusoe makes up schedules and rules in an attempt to impose order.
Even alone, he sets up laws for himself. He designates jobs for the hours
of the day and marks off the days. When Friday, Friday's father, and the
Spaniard enlarge the colony, Crusoe sees himself as "absolute lord and
lawgiver" and always refers to them as "his subjects." He boasts that any
of his settlers would die for him and that he allows liberty of conscience.
Almost at once, he hands down the most basic law in an absolute
monarchy:

> I gave him [the Spaniard] a strict charge in writing, not to bring any man with
> him who would not first swear in the presence of himself and of the old savage
> that he would in no way injure, fight with, or attack the person he should find
> in the island, who was so kind to send for them in order to their deliverance; but
> that they would stand by and defend him against all such attempts, and, wherever
> they went, would be entirely under and subjected to his commands; and that this
> should be put in writing, and signed with their hands.[45]

Crusoe's society becomes stratified early. He makes Friday a slave and
teaches him to say, "Master." Like the American slaveowners, he imposes a new name and new clothes. When Friday's father and the
Spaniard come, the colony is further stratified. The Spaniard becomes
prime minister-overseer, negotiating treaties with future settlers, plan-
ning extra provisions, directing the work of Friday and his father. The
Spaniard is allowed, as Friday never is, to make suggestions, and some
are adopted. In Crusoe's absence, he is governor of the colony.

When Crusoe makes rules for the sailors in danger from the mutineers, he again reveals his deep distrust of men and the basic premise of
his government:

> That while you stay on this island with me, you will not pretend to any authority
> here; and if I put arms into your hands, you will upon all occasions give them
> up to me, and do no prejudice to me or mine upon this island, and in the mean
> time be govern'd by my orders.[46]

He naively insists on complete control of the *weapons* as well as the men. His faith in contracts and promises seems strange when set beside his fear and suspicion of mankind whom he characterizes as ravenous and ungrateful.[47] In 1700, Defoe makes the same point in his own voice in *The Two Great Questions Consider'd*:

> I question whether it be in the Humane Nature to set Bounds to its own Ambition, and whether the best Man on Earth wou'd not be King over all the rest if he could. Every King in the World would be the Universal Monarch if he might, and nothing restrains but the Power of Neighbours; and if one Neighbour is not strong enough for another, he gets another Neighbour to join with him and all the little ones will join to keep the great one from suppressing them. (p. 10)

The men Crusoe fears as ravenous, however, are never part of *his* society and, therefore, owe none of the obligations and receive none of the benefits which bind Friday and the others to him. Throughout his writings, Defoe contrasts the orderly, peaceful societies which could be rich, powerful, and happy with the strife-ridden groups described as like a "raging *Bedlam,* where every (*Lunatick*) Inhabitant is separated from the rest to prevent them from Devouring and Destroying one another; A Great Forrest where the Inhabitants are all Beasts of Prey, the stronger Hunting after the Weaker, the Greater falling upon the Less."[48] Defoe joins with Hobbes and Locke to say that the lack of order and government transforms the world into a jungle and, rather than working together, men without government will be fearful and separated. Man without a well-governed society exists in an anxious state of mind and lacks all hope of progress. He must fortify rather than improve his possessions. Defoe consistently argues that the fundamental purpose of government is to protect property; the Spaniard voices the common opinion, "For all laws and all governors were to preserve society, and those who were dangerous to the society ought to be expelled out of it."

The isolated societies in these works provide an ideal ground for the analysis of the forces pushing men into groups and the relationship between the personality of the leader and the nature of the society formed. In these societies, tension exists because the unstructured situation encourages men's tendency to avoid restraint while the threat to their safety increases their dependence. The conflict, then, finds man's desire for liberty, coupled with the absence of existing laws and customs, opposed to the necessity for respect and harmony which often requires

legislation.[49] In short, Defoe understands that the nature of man determines both a demand for freedom and a weakness and passion requiring
constraint. In his works, we see the working out of Herodotus' idea that
monarchies tended toward tyranny and democracies toward mob rule.
The constitutional states of Aristotle's *Politics* and Plato's *Statesman* could
easily become their perverted ones; these states would then be directed
not at the good of all but the good of the rulers.

Point Desperation in *Captain Singleton* illustrates the competing tendencies in human nature and government. As in the other island societies,
the group's survival is threatened to the extent that there are great
pressures on the members of the community to get along with each other,
and, yet, they are so far removed from English society that none of
England's laws or customs impose on them even peripherally. To a large
extent, they can choose which pieces of civilization's baggage they will
carry with them.

Singleton's rise as a leader can occur because of the special needs of
the group and the unstructured situation. Cast out with the group of
mutineers, he is young and very much a minor member of the crew and
simply remarks that

> . . . the first thing we did was to give every one his hand that we would not separate
> one from another upon any occasion whatsoever, but that we would live and die
> together; that we would kill no food, but that we would distribute it in public;
> and that we would be in all things guided by the majority. . . . that we would
> appoint a captain among us to be our governor and leader during pleasure. . . . but
> the captain was not to act in any particular thing without advice of the rest, and
> by the majority.[50]

Having established a kind of socialism which prevents wealth and in-
equality, and, therefore, a major cause of dissension, the men choose a
democracy as their form of government; again the choice is the one most
likely to prevent division. All men have a voice, the majority rules; the
captain is leader "during pleasure" and each of the men, in theory, will
have a chance to be captain.[51] The terms of the contract between the
leader and the men are carefully stated. Survival is absolutely dependent
on unity both because of their numbers and their skills.[52]

Once the government is established, the men can begin to secure the
immediate needs of the new colony. Until then, the society can accomplish little; for example, there are no huts, there is no plan of action until

a leader is appointed in *Captain Singleton*, and the danger of a literally mortal division shadows each society. In Libertalia, for instance, when the men get ready to settle an argument with force, every leader realizes the consequences and stops it. Jack mentions with great fear the possibility of a slave uprising. All of the societies assume that there must be a great deal of work done and that the leader should direct and divide it according to the abilities of the community members. In all of the societies, stability and survival are the first priorities, and leadership and rules must establish order and direction.

The men divide the work equally and according to their skills, and this arrangement continues throughout the existence of the society; men who fail to do their share are ostracized. As Crusoe's first concern was fortification so is theirs. The camp that the mutineers build on Point Desperation is very much like Robinson Crusoe's. The mutineers choose a place under the shelter of a hill near water, protected from the sun. They set their huts in a well-fortified semicircle, and build a lodge much like the one in *Journal of the Plague Year*.[53] At a later camp, after building their huts, Singleton's men erect an irregular barricade of sharpened stakes over which no animal can leap. They construct a maze-like entrance so no animal larger than a dog can maneuver it.

Danger is so imminent and necessity so pressing that most decisions obviate debate and, therefore, another cause of dissension fails to materialize. Captain Misson's colony in *The General History* organizes in a different way and under contrasting circumstances.[54] Misson has the permission and assistance of the Queen of Johanna to build his colony so that he and his men can live and die in peace and security. With such a purpose, it is fitting that Misson begins with the rule that the men are to be called "Liberi," "desiring that in that might be drowned the distinguishing names of French, Dutch, Africans, etc."[55]

After that auspicious beginning the men build two forts. Besides the fact that this building is evidence of their lurid, threatening past, it testifies to the pervasive feeling in most Defoe novels that the present is *never* secure;[56] at any time a sudden calamity can shake years of quiet and virtuous living. Once the guns are mounted and a battery raised, the men turn to building houses and enclosing fields and pastures, well protected by their forts and ships. Coming with the Queen's approval, Misson has no need for food or clothes at the moment, and he can live on the ship. He has established Libertalia for security, and the military security of the colony is his first concern. Regardless of the protection provided by the Queen, Misson, like Singleton, is more concerned with fortification than with comfort.

From the beginning, Misson's colony is different in its idealistic and humanitarian philosophy; and in that difference Misson and Lieutenant Caraccioli stand alone. The hunters entertain the natives as equals, give them valuable gifts such as axes rather than cheap trinkets, and carefully return them to their villages. When slaves are captured on a pirate expedition, Misson's men order their irons taken off and treat them as free people. The Negroes are even taught seamanship and French; ships are manned with equal numbers of blacks and whites.

The colony cannot continue in this way, however. First, two released prisoners guide Portuguese ships to attack Libertalia, and then the settlers begin to quarrel among themselves. Law and punishment evolve out of necessity. The men agree that "where there were no coercive laws, the weakest would always be the sufferer, and everything must tend to confusion." The form of government which they develop is a kind of democratic socialism on a Greek model.[57] The men group themselves in tens and choose a representative to the assembly headed by an elected governor, or "Conservator," Misson. Misson may call the assembly at any time and must convene it at least annually.[58] All of the cattle and treasure are equally divided with complete disregard for race or previous status. Men rise by industry, ability, and integrity, and the colony thrives for a while with a Council formed of such men who make the ideal "one out of many."

Indeed, Libertalia bears striking similarities to Point Desperation. The form of government and of the organization of tasks and responsibilities, for example, is nearly alike in each. But Misson's colony is utterly razed; its end is unique among Defoe's small societies. The Negroes whom Misson and his men have treated with kindness sweep down from the hills and slaughter the Liberi. Perhaps the ungainly size of the colony makes this inevitable; these Negroes may never have felt part of the society at all; in any event, Defoe probably feared that faction was the nature of man. Furthermore, when compared to Singleton or Crusoe, Misson seems remote from the men. In Libertalia, the men feel none of the constant anxiety that Crusoe and his men do because of the cannibals; the colony is too large for each man to be bound by gratitude; in fact, we know from the beginning that few men share Misson's ideals and goals. When Misson insists on equality, he keeps the colony from becoming sufficiently structured to insure control (in contrast to the stratification of Colonel Jack's plantation slave system or the other settlement on Madagascar organized by twenty-four of Tew's men and based on slave economy), and he fails to bind the entire group of native Negroes to him by gratitude or fear, a strategy which Defoe seems to suggest is essential in the cohesion of a society.

In Crusoe's society, then, laws are made for security just as they are in Libertalia and in Captain Singleton's expedition. Misson's laws, however, are democratic and aimed at preventing fighting and protecting the weak while Crusoe's objective is personal safety and the maintenance of his supremacy. In Libertalia, government and laws insure equality and justice; on Crusoe's island, they are totalitarian, directed toward a class-oriented division of work. Captain Singleton's society begins as democratically for the white men as Misson's, but Point Desperation and the nomadic society in *Singleton* are founded on necessity rather than on idealism. Rebellion and faction would mean the group would not be secure ecologically or militarily and, therefore, never have the chance to develop under such alert leaders as Singleton and Crusoe. It would seem that the extent to which the central character feels threatened determines how democratic the society becomes. Crusoe is afraid to the point that he feels his reason is affected; therefore, his government is totalitarian. Singleton and his men are more desperate than frightened; time after time, they remark that they can do nothing but the most outrageous thing: try piracy, cross Africa on foot. At the other end of the spectrum is Misson who feels most confident and trusting. The parallels between the attitude of the leader and the type of government established anticipate Montesquieu's *Esprit des lois* (1748) which would derive from a comparative study of governments the theory that the structure and function of government is dependent upon the conditions of the people.

V

One of Bunyan's rare specific references to the influence of earthly governments occurs in Part II of *Pilgrim's Progress*. Christina's journey is easier because she has undertaken her trip in "different times." Bunyan's characters are subjects of heaven's government, and earthly politics encroach upon the protagonist's consciousness only when they stand in his way. "The world is therefore in our hand, and disposed by our doctrine, by our faith and prayers, although they think far otherwise, and shall one day feel their judgments are according," Bunyan explains in *An Exposition of the First Ten Chapters of Genesis,*[59] and his tracts reveal a complex mix of other-worldliness, resentment, and practical restraint. William York Tindall concludes that Bunyan "cherished a deep and natural hatred of both king and government" which he expressed freely through allegory and biblical exegesis.[60]

The combination of allegory, fiction-like narrative, and social criticism gives Vanity Fair depth and impact beyond the power of most contemporary allegories.[61] Vanity has the only organized government in *Pilgrim's Progress.*[62] Most of the townspeople reflect the character of "the great one of the fair," and the fair has been designed by Beelzebub, Apollyon, and Legion to cater to the corrupt tastes of Englishmen:

> houses, lands, trades, pleasures, and delights of all sorts, as whores, bawds, wives, husbands, children, masters, servants, lives, blood, bodies, souls, silver, gold, pearls, precious stones, and what not.[63]

Not only does this catalogue expose materialistic values but also the town's equating of whores, wives, and souls with silver. The pilgrims contrast so completely to the townspeople that conflict is inevitable.

Biblical allegory provides the language for criticism of the inhabitants of Vanity.[64] The townspeople label the pilgrims just as Christians in any heathen society are labeled: first as fools, then as madmen, and finally as foreigners. The idea that the pilgrims are citizens of another kingdom is reinforced by their incomprehensible speech, "the language of Canaan." When the pilgrims reject the Fair's goods, the townspeople conclude that if the pilgrims are not mad then surely they are dangerous troublemakers. They handle Christian and Faithful roughly, see them chained, incarcerated, and indicted for sedition.

Faithful's trial explains Christian doctrine, delineates the conflict between the pilgrims and the townspeople, and satirizes aspects of the English legal system. Faithful admits he has won a party of followers, but he insists that they were won by beholding truth and innocence.[65] He admits defying the king of Vanity Fair but excuses himself because of the all-important claim his quest exerts and the difference between stirring up factions and providing an example for a godly life which may create divisions spontaneously. Such a distinction, however, has no meaning in Vanity Fair. His accusers, ironically, describe him accurately; he does not, for example, regard "prince nor people, law nor custom." Envy, Superstition, and Pickthank give testimony entirely based on hearsay, character assassination, and difference of opinion, but they are describing correctly the danger Faithful represents to society. Faithful's answers develop the distinction between inciting rebellion and refusing to conform and make the state of war between the godly and the worldly clear. He is stating Bunyan's position, and, therefore, participating in the debate over the lawful power of the state and the rights of citizens.[66] Bunyan, while insisting upon truth, also advocates discretion.[67] Faithful and Christian represent two ways the pilgrim can be persecuted, and Faithful cannot be truthful and escape.

In instructing the jury to convict Faithful, the judge cites precedents (Pharoah, Nebuchadnezzar, and Darius)—all tyrants who killed God's people and made laws to silence men like Faithful. The judge is correct to align Faithful with Daniel and Moses; here Bunyan candidly reminds the reader that the Christian is a potential anarchist while showing Vanity's citizens exaggerate the threat the pilgrims pose and, thereby, pass a sentence which is unjust, tyrannical, and paranoid. The jury condemns Faithful to the most cruel death it can contrive because it hates him. Faithful has not been tried objectively or convicted on evidence, but rather destroyed because he represents an intolerable alternative to the life of Vanity Fair. The mob, the witnesses, the judge, and the jury demonstrate the danger of Vanity Fair. The wares for sale are not harmless baubles but corruption, hardening their buyers and sellers to truth and tolerance.

The government of exemplary small groups in Bunyan's works prefigures heavenly order. Everyone defers to the morally superior, and he leads effortlessly. Their tranquillity and submission to what Bunyan calls "nature" and reason provide rest for the pilgrim and prepare him for Heaven. The law of nature in The Life and Death of Mr. Badman, Mr. Wiseman explains, "Do unto all men even as ye would that they should do unto you." Similarly, fraud and deceit are "odious to reason, and conscience, and contrary to the law of nature" and drunkenness is a violation of man's nature.

Here Bunyan is close to the Thomistic position that natural law reveals man's paramount duties to God.[68] All men recognize the precepts of the Law of Nature as good and require no persuasion. The opposing conceptions of the law of nature, well established by the fifth century, that justice and good are inherent in man and that man is egoistic, found expression in peculiar ways in religious writings. Many men, like Bunyan, saw no contradiction in the existence of the instinctively recognizable Law of Nature and the nature of man which was evil and required grace to change.[69] Bunyan can write,

> There is uncleanness and pride, I know not of any two gross sins that stick closer to men than they. They have, as I may call it, an interest in nature; it likes them because they most suit its lusts and fancies. . . .[70]

Participation in, in fact, submission to, moral governments becomes a sign in itself of election. Members are joined by common aspirations, common inquiries and their alienation from secular societies. Gaius' inn illustrates most of the characteristics of such a society. Only Christian conversation interrupts the tranquillity and devotion to duty. They recognize the wisdom of Gaius' advice to marry and increase the number of Christians on earth as readily as they solve each other's riddles. They enjoy recounting pilgrims' adventures and manage to convey a sense of well-being and community. Many of the simple domestic pleasures of Bunyan's time serve as the bridge between allegory and the world of the reader. Nuts and apples, riddles, tales of giants and heroes, songs, fireside conversation, and harmonious company create a domestic scene reminiscent of Goldsmith's *Vicar of Wakefield*.

Bunyan's portrayals of earthly government illumine three convictions which he, Swift, and Defoe share. The group itself, the society to which the individual believes he belongs, colors his perception of himself and determines the degree of security he feels. This essential relationship between individual and society assures that the society will influence his behavior. Furthermore, a dynamic relationship exists between an ethical system and the laws the society devises to institutionalize the ethical system. Bunyan sees his religious beliefs more in conflict with societal lawmaking than in harmony and, at the other end of the scale, Swift believes the church's and constitution's will should be all but indistinguishable. Unlike most of their contemporaries, however, none believes that the society's influence is primarily benign, and all are perceptive critics of the travesty of interpretation public policy has become. Rather than being correctives to human depravity, social institutions appear to them to be contributors and reflections of the evil in human nature.

In Vanity Fair, Faithful is executed and Christian is expelled. Defoe wrote,

> To expel men from the Society of a Party or Body of People is the highest executive part of Power any body of People have; all Punishment besides, are inferior to it.
>
> 'Tis the like in Sacred Power, where Excommunication is the severest Censure; and is exprest by casting out a Person from the Society of Christians.

He goes on to explain that the death penalty expels men from the world as unfit for human society, and that banishments are a natural action, similar to the way a person vomits to discharge offensive matter.[71] Expulsion from society is far more common than the death penalty in the works of Swift and Defoe both for artistic reasons and because of the conviction that no man has the power of death over another.[72]

The roots of this punishment are very old. Man was a social and dependent being to the eighteenth-century thinker. Banishment had been the punishment of Cain. Adam, alone in the Garden, was lacking something essential, and Eve was created to make things right. The covenant relationship and the concept of the people of God seemed natural and appropriate; man excluded from the community was depicted as suffering, miserable, wandering. Political theorists from Plato through Locke had pointed out that the community was a mutually beneficial unit with the best chance of producing a good society. Isolated men lived in a state of want and pathological anxiety.[73] The fear of banishment, then, would be a powerful deterrant in a community already cut off from the security of eighteenth-century England and the mark of a man who violated the laws of God and nature. The more threatened the society feels, the more likely it is to try to remove, to obliterate the threat entirely.

Whenever we see the governed come in direct contact with the leader and laws, we are more likely to see the ways the institution can be corrupted and the shadow of an ethical system existing independent of the laws than we are to see a wretch deservedly ousted from a good society. Frightening as banishment and punishment are, they often reveal the way the individual is alienated from society and a legal system divorced from the ideal it was to symbolize.

As allegorical and didactic as Faithful's trial is, Bunyan still criticizes some current English practices satirized later by Swift and Defoe. Vanity's witnesses and jury are of dubious character and obviously operate more for vested interests than justice. The judge has already condemned Faithful and wields absolute power in his court room. Douglas Hay describes the necessity for paying witnesses to appear and the strong influence of prevailing opinion on the jury's decision.[74] Judges ruled their courtrooms in arbitrary and often lordly fashion and made flamboyant speeches much as Hateful does. At Chelmsford a Chief Justice pressured a jury which had found an infanticide insane into finding her guilty, then paradoxically wept as he sentenced her.[75] Faithful, like most of those tried in England at this time, is allowed to speak as a special favor, but his words are largely ignored.

Gulliver's Travels includes several satires of trials. Gulliver feels fairly confident about answering questions because he was "almost ruined by a long Suit in Chancery," which he won, but with costs. The series of questions that the Brobdingnag king asks catalogues the problems in the English legal system. The brevity of investigation,[76] the freedom to plead unjust cause, and the influence of religion and politics remind the reader of Bunyan's description. Furthermore, the king wonders if "precedent" might be used in contradictory ways. In his account to the Houyhnhnm, Gulliver complains that men may not speak for themselves. Fielding's works make many of the same points. In *Tom Jones,* Partridge interrupts the Man of the Hill to tell the story of the stolen horse and observes, "One thing I own I thought a little hard, that the Prisoner's Counsel was not suffered to speak for him. . . . ." Swift makes the point that a special language, incomprehensible to the uninitiated, prevents ordinary men from participating. Hay argues convincingly that the nomenclature of the court was part of its impressive mystique and designed to enhance the court's authority.[77] Gulliver also explains that judges sound those in power and decide very quickly upon the guilt or innocence of the prisoner.

Defoe offers far more extensive critiques of the English legal machinery. In the 1691 *An Account of the Late Horrid Conspiracy,* he wrote

> Were this an Age like such as we have seen which would not bear *Truth,* and at the Tryals such as wou'd force any one who saw or read 'em to wonder how so many *Mad-men* broke out of Bedlam, and got possession of the *Bench* . . . then a true Account of matter of fact . . . from a private hand might be both necessary

and grateful. But now all things have been managed as becomes a *Court of Justice*, not as formerly with the *Decency of a Bear-garden*.[78]

His early opinions of improving conditions (politic language admitted) appear to change; by 1714, he could write, "It is not uncommon to observe some unhappy Offenders voted to the most severe and ignominious Punishments, whilst others, that have been their Associates, are placed in Stations of the greatest Honour and Trust." [79] Moll Flanders' trial, for example, is presided over by a judge who already believes her guilty, depends upon suspect witnesses, and convicts her on circumstantial evidence. Moll's pleading is ignored, and the entire trial and sentencing is over quickly. Both Defoe and Bunyan abbreviate the usual moralistic speeches by judges, but they leave the condemning of criminals until the end of the Sessions.

The life of Anstis in *A General History of the Pirates* contains an extended satire of a trial. Among the diversions of the crew is holding mock trials. The judge (yesterday's criminal) sits in a tree wearing a dirty tarpaulin, tarred yarn cap, and large eyeglasses while the Attorney General argues, "For if the fellow should be suffered to speak, he may clear himself, and that's an affront to the Court." Blackstone and Hogarth both show the judge still attired in heavy scarlet robes and seventeenth-century style wigs. The judge still put on a black cap to pronounce the death sentence.[80] Defoe's perceptive description of the archaic signs of office intended to command respect seem even more ironic in the "judge's" caustic remarks about the legal system:

PRISONER: Pray, My Lord, I hope your Lordship will consider—
JUDGE: Consider! How dare you talk of considering? Sirrah, Sirrah, I never considered in all my life. I'll make it treason to consider.
PRISONER: But I hope your lordship will hear some reason.
JUDGE: D'ye hear how the scoundrel prates? What have we to do with reason? I'd have you know, rascal, we don't sit here to hear reason; we go according to the Law. Is our dinner ready?
ATTORNEY-GENERAL: Yes, my Lord.
JUDGE: Then, heark'ee, you rascal at the bar, hear me, Sirrah, hear me. You must suffer for three reasons: first, because it is not fit I should sit here as judge and nobody be hanged; secondly, you must be hanged because you have a damned hanging look; and thirdly, you must be hanged because I am hungry; for know, Sirrah, that 'tis a custom that whenever a judge's dinner is ready before the trial is over, the prisoner is to be hanged of course. There's Law for you, ye dag! Take him away, gaoler.[81]

In this passage, the prisoner clearly acts as straightman allowing the heavy-handed satiric thrusts which assert that law ignores reason and considers according to convenience. Unfortunately Defoe was not merely embittered; Fielding also mentions a man jailed for "looking like a rogue." The judge finds Captain Jack a likely candidate for hanging largely because of his appearance.[82] The long speeches by judges often described the criminal at great length and were intended to warn the common people. Defoe provides a model in *The General History*. The exemplary Captain Tew allows the traitorous ex-prisoners a trial with witnesses and time to be confessed and absolved by a chaplain of their own faith. He makes clear that "Their blood is on their own heads" because their perjury and ingratitude made them Libertalia's "avowed and obliged enemy."

Slavery, a topic both Swift and Defoe consider, provides another social form that exerts pressure on the governed and the governing. Although slaves do the work of society and know and are subject to its laws and customs, they are excluded from the kinds of participation which we recognize as "belonging." The effects of slavery and the ways men enforce it have implications for the philosophy and ethics of the larger society.

Slavery appears to be necessary for successful colonization in most of Defoe's works.[83] Captain Singleton convinces his cronies that slaves are needed to carry baggage, talk to other natives, and act as guides on the proposed trip across Africa. Singleton, like Colonel Jack, arouses a combination of superstition and gratitude to master them. He discovers a prince among the wounded and by having him healed, persuades the natives that the whites can kill or heal at will just as Mouchat in *Colonel Jack* is convinced that the remote and somewhat mysterious Great Master can have slaves killed or forgiven on command. The prince, like Mouchat, is an extraordinary man. Both are bound by gratitude in a way that ennobles and establishes them as admirable characters. "Never was a Christian more punctual to an oath than he was to this for he was a sworn servant to us for many a weary month after that," Singleton praises him.[84] In the same way that Robinson Crusoe taught Friday "yes," "no," and the rudiments of language, the prince is taught. The other slaves are bound by their prince's life, and a few other promises such as protection from lions. Mouchat, too, was to have been a tempering and controlling model for Jack's other slaves.

Swift offers two parallels to Defoe's study of slavery. The Yahoos and the Irish, as Anne Cline Kelly has pointed out, bear many resemblances to slaves.[85] The Yahoos exhibit the characteristics often ascribed to turn-of-the-century Negro slaves and to the poorest Irish.[86] They grovel, they sneak, they steal, and they are almost unteachable. In addition, they are unusually ungrateful and cannot be trusted. Their groveling is recognized as hypocritical and their violent tendencies can turn on each other as well as on the master. Many of these characteristics were assigned to "savages" whether they were slaves or not. The Yahoos show the results of poverty and bondage.[87] They are dirty, greedy, uncultured, and resentful. They must be driven to work, and, left to themselves, spend their time foraging or brooding. They imitate their captors in the most appalling ways. In the violence they practice on each other, in wanting to eat what the horses eat, and in establishing their own stratification system, they show the corrupting influence of slavery. Like Negro slaves, the Yahoos manage to retain vestiges of their own customs. Until Gulliver comes, presumably the "missing link" between the original colonists and the Yahoos, these practices have been incomprehensible to the horses.[88] The prizing of blue stones and the courtship ritual suggest the corruption of their heritage. So debased are they that they too have forgotten the reason for their actions.

The Irish in the Drapier papers, like the Yahoos and the Aeolists, are both victims and participants in their own oppression. Swift sees a number of problems: the exorbitant power England exerts over the Irish, the submissive behavior of the Irish, and the recalcitrant nature of mankind. For this reason, the Drapier papers repeatedly remind the Irish of their rights, recall incidents when they acted against their own best interests, and urge dignified resistance. Perceptively Swift recognizes that "A People long used to Hardships, lose by Degrees the very Notions of Liberty; they look upon themselves as Creatures at Mercy. . . ." [89] Herein lies the similarity between slaves and misguided men. In failing to see the context of their immediate situation and in forgetting their individuality, they exhibit the peculiar blindness Swift frequently depicts and complains of. By losing sight of self and society, the person is enslaved. The Irish are "apt to *sink* too *much* under *unreasonable* Fears, so we are too soon inclined to be raised by *groundless* Hopes." [90] Such a person is unable to act and betrays himself and his country.

Defoe and Swift were far ahead of their times in linking poverty with slavery. Swift saw the physical and mental debasement in terms of man acting against his own interests; Defoe saw that certain kinds of behavior depend upon security and ease. They show that hunger drives their characters to lose the shape of men and to resemble animals. Despair deprives them of the power to say no. Unscrupulous men exploit their weaknesses and needs until the victims lose their dignity completely. As Defoe lamented in *Caledonia,*

> Afflictions make Men Stupid, Nature winks,
> And *Sense o'erlaid,* he acts before he thinks:
> Subjected Nature fetter'd with Distress
> Dozes, and Bondage does the Soul possess,
> Endeavour Slackness, all the Prospects dy,
> And with the *Hope,* the *Love of Liberty.*[91]

Packs of Yahoos, consenting Irish, groups of homeless boys, thieves in Newgate show the effect of repressive societies bent upon controlling rather than respecting citizens. Moll Flanders' description of her transformation into a Newgate bird is strikingly parallel to Swift's description of the Yahoos who fall into brooding depressions, laugh and claw at each other, and alternately emulate the most successful of their number and yet deny their own similarity to their group to gain favor with their oppressors.

Governments and institutions as presented in the works of Bunyan, Swift, and Defoe point out fundamental differences in their interpretation of the influence of man on his society, and parallel the shifting climate of opinion decade by decade. For Bunyan, governors and governments are facts of life to be dealt with just like all other human institutions. For Swift and Defoe, they came increasingly to be seen as fascinating organisms with various possibilities and varying degrees of influence. Bunyan still interprets man in relation to God and presents man as soul who receives grace from God and who finds weaknesses within. Societies are clearly good or bad, saved or damned, and man relates to them as he does to individuals. Man finds strength or rejection depending on the group with which he is willingly or unwillingly involved. Defoe and Swift incorporate into their works their belief that men require governments and depict various kinds of leaders and organizations. Defoe is fascinated with the rise of leaders and the evolution of societies, Swift with the implications of governmental structures and the personality of leaders. Defoe moves away from Bunyan and Swift, putting man in a world with more possibilities. Swift shows the mores which hold a group together, while Defoe shows the human needs which a society must meet; again, one writer describes situation and the other portrays development. All agree, however, that society contributes to self-perception and a sense of security.

Defoe and Swift have come to see that society is a failed attempt to institutionalize its ethical system. They see the contradiction between conception and practice in everyday life and act as distinct contrasts to Bunyan. For example, Bunyan's *Life and Death of Mr. Badman* offers nearly as complete a guide to methods of deceit and business ethics as Defoe's works, but Bunyan locates the fault in the depravity of man and the nature of a fallen world. Defoe's *The Complete English Tradesman* has dozens of difficult cases which businessmen might face, and his treatment of characters in this work are more similar to Bunyan's than has been recognized. When Defoe wrote novels and political tracts, however, these same problems are made intensely complicated by laws and legal practices. Not only does the legal system necessitate subterfuge and even dishonesty, but it provides additional ways men may cheat each other. The conduct of war, the establishment of colonies, and the treatment of human beings should be extensions of an ethical system. Government for Defoe and Swift, however, has become an impersonal force out of touch with its creators and the reason for its existence. As such it becomes destructive to individuals and as real and monolithic as any other force of evil.

Bunyan's works show that "the world is not our home" while Defoe's and Swift's show the corruption of an ideal. Bunyan's language is allegorical and attempts to free subject in order to address eternal struggle while Defoe and Swift use parody and demand attention to contemporary practice. All three writers remind us of the ideal that men carry in their minds. For Bunyan, the ideal can never exist on earth, but Swift and Defoe brood over creatures that can conceive what they cannot build. Ultimately, they fear that man is too limited and too evil to create the good society he can imagine. In the end, men will always be Lagodans with their houses in disrepair or greedy and destructive like Misson's men. None of the writers allows us to forget the Platonic Form which we carry that contrasts to the disappointing, skewed results of our attempts to translate Idea into society. As different as Defoe's and Swift's focus on the contemporary is to Bunyan's on the eternal, the existence of a world beyond the empirical is equally significant. Biblical typology in *Robinson Crusoe,* historical allegory in *Tale of a Tub,* Moll's childish ambitions, Lord Munodi's anachronistic lifestyle, and many other strategies give us the poignant metaphor Swift creates when Gulliver looks in the water at his own distorted image. In making character inextricable from story and meaning so that character absorbs both setting and event as happens most obviously with Christian, Robinson Crusoe, and Gulliver, these three writers find new ways of presenting truth beyond the empirical world.

CHAPTER III

PIETY, COMMERCE, AND FREEDOM

BECAUSE the impetus of the novel is to encompass reality, it tries to make its subjects, characters, events, and sequence probable and to have its form imitate experienced existence. As Arnold Kettle says, the novel more than any other genre is committed to life rather than to pattern. Much of the history and theory of the development of the novel records the struggle to render nature more directly. Lukács describes the goal of the novel as seeking to uncover and construct the concealed totality of life.[1] In practice, however, the novel selects portions of reality and shapes them into form, but in his efforts to absorb and order, the novelist must also conform to the demands of verisimilitude inherent in our understanding of the genre. Unlike the novelist, the creator of fable, allegory, parable, or satire unabashedly imposes pattern, concentrates on small segments of reality, and creates characters and events never found on earth, sweeping aside the restrictions of verisimilitude and enlisting the reader in his own examination of an isolated movement of the larger society. As the watchmaker can focus all of his attention on a single movement of a wheel, so the allegorist can enlarge and sharpen a detail of a larger part of man's experience. Unlike the novelist, he joyously eliminates the irrelevant and avoids anything that might distract from his theme.

Bunyan, Swift, and Defoe are poised at a particular moment in English literary history. They can exploit the great Renaissance forms while employing in embryo form some of the techniques that the novel will develop in the eighteenth century.[2] The transitional nature of these works has motivated critics such as Sheldon Sacks to disqualify all of Defoe's fiction from his definition of novel because they are not coherent "actions," works organized to introduce characters "about whose fates we are made to care, in unstable relationships which are then further complicated until the complication is finally resolved by the removal of the represented instability."[3] Certainly the novel which developed is a

65

ery different narrative form from anything written in England before the eighteenth century, and our conception of the genre represents the refinement of the definition and the tacit formalization of eighteenth- and nineteenth-century expectations which included emphasis upon characterization and the representation of the actual world and probable events directed toward resolution. Although none of our writers' works satisfies our total sense of what a novel is, most have indisputably novelistic elements. The writers' engagement with and presentation of the world and their concentration on character as complex, individual, and mutable aligns them with novelists. Moreover, the recurring subjects of the great novels engage them: man in society, human alienation, man's pursuit of a worthy goal. This moment of writing balanced the religious and secular points of view, the seventeenth- and eighteenth-century conceptions of man's nature, and what John Richetti describes as "experience and ideology." [4] Montesquieu recognizes this peculiarly English temper in *Esprit des lois* when he writes that the English people had "progressed the farthest of all peoples in the world in three important things: in piety, in commerce, and in freedom." [5] That their art combines the oldest forms of religious and secular narrative and anticipates the modern novel depends upon this moment in history and the-far-from-ordinary awareness shared by Bunyan, Swift, and Defoe of the moment, its tensions and its absurdities.

I

Bunyan's *Pilgrim's Progress,* the most obviously traditional work, represents this phenomenon. From the moment that the man stands at his gate asking, "What shall I do?" he participates in two satisfying literary forms: the *bildungsroman* and the spiritual quest. Christian has all of the characteristics of a Western hero.[6] He is noble, brave, persevering, and strong. He is alone and undertakes a journey which aims at realization of self, and his journey is presented as a pioneering effort and an idealistic quest. As a Christian warrior, he must also serve as a model and, as a hero, embody the values of his culture.

Like Robinson Crusoe and other heroes, Christian can be foolish, he can despair, and he can be comic. While he may fall asleep or appear ridiculous as he does when he runs ahead of Faithful, he also fights Apollyon. Yet he achieves another archetypal quality of the hero, constancy, his most significant and difficult challenge. The demand for constancy within the form of the Progress gives dramatic force to the great temptations, despair and sleep, which combine with those figures who represent moods or characteristics opposed to faithfulness. Bunyan isolates the Christian by putting him in a dream, thereby removing all duties and responsibilities except the Christian quest. He simulates, therefore, a psychological journey in physical terms.

The way to heaven is littered with would-be pilgrims.[7] Those who succeed need to be alert, single-minded, and brave. Early in his journey, Christian meets Simple, Sloth, and Presumption who are asleep. Ironically, he falls asleep in the arbor only a short time later and then laments the waste of time,

> O wretched man that I am! that I should sleep in the day-time! That I should sleep in the midst of difficulty! that I should so indulge the flesh, as to use that rest for ease to my flesh, which the Lord of the hill hath erected only for the relief of the spirits of pilgrims![8]

The New Testament warns the Christian to prepare for the coming night and insists upon distinctions between the duties of the day and the meaning of night. The passage also opposes the flesh, the force pulling down into the earth, with the spirit, the part straining upward. The opposite of sleep is eternal watchfulness made necessary by the man's perpetual state of danger. Christian takes a risk when he sleeps and the consequences seem limitlessly threatening.

The loss of consciousness and the sense of falling into a pit or the center of the earth become the imagery of being swallowed up in *Robinson Crusoe*.[9] Crusoe fears that one moment of inattention will make him the prey of beasts, men, or the sea: he is nearly buried in an earthquake; his sickness seems to hurl him down and encompass him.

Despair is an especial danger for Christian.[10] His psychological condition at the beginning immobilizes him, and the Slough of Despond is only one of many points at which his progress ceases. When his imagination vaults ahead to heaven, he becomes inattentive and begins to struggle blindly. In the Slough, he admits to Pliant that he does not recognize what has happened. Help explains the Slough in terms of a state of mind when the sinner realizes his situation: "there ariseth in his soul many fears, and doubts, and discouraging apprehensions, which all of them get together, and settle in this place." Like sleep, despair deadens, causes delay, loss of confidence in succeeding, and increases the risk of hell.

Primarily dangerous because they encourage sloth or despair, most of
the personages Christian meets represent states of mind.[11] These dramatized versions of temptation and ambivalence convey the sense of the
enemy within human beings and create a realistic psychological experience. The naturalness of a man like Christian believing Mr. Worldly
Wiseman and the effect of Timorous, Mistrust, and the men at the border
of the Valley of the Shadow of Death find recognition in any age. A
number of characters lead man to or are conditions of sloth: Pliable,
Timorous, By-Ends, and Simple, for example. That Christian feels timorous makes his meeting with Timorous threatening. His fears and state
of mind become tangible and undeniable. To acknowledge Timorous is
to acknowledge the reality of his fears. Other characters lead a man
asking "What shall I do" to despair: Formalist, Hypocrisy, Atheist. These
conditions are so threatening because the sense of urgency and of calling
provide the central motives. With calling comes self-respect, the characteristic threatened by sloth, sins such as lust, and, most of all, by despair.
The pattern of Christian's life is to waver between certainty and doubt.
In the Valley of the Shadow of Death and on the Hill Difficulty, for
example, he has been buoyed up by a sense of purpose and of support
from others, but when he is in the dungeon, Hopeful comments on his
wavering strength, "What hardship, terror, and amazement hast thou
already gone through and art thou now nothing but fear?" More than
anything else, he must guard against and overcome his own weakness,
the tendency to despair. The man in the cage represents the emblem of
despair's damning effect, and Christian cannot escape its threat until he
passes the River of Death. The well-known hymn sung by Valiant
mentions discouragement, dismal stories, giants, hobgoblins, and fancies
as shadows swept away by unwavering determination.

For Bunyan and his first readers, *Pilgrim's Progress* had a reality hard
for the modern person to apprehend, a reality based in a sense of the
world as dramatic battleground between good and evil, so that even
characters from biblical times could enter and do battle with modern
gods and devils. Bunyan could use quotations from the Bible in his
characters' dialogue and in his narrations so that they become the medium of thought.[12] He could take a character from the Bible such as Gaius
and imagine him as an innkeeper with a personality and a life. Mercy
could become a living presence. For Bunyan's readers, the pilgrimage
of the soul realized a part of their experience and a way of seeing

themselves. The immediacy of the Bible and Bunyan's subject, however, may be transposed into a comparable search for peace of mind and identity for the modern reader.

The extraordinary energy of the minds in *Pilgrim's Progress*—Christian's, the dreamer's, even the reader's—underscores what Lukács called the "dissonance special to the novel, the refusal of the immanence of being to enter into empirical life." [13] Bunyan's technique loads the most dramatic confrontations with allusions to both states. Apollyon, an external threat coupled to a supernatural, biblical one, blocks Christian's way, and Christian's thoughts are described in the same manner and detail that Defoe uses. First Christian is afraid and "casts" in his mind. He lists the choices, and decides what he must do (stand his ground because he has no armor for his back) and then proceeds to justify his decision in more laudable ways. Apollyon claims to be Christian's king and accuses him of mutiny; Christian answers,

> I was born indeed in your dominions, but your service was hard and your wages such as a man could not live on, "for the wages of sin is death"; therefore when I was come to years, I did as other considerate persons do, look out if perhaps I might mend myself. [14]

A reader unaware of the circumstances and the source might mistake this for one of Colonel Jack's speeches. Bunyan's diction evokes both the temporal and eternal worlds. "Such as man could not live on" and "I might mend myself" are the phrases of economic ambition as well as spiritual aspiration. Christian continues to answer Apollyon as the subject of a king ("how can I go back . . . and not be hanged as a traitor") and as a laborer ("I like his service, his wages"). Apollyon offers Christian rewards and threatens him in language connoting both worlds. After all, Apollyon says, many give Christian's new master "the slip, and return again to me." In a book filled with warnings against backsliding and slipping into sin, and marked by verbal playfulness, the pun unites the inner and outer worlds of the protagonist; such phrases make the point that the man must know two languages and two value systems. Christian keeps his eyes as steadily as he can on the reward of the "City of Zion." The Way, however, offers him every reward the world offers: ease, an end to striving, safety from physical suffering, sensual pleasure, and material objects. These tokens do not merely lie beside the "king's highway" but become active obstacles in his path. He must fight his way past them just as the man of stout countenance fights his way through the door in Interpreter's tableau.

The rhythm of the spiritual autobiography (and of the moods of human beings) include depression and optimism broken by long periods that are mercifully uneventful. Conversion for the Puritan conforms to this pattern. All Christians, in fact, would agree that God's grace and man's faith are the essentials of salvation; conversion usually occurs from two motives—love of God and fear of God's wrath—the first being entirely necessary even though the second might be the easier to produce.

More specifically, the process of repentance demands six steps: an awareness of sin, a sense of both divine wrath and obligation to God, humiliation before God, sincere confession, hatred of sin, and "accepting, receiving, and resting upon Christ alone for justification, sanctification, and eternal life, *by virtue of the covenant of grace.*" [15] Rather than a single epiphany, the saved recollect milestones and experience the feeling of being "called back." [16] Meeting Evangelist, Help, and Hopeful, being relieved of his burden, receiving advice and "arms" (armor, sword, All-Prayer, Promise), and learning to call on Prayer and Promise are not only signs of election but are in themselves a series of salvations. These aids come in the forms of traditional means of grace, of meeting other Christians, and of coincidences and accidents, signs of God's watchfulness. Times of suffering and misery (Slough, the Valleys, Doubting Castle) alternate with the pleasant. Bunyan's is a dramatic definition of "effectual calling." [17] The Westminster Confession reminds men that God sometimes seems to leave his children,[18] and *Pilgrim's Progress* records these times as well as those in which God seems neutral and those when God's help is immediate. Christian is no better than many who died, but the help given and his constancy save him. While salvation is the gift of God, the elect must work faithfully toward heaven. The life of the believer becomes an outward sign of his faith and election.

Christian's most acute suffering involves mental anguish combining confusion over his present situation and of his responsibility for his suffering. A sense of confinement accompanies his periods of suffering. The mind and the earth seem claustrophobic.[19] Moving laboriously, weighted down with the burden on his back, Christian is tangibly struggling. The feeling of moving slower than thought, of rowing against wind and current, heightens most of the narrative. Christian was a captive in the City of Destruction, paced his home and fields restlessly,

felt night and "hobgoblins" close in on the Hill Difficulty, and n
stopped on the Enchanted Ground. The feeling of being closed in, stifled,
held, opposes Christian's desire to move steadily, quickly upward. Although he may not be sure how to escape, he must remember his goal,
and his spirit must strive onward. The goal and his responsibility never
change. Faithful and a series of Christian heroes need not complete the
journey, but those like Ignorance can plummet into Hell from the very
gates of Heaven. The most perilous aspect of the pilgrimage, then,
pertains to the state of mind.

II

The Holy War develops the theme of the individual's responsibility.[20]
Mansoul, "the mirror, and glory of all" that God made with its "castle,"
the heart "a place so copious as to contain all the world," [21] incorporates
biblical history, the theology of salvation, and the experience of an
individual as well as sections on current and church history and millenar-
ian and political theory. Although Bunyan multiplies the allegorical
levels beyond those in *Pilgrim's Progress,* he contracts the Christian experience while setting it in the larger frame of God's design for mankind.

The difficulties and limitations of this ambitious design are immediately apparent. Diabolus rebels and decides to spoil Mansoul, and suddenly biblical myth joins with an account of an individual's sinfulness.
Innocence is killed, Recorder debauched, Diabolus takes Mansoul without a battle, and Swearing, Whoring, Drunkenness, and other evils
become aldermen. That Mansoul is now governed by these creatures
represents both the corruption of the individual, the kingdom of Satan,
and the fallen creation.

The conversion episode is better handled largely because Bunyan
lingers over it a bit more. The doubts and fears that prepare Mansoul for
Emmanuel's coming duplicate the pattern of salvation. Mansoul is miserable and afraid and gradually becomes "broken-spirited." At this point,
she begins to long for God and to learn how to please him. The efforts
to learn to pray and to understand how God acts resemble Robinson
Crusoe's experience in coming to comprehend God's relationships to
man.[22] Both make inappropriate demands, lack patience, and hope God
will do all of the acting. Only after suffering and disappointment do they
learn to please God and to act in ways that improve their earthly and

eternal positions. When Mansoul petitions for mercy and pardon and nothing else, and realizes that Mr. Desires-awake rather than Mr. Good-deed will please Emmanuel, she has gained understanding and, for the first time, acts in a way which will improve her present situation and her future hopes. The celebration which follows Emmanuel's pardon lasts long enough to give a picture of the glory of God and the unmitigated happiness of the Christian life.

Soon, however, Mr. Carnal Security leads Mansoul to fall away from Emmanuel, and the rest of the book is a graphic account of Mansoul's struggle between the forces of Diabolus and the promise of Emmanuel. The struggle also pits the flesh against the spirit, and "Carnal" Security appropriately makes the first advance against the repentant inhabitants of Mansoul. Unlike Christian, Mansoul lacks the concrete vision of an end to a journey. She has only the image of heaven, the brief time when Emmanuel lived in her heart. The battle between God and Satan is eternal for the religious thinker of Bunyan's persuasion, and the experience of the individual often seems closer to the endless battle for Mansoul than to the progressive way of Christian.[23] The variety of foes and modes of attack and the ways war can be waged create a sense of the nearly overwhelming forces pitted against Christian. War comes from Satan, an invading army; from factions springing up within Mansoul (Mr. Benumbing knocks Mr. Conscience down; the narrator laughs to see Mr. Prejudice tumbled in the dirt; and skulkers, survivors from Diabolus's reign, remain in Mansoul to raise rebellion); from Satan's armies which represent dozens of dangers (Rage, Damnation, Past-hope, Doubters, Bloodmen); and from devils who can also use deceit and the temptations of the marketplace against Mansoul. Mansoul is always prey to a hard heart, being "stupefied" or blinded, and exercising too little vigilance. The Holy War frequently alludes to the traditional conflict between flesh and spirit. The body's senses, Mansoul's "gates," open the way for attack on the heart and soul. Diabolus's appeals are to the gratification of the body, and his disciples corrupt the flesh. Although Emmanuel returns to Mansoul at the end, the impression left is one of perpetual struggle, not peace and rest.

What progress Mansoul has made in The Holy War is in understanding. Partly because of the opening episode, the nature of freedom is an important theme. Diabolus insists that Shaddai enslaves Mansoul by holding her in ignorance and blindness and argues that his rule has increased her liberty. The first conditions for surrender to Shaddai offered by Mansoul reflect her rebellious spirit and mistaken ideas of freedom: to keep the same governors, to protect the inhabitants from punishment, to keep their same privileges, and to be guaranteed protection from new laws and officers.[24] Diabolus threatens Mansoul with Shaddai's power, contrasting the liberty she has with submission to God. Diabolus's metaphors define the province of his form of liberty. Mansoul can play with Diabolus "as you would with a grasshopper;" Mansoul has the ball at its foot (72). This freedom is deceptive—Satan is no harmless grasshopper—for it is the careless freedom of a child. In contrast, Emmanuel gives Mansoul a new charter, and she attains adult freedom: forgiveness, "the holy law," a portion of God's grace and goodness, the world, free access to God, power and authority to seek out and destroy all Diabolonians, and exclusive right to the benefits and privileges of Mansoul. The essential nature of pre- and postlapsarian freedom is the same: responsibility coupled with privilege. Implicit in this charter is responsibility, the second theme in *The Holy War*. In the beginning Mansoul alone could open her gates, gates "impregnable, and such as could never be opened nor forced, but by the will and leave of those within." [25] At her trial, she admits she chose to let Diabolus in. The charter increases the responsibilities of Mansoul to include perpetual watchfulness for enemies from within as well as those outside. The fallen human being now can be attacked from within as well as from without. The Lord Secretary reinforces Mansoul's responsibility when he refuses to frame the first petition for her. With the added responsibility, Shaddai grants Mansoul grace.

The hard truths of the Christian paradoxes—only in losing the self can the self be free, only in eternal vigilance can rest be found, only in perpetual warfare can peace reign—are weighed against the promise of salvation, and Emmanuel's last speech encourages them to watch, fight, pray, and make war. Without a vision of the Celestial City and the satisfying entry into heaven, the task of *The Holy War* as apology for the Christian life is much more difficult. The burden rests on the descriptions of the quality of life in Mansoul when Diabolus reigns in contrast to that time when Emmanuel lived within. Chaos, unrest, unhappiness, violence, and distrust characterize such periods. Images of night and clouds and the sound of drums and chants ("Hell-fire! Hell-fire!") contrast to the images of fruitful trees, feasts, and visits, and the colors of gold and white. The darkness and cacophony of Diabolus's entrance contrast with Emmanuel's when Mansoul rejoices, "Lift up your heads, ye gates, and be ye lift up ye everlasting doors, and the King of Glory shall come in."

Here Bunyan is confronted with the necessity of contrasting Diabolus's appeal to the flesh and Shaddai's to the spirit. When Mansoul is under Shaddai's influence the tone and imagery appeal to the imagination in that they are chosen to create an emotional experience based upon the use of the colors of gold and white, of the language of the Psalms, and of descriptions of events such as feasts, all of which have symbolic implications for the Christian and elevate and charge these descriptions. In contrast, the descriptions of Diabolus's appeal refer to lewd servants, towers built to block the sun, fraudulent promises, and darkness. The tides of hope and despair, rebellion and repentance, active war and quiet vigilance capture a realistic part of the Christian experience, but the machinery intended to expand the significance of the allegory overwhelms the individual consciousness. Emmanuel's final speech seems to apologize for Shaddai's ways more than it inspires love and gratitude.

Bunyan attempts to combine his conception of man's free will in relation to God's power in a highly imaginative way. *The Holy War* is surely one of the great works in the tradition of Psychomachia, but it goes beyond that to place the soul in relation to history. The implications of this are that Mansoul can be attacked in several time frames. There are eternal temptations and there are evils determined by specific historical or even supranatural events while there are internal and external stresses which are the perpetual lot of human beings. The soul comes to be the battleground not just for individual salvation but for dominion of the power of good or evil. In raising the significance of the individual soul, Bunyan loses the sense of the individual particularly prone to certain sins. In illuminating the central message of his religion, he obscures the humanity of his protagonist. In *Pilgrim's Progress,* Bunyan introduced time frames and sources of conflict not only within the narrative but also in the marginal glosses which may cite scripture and which habitually use such grammatical forms as present tense which contrast with the dreamer's use of the past tense. The marginal notes keep the reader continually aware of the eternal pattern of the narrative and, by the use of verbs and pronouns, blur the distinctions between characters, dreamer, and reader.[26] Sacvan Bercovitch describes the *exemplum fidei* as resting upon the principle that any Christian's life opens, as did the

New Testament, a history of the Christian experience and can be called "*microchristus.*" Furthermore, this life is the story of the self trying to make sense of his nature by "proving that the terms of the conflict are predetermined, certified, and sealed from eternity under the signature of Another." [27] This paradox determines that Mansoul is responsible for her gates and yet the forces against her and the outcome are given. The communication of theory in ambitious forms seldom grips the imagination as well as simple narrative, and the contrast between *The Holy War* and *Pilgrim's Progress* with a recognition of the similarity of their purposes and themes suggests why Bunyan himself returned to less allegorical ways of describing the self's experience in its material and eternal societies.

Such concentration on the mind and the interaction of situation, emotion, and responsibility invigorates spiritual autobiographies whether they be Anglican or Puritan, lives of sober women or late eighteenth-century Methodist ministers.[28] As Starr and Hunter have demonstrated, much of the power of *Robinson Crusoe* comes from the use of the conventions of this subgenre.[29] The tension between confined body and aspiring mind make some incidents in Defoe's novels unforgettable. Crusoe, a prisoner on his island, struggles as Christian does. He must make the best of his situation, and, more crucially, he must master his emotions. *Moll Flanders* contains numerous scenes of confinement, too. The house of her childhood, the bedroom in her seducer's house, the streets of London as she flees, Mother Midnight's house, Virginia, place after place traps her and retards the realization of her ambitions. Her introduction into Newgate especially draws upon the familiar experience of spiritual autobiography. The physical setting is alien and horrifying to her. She plunges into it, devoured, every sense assaulted. She must do what she can to accommodate herself to the physical environment—pay for food, straw, and some privacy, make peace with the other inmates, but, more crucially, she must master her emotions. The risks of becoming "raving mad" or sinking in despair confront her over and over. The intense interaction of self and setting, the clear, hard focus on the psyche upon which salvation or death depends is the peculiar legacy of the religious tradition to fiction.

Part II of *Pilgrim's Progress* offers an alternative Christian experience. Conversion here emphasizes the sure, constant knowledge of God's love rather than the repeated drawing back to God and his admonitions which

Christian experiences. Where Christian nearly forgets his Key Promise, Christiana never doubts. Her way is easier because of her trust, the examples of those who went before her, and, most of all, because of companionship and circumstances. While Christian is driven, searching, and afraid, Christiana is matter-of-fact, begins by choice, and uses landmarks to anticipate temptations. Some pilgrims will die like Faithful, others struggle like Christian, and others move gracefully through life like Christiana. Bunyan conceived her not only to expound certain theological points and represent another type of Christian life, but also to illustrate how the Christian is insulated from many of the frequent sources of human suffering. Many more of the ordinary events of life— loss of spouse, threat of spinsterhood, marriage, birth, deaths of loved ones—occur in Part II. Faith tempers joy, fear, and unhappiness over these events. The dignified, almost ritualistic way the group members are called over the River one by one underscores the acceptance and even understanding of death's relationship to life. The time to die is fitting and to be regarded as another, more important passage. Those left feel joy for their friend, longing for their passage, and some deprivation because of the loss of a companion. Each leaves with dignity, order, and obedience. Stand-fast, the last described, ends the book with a prose hymn of praise. He has "lived by hearsay and faith" and now goes where he will "live by sight . . . with him in whose company I delight myself."

The themes of understanding more and more coupled with the increasingly felt absence of even the voice of God bring the hymn and the book to a fitting close. The metaphors of the final speech bring together the ideas and perils of the journey. Terror and anxiety as recurrent feelings take active expression in the river, bitter to the taste and cold to the stomach. The feeling of fear, traditionally explained as cold to the stomach, melts beside the "glowing coal" of his heart. The contrast between earth and the journey on the one hand, and heaven and "the conduct" (the escort), and companions on the other are united by descriptions of Christ. The reader is reminded that Jesus, the first pilgrim, was persecuted but left footprints for others to follow. That Christiana benefits greatly from Christian's, Christ's, and other path-breaking gains significance by the joy Stand-fast describes in following the footprints. Stand-fast's speech ends in a paragraph rich in images of light and reminiscent of Old Testament Psalms, ". . . his countenance I have more desired than they that have most desired the light of the sun . . . yes, any step hath he strengthened in his way." The narrator controls the tone by maintaining the pace and describing the event as natural, easy, and pleasurable to watch.

III

Bunyan's contemporaries, Richard Baxter most notably, pointed out that Bunyan's narratives concentrated on the "heart-occurrences" of individuals and warned that this technique worked against universally applicable lessons. As allegorical as Bunyan was, he was also psychological and, by being so, able to portray an individual who represented mankind and to construct an eternal journey through contemporary English trials. The separation of self and society inherent in Bunyan's religious view of man ironically finds more parallel in modern novels about man's alienation from society than it does in the moderate Puritan spiritual autobiographies Baxter preferred or in the purely secular novellas produced in France and England a few decades later.

Bunyan's narrative strategies, then, bear the weight of one of the major themes that will come to dominate English and American fiction: the discrepancies between the narrators and the society around them. Defoe's narrators, although placed in more concrete worlds, do the same. His narrators dominate the reader's experience and judgment; their voices are so distinctive and pervasive that all other viewpoints fade in the background.[30] Moreover, they find their actions and opinions more influenced by external forces. John Richetti explains that Defoe's readers must be willing "to participate at one and the same time in thoroughly observed fact and in extravagant fantasy."[31] The narrator juxtaposes a series of subtle choices against a traditional ethical system. The confusion of which critics sometimes complain in Defoe's novels often results from the character's multi-dimensional consciousness and the ambiguity of the situation in which he finds himself.

The narrator/protagonist expresses this multiplicity of perceptions and its resulting anxiety through his sense of his uncertain position in society. He feels both different from those who share his own situation and yet central to this same group. At the same moment, he may feel isolated and even threatened, yet also capable of exercising control and, more significantly, may even see himself as the person upon whom attention, human and providential, is focused. His loneliness and unhappiness motivate his ceaseless movement.

The attitude Defoe's characters most often project toward the external world is one of suspicion. Crusoe and Singleton might be expected to be suspicious in their situations, but the scope knows no limits.[32] Although Crusoe "thought himself very rich in subjects," he and his "subjects" always bear arms and are "under continual apprehensions." When he hears that other Europeans are marooned, he says,

> I fear'd mostly their treachery and ill usage of me, if I put my life in their hands: for that gratitude was not inherent virtue in the nature of man; nor did men always square their dealings by the obligations they had receiv'd, so much as they did by the advantages they expected.[33]

He does not think that there may be safety in numbers; he expects that each new colonist will be a new threat. The distrust which characterizes these societies pervades the ordinary world of the characters, too.

We would expect Moll to be secretive and devious in the Mint, but she is equally devious and wary in normal situations. Moll never tells any of her husbands and certainly none of her "friends" her complete assets. With the men that she most trusts, her money serves as a kind of material striptease. She hands them a little at a time and imagines that they are eagerly asking, "What next?" Similarly, the Governess passes herself off as a respectable business woman and confides to no one the mechanics of her operations;[34] Jemmy and the lady impersonate gentility to deceive Moll. The family that Moll lives with in Colchester is permeated with jealousy and distrust; the older brother dupes Moll and his family while the sisters, brothers, and parents take turns being suspicious of each other and of Moll.

The projection of distrust may be found in other novels as well. Jack thinks everyone is after his money, likely to get him in trouble, or ready to accuse him of theft throughout his early years. He and Roxana spend much of their energy protecting their wealth. The queen in Captain Misson's life is not at all sure she wants a colony near her even if a former ally is the leader. In no society are alliances liberally made. Groups trade when they see clear benefit, but do not seek contacts. Interest is always considered the most certain security. Friendships form in much the same way: alliances begin with mutual advantage (as between the Governess and Moll, Roxana and the Quakeress); when benefits cease, the acquaintance is quickly dropped. Moll Flanders, for example, looks to her advantage in each relationship, and she is quite successful in using people.

Almost every marriage leaves her with more stock; nearly every criminal teaches her more about her trade; even a chance encounter with a usually respectable gentleman increases her wealth. On the few occasions when she meets her match, she shifts ground and tries to get around them. When the older brother in Colchester simply cannot be made to marry her, she lets herself be persuaded that the only choice she has is to marry Robin and accept £500 reparations. Moll and the Governess have a mutually profitable arrangement, but they never share the trusting, intimate talk that Clarissa and Anna Howe or Amelia and Mrs. Atkinson do.

The characters' expectations about life further emphasize the isolation and threat that they feel is inherent in society. Jack articulates this notion most directly:

> It would have been a singular Satisfaction to me, if I could have known so much as this of them before, and had saved me all the Fatigue, Hazard, and Misfortune that befel me afterwards; but Man, a short sighted Creature, sees so little before him, that he can neither anticipate his joys, nor prevent him Disasters, be they ever so little a Distance from him.[35]

Jack's life is a series of ups and downs; an inescapable pattern of settled life followed by calamity dominates the book. Colonel Jack remarks several times,

> And now I began to think my Fortunes were settled for this World, and I had nothing before me, but to finish a Life of infinite Variety, such as mine had been with a comfortable Retreat, being both made wiser by our Sufferings and Difficulties, and able to judge for our selves, what kind of Life would be best adapted to our present Circumstances, and in what Station we might look upon ourselves to be most compleatly happy.[36]

Each time, however, an "unseen Mine" explodes his tranquillity, and he goes on another trip or marries another woman. He epitomizes the characters' anxious belief that all others, and even they themselves, can be catalysts without warning and precipitate a crisis. Life, in Defoe's vision, is profoundly unpredictable.

As diverse as are the circumstances of Crusoe on his island, Jack in Virginia, Moll in the Mint, and John wandering the London area as a refugee from the plague, the characters' perceptions of themselves and their relationship to their immediate environment are the same. Each one feels he is singled out, special, and must insist upon explaining how he is different. Several of Jack's youthful companions notice his reluctance to try new schemes, and their swearing, threats, and violence offend him. Day after day, he says little, and Will chides him for his want of eagerness. Besides this continual feeling of not belonging, or perhaps of belonging elsewhere, Jack insists on his alienation and greater sensitivity. He writes of crying as he robbed the old woman of twenty-two shillings in much the same way that MacKenzie might describe a lower-class man of feeling.

Jack is the same kind of misfit in Virginia. Immediately he tells the overseer his story with favorable embellishments so that he will not be mistaken for a felon (although he is more guilty than some). He feels that the master of the plantation is speaking to him and has special knowledge of him, although it is another young transport whom the master has drawn aside. Jack draws attention to himself.

Moll Flanders experiences a greater degree of dissociation. In almost every society she gives clues to the reader that she is an outsider; for instance, she explains metaphors and "hard words," indicating that they are strange to her. Even though it is the expectation of all the girls who live with Moll's Colchester nurse that they will go out to service, Moll cries and pleads until her nurse worries about her health. Moll has already made it clear that the care she got in this home was different from that given most parish charges; she says she was reared with "a great deal of Art, as well as with a great deal of Care" and as "Mannerly and as Genteely as if we had been at the Dancing School." Like Jack, she believes she receives special attention. Furthermore, just as Jack fails to see that the master suspects his ignominious past, so Moll fails to see that the ladies are amused by her pretensions. Even more telling is the fact that at no point does Moll think of herself as a servant; she thinks that, after the death of her nurse, this family has taken her in solely because of her merits. Yet more significant is the fact that Moll never tries to explain herself or test her perceptions of her position with those around her. She has encountered ridicule and indifference and feels superior. In contrast to Jack who tries to explain his differences and disagreements to other characters, Moll addresses the reader. Not only does this indicate Moll's greater degree of alienation from others in her society, but it underscores the theme of Moll's relative lack of self-awareness. Jack *is* different, and his actions prove it. Moll, however, is more like the society than she is different from it. She is, after all, a Colchester child supported by the parish.

Comparably, when Moll supports herself entirely by theft, she not only considers herself different from the other thieves but also points obsessively to her distinguishing characteristics. How different she considers herself is made most explicit in her reaction to Newgate's other inmates. *They* are "harden'd Wretches," "this Crew," "wicked and outragious," and soon she, as they, has no vestiges of the "Habit and Custom of good Breeding and Manners." Their taunts are those of persons who have recognized Moll's snobbery and airs:

> what! Mrs. Flanders come to Newgate at last? what Mrs. Mary, Mrs. Molly, and after that plain Moll Flanders? They thought the Devil had help'd me they said, that I had reign'd so long, they expected me there many Years ago, and was I come at last? then they flouted me with my Dejections, welcom'd me to the Place, wish'd me Joy . . . then call'd for Brandy, and drank to me; but put it all up to my Score, for they told me I was but just come to the College, as they call'd it; and sure I had Money in my Pocket, tho' they had none.[37]

Their jeers, such as putting the cask of brandy "up to her Score," demonstrate to her that she is no better than they and that the other inmates know her pretensions. When she recognizes that she has become like them, a "meer Newgate bird," her courage evaporates. Jack's fellow thieves laugh at him, too, and emphasize his unassimilated status.

Moll's obsessions with pointing out the ways in which she differs extend to all areas of life. If we believe Moll, she is more dexterous, prudent, and ingenious than her peers. She comments that the Governess and she agreed that she should always steal alone because she always has the best luck that way:

> and so indeed, I had, for I was seldom in any Danger when I was by myself, or if I was, I got out of it with more Dexterity than when I was entangled with the dull Measures of other People, who had perhaps less forecast, and were more rash and impatient than I; for tho' I had as much courage to venture as any of them, yet I used more caution before I undertook a thing, and had more Presence of Mind when I was to bring my self off.[38]

Moll describes her victims as less intelligent than her peers ("but the chief was, that the Woman whose Watch I had pull'd at was a Fool: that is to say, she was Ignorant of the nature of the Attempt." Ironically, Moll is unable to steal that watch).

Such characters' double vision is based in part upon their belief in their own basic goodness and moral intentions. At the end of the novel, Moll confidently manages an ostentatious plantation, dresses Jemmy up as "a very fine gentleman" complete with fowling pieces and a scarlet cloak and brags that he loves shooting more than working. She, like Jack, has come into her own. At the conclusion, she has found both the social place and self-respect that allows the "sincere Penitence" which she equates with their "settled life." Reputation holds an equally significant place in Jack's perception of himself as superior. He is proud that he "got some Reputation, for a mighty civil honest boy," punctual, careful, quick, and tractable, and quick to learn while his brothers were "surly, ill-look'd, rough," forgetful, disobliging, and thoughtless. His virtues are the stuff of the middle-class work ethic. Furthermore he speaks for all the Defoe characters reaching for self-respect when he says, "it was Honesty, and Virtue alone that made men Rich and Great, and gave them a Fame, as well as a Figure in the World, and that therefore I was to lay my Foundation in these, and expect what might follow in time." Because the characters hold this particularly Renaissance view of honor[39] and because they see themselves as striving for these virtues, they are able to set themselves apart.

Conversely linked to these feelings of isolation are the characters' feelings of control and centrality. Although Moll is penniless and a fugitive in the Mint, Jack an indentured servant whose treatment is little better than that given Negro slaves, Crusoe a castaway and John an illegal, feared emigrant from London, all have the impression that they are in control of themselves and can effect a better future. Moll, for instance, never stops scheming in order to get a settled life. Marriage after marriage is undertaken with just this objective, and her marriage to the banker and her brother attest to the sincerity of her desire. With the banker she lives "retired, frugal, and within ourselves," keeping no company, making no visits, minding her family, and obliging her husband until he dies. Had her Virginia husband not been her brother, Moll might have lived the quite ordinary life of a middle-class matron. Robinson Crusoe regulates his life, builds comfortable homes and, after the early periods of despair, believes that he can provide for himself, defend his island, and eventually escape it. John, too, is certain that he is the center of his small society even when the larger group joins his. Although he is met by hostile villagers and confronts seemingly insurmountable problems (such as the constable's refusal to let them pass), he never doubts that he can keep his band fed and sheltered. He feels in command even in the face of the law, the angry fear of the villagers, and the approaching winter.

Defoe expresses the tangled threads of seventeenth- and eighteenth-century thought. The Puritan mind had to reconcile the sense of man's isolation before his God with the promise of a community of the Elect.[40] Man was both demoralizingly sinful and yet destined for Heaven. He was encouraged to see himself as a depraved sinner, ruthlessly cataloging his shortcomings, and yet to think of himself as "a little lower than the angels" and created in God's image. He was both estranged and central. Besides the felt religious duality, an almost purely secular discussion of personality had been blossoming. Those in agreement with Hobbes or Calvin about the nature of man found themselves opposed and perhaps outnumbered by those who agreed with Hutcheson and Shaftesbury. Both the religious and secular tended to pit basically contradictory impulses against each other. The age had begun to shift its concentration from discussions of the body and soul as a battleground to questions of what personality is. Locke, for instance, felt compelled to raise what seems to us to be an elementary issue: ". . . we must consider what person stands for; which I think is a thinking, intelligent being, that has reason and reflection, and can consider itself, the same thinking thing, in different times and places."[41] This implies a self separate from society, a somehow inviolable and unique identity, conscious of itself as existing within a shaping society. The consciousness of such a self by necessity separates the character from all others and from the situation itself. The character becomes central because of his perception of himself and alienated because of his awareness that he is separate and must always be so. A new element of uncertainty comes into being. Not only does the individual have to ask whether he is among the Elect, but he must ask what core identity marks him as different from all others.[42] The Defoe character is suspended between the horns of contradictory modes of thought. At no time before had the question, "What have I become?" had such resonance. When Moll asks this question in prison, when Jack asks it in Virginia, and when Roxana asks it after the suspected death of Susan, the characters have inseparably fused ethical self-concept and social judgment. The confrontation of shaping society with aspiring will becomes the novel's subject.

The characters, then, exist in uneasy circumstances. Their world is unpredictable, their society suspicious, and their peers suspect. They feel isolated and threatened. Defoe himself recognized the difficulty of interpreting events and assigning causes. In 1706, he wrote,

> But Fate, that makes Footballs of Men, kicks some up Stairs and some down; some are advanc'd without Honour, others suppress'd without Infamy; some are raised without Merit, some are crush'd without Crime; and no Man knows by the beginning of things, whether his Course shall issue in a PEERAGE or a PILLORY. . . .[43]

By 1714, he assigned a great deal more responsibility for calamity to man's "wickedness" and "want of sense," but he continues to admit causes outside "natural influence." In *Tories and Tory Principles Ruinous to Prince and People,* he explains,

> there are some Things so unfortunate and fatal, as to communicate their destructive and pernicious Effects, that is, to be the Bane and Ruin of all those who possess or have to do with them. Whether such Events are meerly accidental, or guided by a more immediate Providence is hard to determine, and not requisite to the matter in Hand. Men of loose Principles assign all to Chance, and the more religious endeavour to persuade, that even the most inconsiderable Transactions come directly from the Disposition of the Supreme Being. When the Fatality, or ill Fortune here spoken of, seems to be annex'd to brute Beasts, as in the Case of *Sejanus*'s Horse, or to Things inanimate, as the Gold of *Toulouse,* the Calamities observ'd to follow them wheresoever they are, must certainly proceed from other Causes, than any natural Influence there can be in such Beasts or Things; but when they are the Concomitants of rational Creatures, there is no Question to be made, but that either their own Wickedness, or want of Sense, are the true Occasions of the Disasters and Misfortunes that attend them.[44]

This carefully unified pamphlet concludes that the Tories are a turbulent and unruly people who bring about their own ruin. The shifting and weighing of mere accident, Divine Providence, and human responsibility as explanation is most obvious in the themes of *Robinson Crusoe* and *The Journal of the Plague Year,* but invigorates *Moll Flanders, Captain Singleton,* and *Colonel Jack* as well.

The sense of wandering and searching which is so much a part of Defoe's novels comes from the character's warring sense of centrality and alienation, of significance and irrelevance. Relationships are unsettlingly temporary; when Crusoe leaves his island, Jack the plantation, and the

Cavalier his home, no painful hollow remains; when H. F. stays in London or Roxana in Paris no one rejoices. The protagonist's existence matters to himself and, strikingly often, to no one else. The tensions between the needs for respect and centrality on the one hand and for self-respect and specialness on the other leave the character searching and dissatisfied. The moments of contentment often come in the isolated societies. For a time, Crusoe is perfectly content on his island, Roxana with the Quakeress, and Moll in Virginia. These intervals cannot last and exist self-consciously as "islands," as artificial constructs, even for their inhabitants.

Defoe's most complete definition of happiness in his fiction is found in *Robinson Crusoe.* Crusoe's father describes the happiness of the middle state and contrasts the other stations of life. He finds his son's desire to leave incomprehensible:

> He told me it was for men of desperate fortunes on one hand, or of aspiring, superior fortunes on the other, who went abroad upon adventures, to rise by enterprise, and make themselves famous in undertakings of a nature out of the common road. . . .[45]

He describes the middle station as safe from misery and hardship yet spared from "pride, luxury, ambition and envy." Much that Crusoe learns on the island reinforces the image of happiness in the middle station of life. He learns contentment with what he has, to value food and security and good health; the value of objects changes. Later the Czar of Muscovy repeats the same pattern of discovery, of accommodation and, finally, of the attainment of peace of mind. By the end of *Farther Adventures,* the definition has been dramatized and reiterated.

The narrator of *A Tale of a Tub* remarks that happiness is the state of being well deluded. Although this is not in itself an original idea, Swift transforms it into satiric engravings of scurrying and stumbling. Peter and Jack rush about like the Lilliputians. Gulliver leaps into manure and exhausts himself at the Brobdingnag piano. As long as the delusion of happiness lasts, the individual has peace of mind. Spleen usually accompanies enlightenment. When Jack recognizes his folly, he wants Martin to tear his coat. Gulliver sees England through Houyhnhnm eyes and cannot bear human company.

Much has been made of the gloom and indignation in Swift's satires. But a consistent picture of the contented life opposes this dark vision, however, and locates Swift in the mainstream of early eighteenth-century thought. For Swift, set against the ravages of time and the frustrations of civilized man, are ease of body and quiet of mind. Amid the confusion, hurry, and crowding of Swift's Hogarthian scenes appear interludes of tranquillity. The number of characters and events decreases, the pace of the narrative slows. Lord Munodi's estate comes as a haven after the series of islands filled with grotesque beings whose thoughts scurry like rats. Mendez's leisurely meals temper Gulliver's frantic disquiet. The Houyhnhnms are never sick, and their lives proceed in sedate undertakings. The chattering and striving and activity of the Yahoos make them more of a contrast to the horses.

Swift's sermon "On the Poor Man's Contentment" discusses three topics: the advantages of the poor, the problems besetting the rich, and, finally, happiness. Health, sleep, and pleasure in good food immediately come to Swift's mind and seem to be found in the simple lives of the poor. Furthermore, the poor seldom suffer from such destructive forces as envy, ambition, and faction. They do not lie awake scheming nor are their desires limitless. Swift then quotes Agur's prayer, part of which is familiar to all Defoe readers:

> Give me neither Poverty nor Riches; Feed me with Food convenient for me. Lest I be full and deny thee, and say, Who is the Lord? Or, lest I be poor, and steal, and take the Name of my God in vain.[46]

The Middle Way, the commonplace of the eighteenth century, receives theological endorsement. The poor find the path to heaven more easily than the rich because they have fewer temptations and acts of charity and diligence come easier to them. Their lives prevent the kinds of self-destruction that stress, rich food, and alcohol practice on the rich. Finally, quiet of mind is more likely to be theirs. Not only do they work hard, but they are seldom in a position to do much evil.

Bunyan's treatment of the blessings of poverty offers an historically telling contrast to Defoe's and Swift's. Mr. Wiseman offers comfort to a bankrupt in The Life and Death of Mr. Badman by making four points: it is God's will; the poor can see himself preserved by God more clearly than the rich can; God may have reduced him in order to save him; and the poor cannot commit some of the sins against God that the rich can. Here we have an unmistakable contrast in focus. Bunyan thinks about the eternal world. Mr. Wiseman leads the bankrupt to consider how he became poor:

> [if he] can say with good conscience, I went not out of my place and state in which God by his providence had put me; but have abode with God in the calling wherein I was called, and have wrought hard, and fared meanly, been civilly apparelled, and have not directly nor indirectly made away with my creditors' goods; then has his fall come upon him by the immediate hand of God, whether by visible or invisible ways. For sometimes it comes by visible ways, to wit, by fire, by thieves, by loss of cattle, or the wickedness of sinful dealers, etc. And sometimes by means invisible, and then no man knows how. . . .[47]

Bunyan, unlike Defoe, includes human actions—thieves and sinful dealers—in the category of acts of Providence. He spends far more time explaining the biblical injunctions and promises: " . . . hath not God chosen the poor of this world, rich in faith, and heirs of the kingdom which God hath promised to them that love him?" Furthermore, Bunyan gives Psalm 49:6 as the example of the kind of sin from which poor men are exempt (trust in wealth). Bunyan emphasizes man's relationship to God; Swift sees the poor free from sins associated with earthly ambition and emphasizes man's relationship to men. Bunyan exhorts men to submit to the will of God; Swift writes of charity, diligence, enforced moderation, and political powerlessness.

Although Swift agreed with Defoe that "nature directs every one of us, and God permits us, to consult our own private Good before the private Good of any other person whatsoever," [48] most of his surviving sermons and other writings insist upon man's obligation to his fellow men. Regardless of poverty, people were to do what they could for others, and he frequently satirizes or describes lack of charity. Although he blames most of the Irish beggars for their own miserable condition, he urges all men to be responsible for relieving them. The birthday poems to Stella and the letters to Arbuthnot offer a working relationship with implications for the interpretation of group dynamics in Swift's other works. The delicate relationship between "quiet of mind" and "ease of body" especially fascinated Swift.

Esther Johnson and Swift shared a rare level of understanding and conversation, created a relationship somehow immune to invasion, and coped with physical discomfort. She, like Swift, suffered nagging bouts of bad health; she had headaches, poor vision, neuritis, and perhaps

asthma, and died an emaciated invalid. The birthday poems and journals
he wrote her leave us his most personal description of happiness. In the
poems, she is cheerful, intelligent, witty, brave, familiar, and devoted.
In a poem ascribed to her, she thanks Swift for teaching her to accept
the infirmities of age, for the alternative is antic painting. Corinna aches
physically and mentally as she sees the mouse-hair eyebrows and wrecked
plumpers;[49] Stella will never experience the need for such deceit. He calls
her "Best Pattern of true Friends," [50] and their relationship is a model
of social order. Stella's character is distinguished above all by honor,
which Swift defines as disinterested virtue and sense. Her wit, composure,
and concern endear her to Swift and make her companionship a joy. The
esteem and concern they had for each other resists the depressing effects
of increasing references to gray hair, deafness, pills, and spectacles. Swift
finds security and variety in her, qualities he says other men continually
seek in women. That he compares her to a familiar tavern associated with
warmth, old friends, and good times and contrasts her with the virgins
in conventional pastorals contribute to a recurrent theme in the poems.
Their friendship has an immutable core which resists the battering of
age. In 1725, he describes the couple, Wit and Beauty, and pretends they
must renounce these qualities for Gravity and Wisdom. His poem,
however, affirms their permanence even in the renunciation. His poem
to her is witty—the shadow of Donne and the Metaphysicals lurks as
surely as it did in the 1719 play on halving. That Nature dims his eyes
as Stella finds wrinkles clothes truth and sentiment in wit. That she will
be young to him as long as he can hear confirms the beauty he never
ceases to find in her and completes the witty compliment. Among her
virtues, Swift often mentions her distaste for vice and disgust at "Enslav-
ers of Mankind," qualities he prides himself on.

Swift and Stella provide a touchstone for identifying what goes wrong
in social relationships. Time after time, interest and egoism efface esteem.
Swift and Stella listen to each other; Swift's journal puts them in a single
room and creates a dialogue which at times approaches monologue, so
close are they in point of view. In contrast, Gulliver is usually in
competition with those to whom he speaks. He postures and brags on
each island, and the pattern of each part of Gulliver's Travels becomes a
description of Gulliver's England, a description of the island (although
these parts may be reversed or given in alternating sections), the island
king's judgment of England, and Gulliver's opinion of the island. The

tolerance and mutual respect found even in the jests and illnesses described by Swift in the Stella poems are significantly lacking in the small societies. The contentious life of the brothers in *A Tale of a Tub* and those who would proselytize other people find outlets in self-destructive behavior. The Irish tracts also tell of domestic conflict. The English ignore the rights and needs of the Irish, and neither side displays compassion or a sense of humor.

For Swift, the extension of social disorder is individual destruction. The person loses first his dignity and finally his self-esteem. The catalogue of madmen in Book IX of *A Tale of a Tub* illustrates this point. The antisocial behavior of the first two men defeats conversation. One rants and foams; the other sputters and babbles. That they should be soldiers and lawyers, respectively, both occupations supported by social disharmony, emphasizes the communication and dignity of Swift's relationship to Stella. Each madman loses the shape of man and becomes a parody of social predators. Social disorder sends the brain galloping, and Aeolists, factions, and opportunists spring forth. The petty whisperings and inane innuendoes in Lilliput could not happen in the secure society of the Houyhnhnms.

Swift appears to equate loss of the responsible self with loss of soul. Bunyan inverts the process by describing the protagonist's discovery of his moral destiny and then his interactions with individuals and society. Defoe recognizes the forces that natural accidents and society can bring to bear on the individual and describes the complexity of considerations and the variety of possible courses of action. His characters manage to separate even despicable action from the moral self.[51] Nevertheless, his characters no less than Swift's and Bunyan's maintain self-respect only when the self exerts itself, insists upon its independence, its existence, apart from society.

IV

In recognizing the exertion of the nuclear self against the impact of society and other people, each writer recognizes the essential union of secular and religious considerations in the individual's life. Furthermore, each insists that fulfillment depends upon the examination of the implications of action and the exercise of moral choice. Each distinguishes between life and mere existence, and between happiness and the condition of stupefied delusion. The forces most dominant in civilized society are the norms, aspirations, traditions, and sentiments that make up the common mental life rather than, for instance, their physical environment.[52] The society itself has an identity formed in part by each member's apprehension of the other members, of the society as a whole and of his place in it, and of the whole group's value system. In the prose works of these writers, this group philosophy extends into the work and comprises the substructure for many actions and judgments. As such it contributes a criterion for what is valuable and useful and provides specific ideas and objects which the characters cannot ignore or avoid. The realities of wartime finances, the changing economic base, and the traditional uses of coins as literary symbols explain the frequent references and extended anecdotes about money in Defoe's and Swift's works, for money provides an obvious vehicle for the exploration of the individual's confrontation with society's realities.

"With Money in the Pocket one is at home anywhere," Moll says. With money Moll can even make herself comfortable while being transported as a felon. She feasts on brandy, lemons, and fresh poultry at the Captain's table. Roxana is equally at home in France, Holland, and England once she has made her money. Money helps open the mind of the Captain who has kidnapped Jack as well as the mind of his plantation master. With money and craft, Jack can be English in France, French in England, and respected in both countries. In Virginia, he is a plantation master and in the Gulf, an honored guest. Likewise, Robinson Crusoe holds court throughout Asia and northern Europe.

Defoe's nonfiction tirelessly describes the uses of money, the way it transformed the conduct of war in his lifetime, and its advantages and dangers.[53] In the *Review* for 16 October 1707, Defoe lists avenues of influence for money. Calling money "the God of this World" and "the Pole Star of Affections," he finds money's influence behind great and noble actions. With compelling cynicism, he writes,

> For Thee, the Kings of the Earth raise War, and the Pot-sherds dash against one another. Thou art Ambition, for Pride is really nothing but Covetousness; 'tis for Thee the Mighty sell their Rest, their Peace, and their Souls in Quest of Crowns and Conquests. They talk sometimes of other Trifles, such as Liberty, Religion, and I know not what; but 'tis all for Thee, I never knew but two Exceptions in our Histories, *viz, Gustavus Adolphus,* and *King William.* . . .

That money brings about a satisfactory existence and becomes a necessary condition for a moral and happy life cannot be denied. "Give me
not poverty lest I steal" may be the best known quotation in Defoe's
works. Defoe wrote about the effects of poverty as skillfully in his
expository as in his narrative prose. He insists that

> Indigence and Want are always the Parent of Uneasiness and Disquietude; 'tis
> natural to Persons under straight and difficult Circumstances to be restless and
> projecting Minds, still casting about in their Thought how to extricate themselves
> from such Misfortunes. . . . nor can all the Rhetorick that the World is Master
> of stop the Mouth, or silence the Clamors of an empty Stomach.[54]

Each novel ends with the protagonist comfortably and securely prosperous, and for Defoe the necessity of material well-being for moral reform
appears indisputable.

Several of Defoe's novels establish characters who are ambitious and
materialistic, but who find themselves in new situations where money
is useless and may even be burdensome. Captain Singleton finds that his
shipmates' money is "mere trash" to the natives from whom they want
to buy food until they learn to beat coins into trinkets. "For gold or silver
we could get nothing," he ponders; "we were in a strange consternation."
Later he calls a halt to the gold and ivory hunts; the men have all they
can carry and more than they need to establish themselves in western
society. Robinson Crusoe, too, muses about the uselessness of the gold
he saves from the ship and learns to cultivate only enough land to feed
himself and provide a safe larder. The Cavalier takes only what he can
use, and John in *Journal of the Plague Year* carries the bare necessities for
camping outside of London. Anything beyond the immediately useful
becomes a burden.

Perhaps the best section of *Colonel Jack* initiates Jack into the draw-
backs of having money. He has no pockets, he has no bank or strongbox,
he loses his money in a tree, he is afraid he will be thrown out of the
Glass-house. Jack observes that for his errands he was better off being
given food, and one of the Coffeehouse men observes,

> . . . how naturally Anxiety and Perplexity attends those that have Money; I
> warrant you, says the Clerk, when this Poor Boy had no Money, he slept all Night
> in the Straw or in the warm Ashes in the Glass-House, as soundly and as void of
> Care as it would be possible for any Creature to do; But now as soon as he has
> gotten Money, the Care of preserving it brings Tears into his Eyes, and Fear into
> his Heart.[55]

Crusoe experiences the same dilemma and anxiety when he returns to civilization and must find a way to keep his money. Both Moll and Roxana compare themselves to bags of money dropped on a roadside, and they need a friendly banker.

Enough money can cushion a character, however. Moll and Roxana acquire and count their money in the ways that Crusoe and Singleton inventory and obsessively feel what stands between them and the next attack. Moll touches her coins and Singleton his wooden stakes. The coins and posts cease to be material objects and are transformed into psychological provisions and become part of the imagery of fortification prevalent in all Defoe's writing. Several passages in *The Storm* combine the kind of recognition of God's benign relationship with His world and the attention to security found in *Robinson Crusoe*:

> It pleased God so to direct things, that there fell no Rain in any considerable Quantity, except what fell the same Night or the ensuing Day, for near Three Weeks after the Storm . . . which gave People a great deal of Leisure in providing themselves Shelter and fortifying their Houses against the Accidents of Weather. . . .[56]

This passage is highly characteristic of Defoe, the specific references to time and the interpolated qualification "except what fell the same Night or the ensuing Day" link material event to psychological experience, represented by the selection of the words, "Accidents," "providing," and "fortifying."

In another type of writing, Defoe describes the Church of England as "Fenc'd about with so many Acts of Parliament, as the Test, the Conformity, and Schism Acts."[57] Attention to barricading, protecting, distancing threats is never far from the narrative consciousness. At times no provisions for security can be adequate, but the external cushion tends to soften the internal dilemma.[58] Every important Defoe character "takes stock" before and after each enterprise; each one at some time collects more plate, more money, more jewelry than he can possibly use. Moll even collects a horse she cannot use.

But the objects themselves are not the end, and, therefore, we must look beyond them. Each character has good reasons for his anxieties over possessions and these reasons illuminate a view of the world. Idealistically and foolishly, the narrator of Misson's tale says that money is "of no use where everything was in common and no hedge bounded any particular man's property." Unfortunately this does not prove to be true.

Everything is divided, and in a few weeks, ability and diligence establish the rich and the poor. In contrast, Moll's banker husband and the English factor in *Captain Singleton* die when they lose their money. Like Swift's Yahoos with their little blue stones, they have lost perspective and the sense of money as symbol rather than as a good in itself. Avarice replaces necessity for Moll, Roxana, and Jack in the course of each novel, and, in every case, calamity results. At the height of his spiritual balance, Robinson Crusoe says,

> In a Word, The Nature and Experience of Things dictated to me upon just Reflection, That all the good Things of this World, are no farther good to us, than they are for our Use; and that whatever we may heap up indeed to give others, we enjoy just as much as we can use, and no more.[59]

This philosophy is easy enough to remember in the isolated societies where self-respect is free from external influence and possessions rust or rot. But in every other world, those men who covet more than they can enjoy are ensnared in the act of acquisition and are punished for their lack of restraint. When Jack works diligently in America, it is not greed which pushes him but the desire to have enough to live comfortably. Just as Crusoe produces enough and no more, so Jack reaches that point and knows he should go on to other things. Just as Walters said in *Captain Singleton*, no reflective man acquires for the mere sake of acquiring.

Jack's experience in the Virginia society has important implications for the world of the novels. At one time, both Jack and Crusoe have worked very hard to establish thriving, prosperous plantations. They feel satisfaction but no greed when they succeed. At this point, the contrast between these particular societies and the ordinary societies becomes marked. Necessity for survival and self-respect motivate the characters in both situations, but in the ordinary world of the novel, as Moll says, "Avarice stept in and said, go on, go on." Yet, it is not pure greed for the sake of miserliness; the circumstances differ in three ways and thereby change the character's needs.

First, limits inherent to the small societies control the characters' ambitions for position and possessions. Although Crusoe can be king of his island, Moll the most elusive and famous rogue in Newgate, and the mulatto the king's personal servant with all the freedom he could hope for in Magadoxia, Jack, Moll, and Roxana have continents to conquer in their ordinary lives. Within their confined environments, Crusoe and the mulatto cannot improve their status. Not so Jack, Moll, and Roxana who want to "cut a figure" in England where someone can always climb higher than they. Possessions become the signs as well as the means of attaining success. How easy it is when reading a Defoe novel to mistake token for object. How easy it is to condemn Roxana for taking the Prince for all she can get while overlooking the pleasure she takes in having sufficient, appropriate plate to entertain him. How easy it is to see hers and Moll's fascination with clothes as vanity and materialism, rather than the satisfaction that at last they can dress attractively. Jack's pleasures in such frivolities as cards, horses, and good lodgings are not signs of decadence but of hard-won status. Once having tasted the "good life" and settled circumstances, the characters are even more determined to remain at that level or even rise. But, as Robinson Crusoe says, there is a tendency to "leave the happy view I had of being a rich and thriving man in my new plantation, only to pursue a rash and immoderate desire of rising faster than the nature of the thing admitted." Because there is always some higher position outside of the small societies, the character's acquisitiveness pushes him beyond prudence and safety.

Second, in the isolated societies the only standards that matter are those of the protagonists. If carriages are unknown, if no one dresses in black silk or carries a gold watch, no one wants them. In a small, rigidly stratified society, fewer "desirables" exist toward which they want to strive. Although manners and breeding are important, and rather strict conventions exist, material possessions do not distinguish men in these worlds. Because survival and ingenuity are more immediate, stratification comes more quickly and obviously. Crusoe can refer wryly to his summer house and fine hat, Jack can take pride in his clothes and aspirations, Misson can remark on his well-provided ships, but it is none of these things that makes each one "monarch." While natural ability is the chief criterion for success, it may have almost nothing to do with social position in the outside world. As the girls say to Moll, ". . . if a young Woman have Beauty, Birth, Breeding, Wit, Sense, Manners, Modesty, and all these to an Extream; yet if she have not Money, she's no Body, she had as good want them all, for nothing but Money now recommends a Woman. . . ." Moreover, without a settled, secure protector, Moll has no place at all in London.

Regardless of how carefully Jack imitates gentlemanly behavior, he can never be a gentleman without money and position. That he can have his nose slit and be beaten up by his wife's creditors indicates the distance between his real position and his aspirations, or even his conception of his place. Whenever he goes to England, his relative insignificance is made clear, and perhaps as a response to this heightened consciousness of his inferiority, Jack commits some foolish act: marrying an extravagant wife or rushing off to a battle. When confronted with external signs of success, Jack, like the other Defoe characters, falters, and in his insecurity, reacts rashly.

The third difference between the real world and these societies is that as threatening as the conditions of the small societies are, those of the ordinary world are more so in relation to the value system of the protagonists.[60] Although Robinson Crusoe lives in terror of cannibals and lack of food and shelter, he does have some means by which to control his environment; he builds elaborate and imposing fortifications and develops a successful scheme for providing for himself. Back in the world of commerce, he cannot rise fast enough, for something is always lacking.[61] As hard as life is on the plantation, Jack is never at the loss he is in France when challenged to a duel, nor does he acquit himself as badly in America as he does with his first wife. Misson and the other pirates are continually in danger on the high seas, but they are not in danger of being treated with the callous disregard reserved for most English sailors.

Given the constant temptations of supernumerary marks of success, external standards of judgment, and a more threatening environment, the loss of perspective and restraint can be expected.[62] Just as Crusoe's behavior becomes less rational and more extreme when he sees the footprint, so does the behavior of men who are convinced that a certain social status rightfully should be theirs and who can never be "settled" until they have attained it when they face the threats of the larger world.

Preoccupation with things, then, in Defoe's works is thematic. These material objects amount to the frame of reference which serves as a paradigm for the individual internalization of the norms, values, and standards of the culture. In the isolated societies, ability and usefulness determine the position; in the ordinary world, possessions and birth do. The characters are brutally taught this lesson: Moll at Robin's house, Jack on board ship—and if they have difficulty judging how much is enough for security, they can hardly be blamed. Money would be of no use in England were England like Libertalia or Point Desperation; gentle birth would be of no use if England required the capabilities of Virginia or Madagascar. When Moll says that "Diligence and Application have their due Encouragement, even in the Remotest Parts of the World," she might be voicing the controlling premise of the works: whatever tokens that society gives for industry will be collected diligently, and it is not the collecting that is important; it is not even the collection, but it is the "Cast for his Life," the risk taken in the hope of a better life, that matters.

For Swift, money most often symbolizes a social force capable of enslaving the mind and engaging the body in ignoble pursuits. He locates money as a secret spring or nearly invisible figure in education, politics, religion, and other professions. Gulliver complains that he has a great deal of trouble explaining money to the Houyhnhnms,

> the Materials it was made of, and the Value of the Metals. That when a Yahoo had got a great Store of this precious Substance, he was able to purchase whatever he has a mind to; the finest Cloathing, the noblest Houses, great Tracts of Land, the most costly Meats and Drinks, and have the choice of the most beautiful Females.[63]

In a simple phrase, Swift reminds the reader of the intrinsic worthlessness of coins. The rest details the effects of money and lists the objects prized by his society. Wisdom, conversation, even comfort fade before beautiful women and costly meat. The economic operation of the country rests on a few unpleasant principles: most people labor so a few can live a life of luxury, the intemperance of men and the vanity of women cause a disastrous balance of trade, and everyone depends on dozens of others. All are departures from natural order. Here Gulliver's account is hardly exaggerated. A cup of tea requires trips around the globe for tea, sugar, and, in some cases, the cup. English clothing requires the work of dozens. Gulliver tells his Houyhnhnm master, "When I am at home and dressed as I ought to be, I carry on my Body the Workmanship of an Hundred Tradesmen; the Building and Furniture of my House employ as many more; and five Times the Number to adorn my Wife" (XI, 252-253). Gulliver has undertaken his last voyage to make money, and it serves as motive for many of his sailors and most of the vices he describes. In the Houyhnhnms' parable of the Yahoos, Gulliver's point that money becomes an insatiable end in itself appears in their hoarding the worthless stones.

Swift's greatest quarrels with the Irish often involved money. In *Some Arguments Against Enlarging the Power of Bishops* (1723), he compares the value of money to real goods again. Several Oxford Colleges based their rents on the price of barrels of corn "For a Barrel of Corn is of real intrinsick Value, which Gold and Silver are not...."[64] The material from which coins were made allowed Swift to argue the relative worthlessness of money. He calculates values and effects over and over in the Drapier letters taking special pleasure in comparing equivalents in different periods of history.[65] The Irish seem ignorant and whimsical to Swift, and he belabors them over the nature and use of money throughout his career. The sermon, "The Causes of the Wretched Condition of Ireland," describes the woman as carrying the "whole yearly Rent of a good Estate at once on their Body." The translation of value into the concrete terms of labor and of consumption convey moral outrage more concisely than any other technique. Swift felt a sensible nation would overcome a lack of silver, but a nation of perverse sheep like the Irish ruin the balance of trade, chase luxury, and even support policies opposed to their own best interests.

While the projectors work to improve agriculture, building, trade, and manufacturing, the masses live in rags. Pat Rogers has argued that the Lagado academy is closer to Exchange Alley than to Gresham College,[66] and, while this is an overstatement, certainly the aims of the projectors fall closer to the motives of produce and profit than to the Royal Society's collection of information for information's sake. The projectors want to grow vegetables out of season, make food, build houses, make silk, make pillows, prevent horses from foundering, and invent an universal language. These are the plans of a trading society, and Swift's contempt for the idea of improvement through inventions encompasses the notion that profit brings happiness. The specific identification of scientific speculation and the market economy blends the late seventeenth-century objections to the new science with the reservations of the early eighteenth-century thinker contemplating the bustle of commercial England.

Swift's uneasiness concerning the arbitrary value of money increased as a result of his experience with the relationship between worth and those in power and with his growing familiarity with the change in the foundation of the English economy. In a number of ways, Swift expresses Tory distrust of credit and stocks in the *Examiner* papers.[67] Now unscrupulous men could manipulate the value of money even more readily. In one of his earliest papers, Swift complains of the "knavery," "couzenage," and "unintelligible jargon of terms" connected with credit. He insists that stockjobbers, Whigs, and "dextrous" men scheme to use credit for their ends and depicts Harley as virtuous and intelligent, a man who successfully defeats each plan. The Drapier conflict acts itself out in a similarly dense environment. Wood, interested parties, and part of the press manipulate words and terms while the Drapier and a few others see through the smoke screen. The full oppression and injustice of the English toward the Irish can be seen in economic policy. The English try to legislate what conquerors impose. They assign value to currency and interpret events which contradict the Irish reality. Wood's coins, the tax system—wherever Swift looks he sees English rhetoric out of phase with Irish experience. The *Letter from a Lady in Town to her Friend in the Country, Concerning the Bank* (1721) attributed to Swift[68] describes the operation of the moneyed interest. The "friend" recommended to the lady combines promises of extravagant profit, testimony of "Eminent Persons," specious comparisons of the directors to Moses and the prophets, and fantasies of benefits with imposing jargon and threats of the lists filling immediately.[69] The lady discovers each promise to be false and exclaims in wonder to her correspondent in the country.

Aside from the deceptive worth of money, it can change the behavior of people in unpleasant ways. The Drapier observes ironically that "*Money,* the great *Divider* of the World, hath by a strange Revolution, been the great *Uniter* of a most *divided* People." [70] With money come many of the troubles of the world: anxiety, fear of robbers, avarice, and insecurity. The wealthy are the common prey of governments and thieves, " . . . oftentimes of no Use, but to be plundered; like some Sort of Birds, who are good for nothing but their Feathers; and so fall a Prey to the strongest Side." [71] One ostentatious possession leads to the next. Most perverting, however, is the necessity of exploiting others to become and stay rich. The change in the farmer who exhibits Gulliver and the insatiable collecting of objects by the Irish aristocracy appear as the inevitable results of capitalism. The sermon "On the Poor Man's Contentment" compares the conditions of the rich and poor arguing that "the Desire of Power and Wealth is endless, and therefore impossible to be satisfied with any Acquisitions."

An aspect of Gulliver's personality is his being an "economic man." He undertakes three of his four voyages because they appear to be "advantageous," and he often sets out with a "prosperous" omen. Even knowledge seems to him to be a potential source of wealth and advancement. He describes his youth as a time spent in education, apprenticeship, and "in reading the best Authors, ancient and modern" and observing people and manners on shore. When he describes what he would do as a Struldbrugg, he begins with acquiring wealth, then studying which would allow him to excel all others in learning, and finally to recording public events. He would then become "a living Treasury" and "the Oracle of the Nation." He would gather a colony around him, oppose the degeneracy that is often part of a government's history, and participate in the advances of science. Gulliver the projector, the prophet, and savior explains his reliance on science and economics. Besides offering the Brobdingnag king gunpowder and reminding him that it is cheap to produce, Gulliver admits that he was "a Sort of Projector in my younger days" in Laputa and tries to help the Houyhnhnms increase their control of and profit from the Yahoos by explaining the advantages of asses over Yahoos. Gulliver uses the jargon that Swift ridicules in the *Examiner* papers. He takes things "into account," he "acquires" the respect of others, he sees his "interest decline," and "tallies" characteristics and vices.[72] His desire to be respected, to climb to the top, to influence, rest upon the kind of market mentality that Swift saw in the Whigs in 1711.

V

A Tale of a Tub and *Gulliver's Travels* portray the impact of society on the individual. In these books, the characters attempt to understand the mores of particular social orders and collect their tokens in order to gain acceptance and respect. They willingly subordinate themselves to the culture. In his most unified political propaganda, Swift finds influence spreading from society to individual and back to society with increasingly vicious effects. The emphasis in the propaganda is upon the latter half of the movement. Swift assigns a motive to a man and then presents motive becoming defining label for a group. This theme exists as early as *A Tale of a Tub* in such passages as those describing Peter's and Jack's assumptions of power and in Section IX, "A Digression concerning . . . Madness."

The *Examiner* papers considered with Swift's other political writings about the last years of Anne's reign reveal the extent to which Swift could exploit the idea that single men could draw others into their company and become serious threats to the larger society. When Swift explains the downfall of the Godolphin ministry, he exploits the possibilities in rival economic theories while explaining motive and outcome in terms of greed and acquisitiveness. Although Godolphin and the others were initialy well-intentioned, they became avaricious, and the change in them visited evil back upon their country. Swift recalls that Godolphin once gave up his employment on principle but became the instigator of the Act of General Pardon, an Act in his opinion which no innocent man would think to create. In opposing the peace, Godolphin is part of a group which distributed money "where Occasion required." Such subjective interpretations contributed to Harley's, Lewis's, and other friends' opposition to the publication of *The History of the Four Last Years of the Queen,* but testify to the relationship Swift believes exists between personal honor and public well-being and the ways he saw avarice corrupting human beings.[73]

Swift fully understood the advantages of making the same point several ways. Like the other Queen Anne journalists, he discusses a limited number of issues and, therefore, needs to repeat a position in a variety of ways. Throughout the months in which Swift wrote the *Examiner,* his principle work was labeling the Godolphin ministry, its policies, groups of English people, and his own group. To some extent, the forms of satiric wit depend on labeling and naming: irony—the mingling of the valuative meanings of words—innuendo, allusion, fable, allegory, and metaphor. A substantial bond unites name and man in such a way that power over names quickly becomes power over men.[74] It is such a power which Swift wields in the *Examiner.* Using a number of indirect methods and recurring themes, Swift defined these groups through the labels he affixed, and many of these labels draw their acid from their associations with money.

Swift's political satire is so good and so effective because he appears to present facts and reasoned arguments while employing fictional and satiric techniques.[75] "Sharper" is the name Swift assigns to the Godolphin ministry and the Whig party, which is the basis for a cohesive characterization. A sharper is a gamester, a gambler who relies on cunning, a person who lives by his wits and by taking advantage of others (*OED*). The charge of mismanagement, the most frequent against the ministry in the

Examiner, is specifically linked to "sharper." The ministry is like a gambler who has not known when to quit, leaving his debts to his heirs.[76] A sharper has held England's cards all evening, "played Booty" (plundered), and lost England's money. Again, the aphorism of the ministry has been "if you cannot cheat as well as he, you are certainly undone." [77] To their shrewdness, Swift lays their invulnerability to prosecution. Swift progresses from assertion of the suitability of the label through descriptions of their actions demonstrating the charge to the assumption of its accuracy and of the nation's recognition of them as cheats. In assigning motive, Swift frequently draws upon this consistent picture. "They desire to reap the Advantage, if possible, without the Shame, or, at least, without the Danger." Such are men who live by their wits rather than by honest labor. The adjectives describing the Whigs and their actions reinforce the name. "Dexterous" and "deluding" are favorites. Whether he is describing the maneuvers of the political liar or pretending to puzzle over man's capacity to devise evil uncontrolled by law, Swift keeps the cunning of the ministry before the reader's eyes.

Using a second favorite tactic, Swift condemns men by the company they keep. The ministry's ability to circumvent the law resembles that of "A Scrivener, an Attorney, a Stock-jobber, and many other Retailers of Fraud." [78] Swift is able to implicate the whole Whig party. Again the attack is partly economic; these people are *retailers* of fraud; each occupation named was associated in the eighteenth-century mind with money made apart from honest work. From a stance hostile to political parties, he posits that the explanation of Whig unity is that of "Troops of *Banditti,*" "Knots of *Highwaymen,*" and "Tribes of *Sharpers, Thieves,* and *Pick-pockets.*" [79] In two paragraphs, Swift links the Whigs not only with thieves but to the enemies of the Church, the Catholics and Dissenters. "Interest" supplies the primary motive for unity and action. Continuing the war has been in the interest of the group, decisions have been made to benefit them, the "moneyed interest" has ridden on the backs of English land owners.

Examiner #14 on political lying encompasses many of the themes and charges against the Godolphin ministry.[80] The essay begins with Swift's reflecting on the saying, "The Devil is the Father of Lyes" and noting that the first lie was political. By reminding the audience of *Paradise Lost,* Swift casts the politician as Satan, surrounds him with rebellious followers, raises the specter of rebellion against a just and good monarch, and gives voice to ingratitude, grumbling, cowardice, and ambition. Satan, as deluder, power-monger, and self-seeker, becomes a portrait of the leader of the fallen Whig party. Godolphin, the Marlboroughs, and the Whigs look haughty, ungrateful, and usurping in their relationship with Queen Anne. Indeed, Swift insists this was one of the chief reasons Anne had to put them out of their employments.[81] Cromwell and the Commonwealth lurk behind this allusion. Swift blames the Dissenters for the Cromwell era and alludes to the Whig-Cromwell similarities repeatedly, even accusing the Whigs of wanting "to build a Commonwealth, or some new Scheme of their own" upon the ruins of the present government.[82] At another point, he refers to them as an "oligarchy." Furthermore, Swift had enraged Maynwaring and other Whigs by habitually referring to their party as "declining," "ruined," "fallen," "desperate," "wholly out of Employment," and "out of all Hope of reestablishing themselves."[83] The image of the sprawling, beaten followers of Satan becomes the condition of the Whigs. In calling lying "the last Relief of a *routed, earth-born, rebellious Party* in a State," Swift reinforces the Miltonic parallel.

The essay reflects on the way men have surpassed Satan as liars and compares political lying to other kinds of lying. In so doing, Swift is able to characterize and distinguish political lying in great detail and explain its special dangers.[84] A series of metaphors, the genealogy and character of political lies, and reflections on "Truth will at last prevail" devastate the Whigs. Such lies, those born "out of a discarded Statesman's Head" as well as those which are "the Spawn of a Stockjobber" have been the guardian spirit of the Whig party and have dazzled the eyes with a mirror which shows the true friends of England with "their Girdles hung round with *Chains* [slavery] and *Beads* [Popery] and *Wooden Shoes* [subservience to the Allies]." Swift describes them as "Being of dextrous Artifice and Management," thereby using phrases suggesting enterprising economic methods which the ministry has deluded the people into tolerating.

This, Swift's second *Examiner,* brings together the most damaging of the charges against the Godolphin ministry—mismanagement, deviousness, scheming, profiteering, acting according to expediency, apostasy— and implicates their followers as those willing to profit from the spoils of the corrupt or as deluded and dazzled men.

The names Swift assigns the Whigs as a group are "faction" and "cabal." The Whigs are a "patched up" conglomerate of "heterogeneous, inconsistent Parts, whom nothing served to unite but the common Interest of sharing in the Spoil and Plunder of the People." [85] The image of highwaymen and banditti rears its head. Both faction and cabal are strongly prejorative terms. Among the definitions of faction are

A party in the state or in any community or association. Always with opprobrious sense, conveying the imputation of selfish or mischievous or turbulent or unscrupulous methods.

"Party" in the abstract; self-interested or turbulent party strife or intrigue; factious spirit or action; dissension.

To act in a factious or rebellious spirit; to intrigue; to mutiny. (OED)

Even Bolingbroke, a committed party man,[86] wrote "Faction hath no Regard to national Interests." [87] "Cabal" referred to a small group of intriguers meeting for their own interests. By emphasizing the disparities of those under the Whig banner, Swift eliminates common principles as motive and substitutes common hopes of influence and profit.

The English were party extremists and would remain so for another hundred years. In 1831 Croker wrote, "Party is in England a stronger passion than love, avarice, or ambition." The excesses of party politics, however, were deplored and satirized in the early eighteenth century.[88] A fairly consistent distinction was made between party and faction. Swift compares faction to parties and to the best interest of the nation habitually. Generally, party referred to people united to maintain a cause or policy and did not necessarily carry the connotations of selfishness, lack of principles, or spirit of rebellion or factiousness. Swift makes it clear that the Whigs are faction, not party.

If these two Rivals were really no more than *Parties*, according to the common Acceptation of the Word; I should agree with those Politicians who think, a Prince descended from his dignity by putting himself at the Head of either; and that his wisest Course is, to keep them in a Balance; raising or depressing either, as it best suited with his Designs. But when the visible Interest of his Crown and Kingdom lies on one Side; and when the other is but a *Faction*, raised and strengthened by Incidents and Intrigues, and by deceiving the People with false Representations of Things; he ought, in Prudence, to take the first Opportunity of opening his Subjects Eyes. . . .[89]

Adjectives, descriptions of actions, and assignment of motive work together to develop the equation of Whig = faction. The "inveterate Faction" published its fears of impending disasters while secretly working to bring about those disasters—even to ruin credit—so that they might return to power.[90] Collected under the factional banner are old Whigs, Presbyterians, Socinians, Deists, Free-Thinkers, and others with a variety of philosophies of government ranging from Machiavellians to republicans. The conclusion that must be drawn is that personal gain and secret deals unite such diversity.

Small groups and individuals are characterized and attacked in the same ways. The "moneyed interest," [91] for example, Swift calls a "Species of Men quite different from any that were ever known before the Revolution." "Species," an obvious pun, sets them apart from ordinary men, makes them creatures yet unclassified while giving the very basis (specie) of the classification. In addition, "Species" has a third meaning, the outward appearance of an object. The deceptive and masking exterior fits in with the "Knavery" and "Couzenage" used to shift the reckoning of wealth from land to stocks and with the "unintelligible *Jargon* of Terms" used to befuddle the quarry. Such a group would be comfortable in an intriguing faction.

The military interest and the press are treated as small groups within the Whig party. Several numbers of the *Examiner* portray the Whig press as conforming to the image of the party. The Whig journalists lack skill; it is often unclear whom they are describing, they have little to write about except the *Examiner,* and "so weak a Cause, and so ruined a Faction, were never provided with Pens more resembling their Condition, or less suited to their Occasions." The antithetical phrases emphasize the weakness and party prejudice on the one hand and the dire straits of the party on the other. Each time he uses "ruined," he brings the image of the bankrupt to mind. In the last *Examiner,* Swift has the press condemn itself in a mock petition.[92] They admit to "false Quotations" (a favorite charge of Swift's), "noted Absurdities," libel, and dependence upon the *Examiner* for subsistence.

Furthermore, the Whig journalists are impotent, they are doomsayers and carpers, they cry out "the Pretender" in an attempt to bring him in. Swift is careful to associate them with the Whig party at all times. They represent the condition, the members, and the methods of the Whigs. In *Examiner* #17, he uses a series of parallels to members of a lord's estate. Each one represents a Whig notary or group. The final one, "if my Neighbour and I happened to have a misunderstanding about the *Delivery of a Message,* what could I less than strip and discard the *blundering* or *malicious* Rascal who carried it?" Part of the household, they cannot be separated from the party which is out to cause Englishmen trouble.

As well as characterizing the party, the ministry, and groups within the party, Swift attacks individual Whigs. Thomas Wharton is the object of a vicious personal attack. He has profited, Swift says, from his post. He has exercised power arbitrarily. He has not respected religion or law. He is a "defiler of altars." Swift calls him this in the 30 November *Examiner,* translating the episode into an ironic and perverted act of generosity in the 4 January issue:

> That worthy Patriot and *true Lover* of the Church, whom a late *Examiner* is supposed to reflect on under the Name of *Verres,* felt a pious Impulse to be a Benefactor to the Cathedral of *Gloucester;* but how to do it in the most decent, generous Manner, was the Question. At last he stole into the Church, mounted upon the Altar, and there did that which in cleanly Phrase is called *disburthening of Nature. . . .*[93]

The thousand pound fine was employed to support the church, "as no doubt, the *Benefactor* meant it." The irony of "true lover" of the church is especially heavy. In the 18 January *Examiner,* Swift corrects the location. "*Defiler*" is literally true. In the winter of 1680–81, Thomas Wharton and his brother Henry broke into a village church in Barrington, destroyed Bibles and furnishings, and defecated on the altar.[94] In Swift's opinion, the description was figuratively true also. Wharton continually supported the Dissenters and threatened the Church of England. Wharton's support for the Occasional Bill, the Scottish Union, his free spending in order to influence elections, and his suspected lack of support for the Test Act joined to his work against the new ministry provoked Swift's attacks.[95]

The letter, modeled on Cicero's to Verres, who as *praetor urbanus* and legate had sold justice, exploited his subjects, and used his wealth to retain power, is one of the most direct *ad hominem* attacks in the *Examiner.* The characterization of the Whig party, their ministry, and groups and individuals associated with the party develops a consistent and damning image of mismanagement, scheming, self-aggrandizement, deception, and impiety.

Swift's treatment of Matthew Tindal exemplifies the recurrent rather than the direct attack which Swift also employed. Tindal, a Catholic during the reign of James II, had become a Deist and written *The Rights of the Christian Church established* in 1706. *The Rights of the Christian Church* attacked the High Church and was ordered burned in 1710 with Sacheverell's sermon. Tindal became a synecdoche for those who attacked the established church. In *Examiner* #19, Tindal is called a Projector and a Garbler of projects and quoted derisively.

Tindal represents the hands into which the Godolphin ministry delivered the Church. In a passage insisting upon the presumptuous usurpation of power by the Whig ministry, Swift accuses them, saying that they took the care of the church

> intirely [*sic*] out of the Hands of *God Almighty* (because that was a *foreign Jurisdiction*) and made it their own *Creature,* depending altogether upon them; and issued out their Orders to Tindal, and others, to give publick Notice of it.[96]

Tindal is both a hired hand and a heretic; he is the type of clergyman encouraged and rewarded by the ministry.[97] Swift satirizes Tindal with offhand anecdotes, implying that he is unworthy of sustained attack. Not deigning to use the common protection from charges of libel or even the transparent Sibyllic mode, Swift habitually associates Tindal with the repeal of the Test. If the Whigs were restored, a petition by Tindal, Collins, Toland, and others would be brought in to qualify "*Atheists, Deists,* and *Socinians,* to serve their Country in any Employment, Ecclesiastical, Civil, or Military." [98] By using Tindal as symbol and placing him in hypothetical situations, Swift can condemn a whole party through a "typical" member.

In order to justify the change of ministry and discredit the Whigs entirely, Swift had to provide an image of the Harley ministry. He abandons fictional and satiric devices and adopts the most direct, uninflected prose in the *Examiner.*[99] The motif is the constancy of the party. In a time of political upheaval and national uncertainty when the Whigs revolved like dogs at bedtime, the new party is consistent. The Whigs roar like "Men in the Gout, or Women in Labour," ineffectually and blindly, but the "Bulk of *English* Gentry kept firm to their old Principles in Church and State." [100] The difference between the two is grounded in the core of their characters. The Tories are the same whether they are in or out of power except for "a little Cheerfulness or Cloud in their Countenances; the highest Employments can add nothing to their Loyalty; but their Behaviour to their Prince, as well as their Expressions of Love and Duty, are, in all Conditions exactly the same," but the Whigs in power "grow into good Humour and good Language towards the Crown, profess they will stand by it with their Lives and Fortunes; and whatever Rudenesses they may be guilty of in private, yet they assure the World, that there never was so gracious a Monarch. . . ."

The closest that Swift comes to satire is the transparently ironic comment, "to the Shame of the *Tories,* . . . nothing of all this hath ever been observed in them." Such men as the Tories form the foundation and anchor of English stability.[101] The Church, the constitution, property, and the monarchy are safe in their hands. Time after time, the Whigs are shown acting intemperately and angrily; each time the candor and constancy of the new party, reinforced by the straightforward prose, counters their threat to the people. The Whigs are compared to women, animals, tempests, girls at Bartholomew Fair, and revolutionists while the Tories are placed quietly beside them.

Swift's discourses on political parties show the pressures exerted by circumstances and other men on human beings. Intensified by the individual's ambitious yearnings and personal insecurities, the social forces become nearly overwhelming. Bunyan treats these social aspects in Vanity Fair and transforms its wares into personifications of earthly values potentially able to occupy and finally possess the soul. The temptations and milieu of Vanity Fair have matured and become more seductive by the early eighteenth century, and Defoe and Swift encounter them everywhere. While Christian and Bunyan's other protagonists must retain their visions of heaven, Defoe's characters must attain material security in order to climb out of despair to middle-class status and freedom from sinning, and Swift's protagonists must hang on to reason, resisting the blinding, submissive apathy of the Irish and the zeal of the reformer. What is an episode called Vanity Fair for Bunyan becomes a major subject for long works by Swift and Defoe. But all three writers are intensely conscious of the striving self attempting to realize its fullest potential in an environment threatening to define it by the world's hostility and difficulty. In describing the struggle of the individual to maintain his essential integrity, the writers use such external forces as money to represent the attacking forces but also explore the validity and influence of various kinds of experience as no writers had done before.

CHAPTER IV

THE LIFE OF THE MIND

THE writer of fiction builds a bridge between the external world as known by his readers and the world he conceives. This bridge is crucial. Without it the reader becomes confused and the fiction is unconvincing, yet the bridge must primarily serve to bring the reader into the world of the fiction. Because Bunyan, Swift, and Defoe want to change the reader's perception of his society and his part in it, and, perhaps, even change the reader's behavior, their task is more demanding than the writer's whose end is to use external reality as setting for plot. To build a bridge back to the reader's world defeats their purposes. They must consume the reader in their constructs. Regardless of which end of the bridge the reader occupies, he must recognize the fictional world to be like the real world or the possibility of its effect upon behavior is lost. The difficulty arises when the author's understanding runs counter to the interest or expectations of the reader (as the endings of *Gulliver's Travels* and *Pilgrim's Progress* do). Here, the world presented must be separate from the daily world of the reader to allow the author a convincing say. Separate, yet linked.

By creating island kingdoms and dream journeys, Bunyan, Swift, and Defoe solve a number of narrative problems. They present worlds which are self-sufficient, thereby imposing coherence and freeing them from troublesome external restrictions inherent in the world as we know it. They become free to explore and represent their perceptions to the reader as truths. They avoid denying the reader's initial opinions and conceptions. Above all, what is presented becomes the whole and essence of the world. Bunyan and Swift largely work within hagiographic and satiric parameters. Defoe inherits their forms and adds realistic techniques of his own.[1] In constructing their worlds and presenting the inner lives of their protagonists, they accomplish astonishing feats. Bunyan, for example, conflates time, Defoe builds a human psychology in which virtues are complex and ambiguous, and Swift leads reasonable men to doubt reason while he cancels time.

Clearly the independence of the created worlds can be pushed too far. Bunyan, Swift, and Defoe did live in the same world as their readers and shared most of the same conceptions which shaped and governed that world. Had Bunyan not, the dream in *Pilgrim's Progress* would have had little meaning. Still, in the societies the authors present, the reader can step away from where he has lived and even turn around. He is able to participate in the writer's vision that "This is the world as it really is" because he sees beyond symptom to cause, beyond surface to meaning, and understands the experienced world's relationship to individual consciousness and action more fully. The large is captured in the small and not attenuated by disorder on the periphery.

The significance and presentation of the inner and outer reality of the protagonist determine the relationship between motive and action, between society and self, and even imply the validity and influence of various kinds of experience. Imaginative writers of the seventeenth and eighteenth centuries, like philosophers, speculated about the inner life, individuality, and personality, but because they had to embody their opinions in characters whose realism could be accepted yet whose personality and behavior might not be possible, their job was more difficult.[2] Leo Braudy has pointed out that Swift in the creation of Gulliver "seems poised between the satiric and fictional view of character, between character viewed from the outside, in analogy and painting, with the goal of caricature and simplification, and character expressed from within, through an essentially nonvisual exploration of the potentials of inconsistency and uncertainty."[3] This statement poses the position and the great problem of developing fiction. In the struggle to present character and theme, the writers confronted and solved the narrative problems which would find their fullest expression in *Tristram Shandy*.

I

Bunyan saw that he could use the form of dream narrative to exploit Biblical tradition and contemporary possibilities for interpretation; for him dreams were powerful experiences, and his story gained considerably from the mysterious aspects of dreams. He insisted that *Pilgrim's Progress* "delivered under the Similitude of a DREAM" came to him in a compelling dream and "fell into Allegory." The account of Christian, then, becomes doubly true. Bunyan purports to tell an actual dream, and the tale partakes of the special truth of dreams because they are free from conscious direction. The necessity of limiting expression to common events disappears.

No one in the seventeenth century denied the potential of dreams as messages or prophesies from God. Richard Burthogge in *An Essay upon Reason* (1694) explained that the believer's grasp of Old Testament prophecy could be so vivid that it was immaterial if the content was experienced or read. Bunyan simulated a dream and the immediacy of belief in Scripture. Furthermore, he must have felt the same force of the Scriptures and communicates its reality in his prose. The integration of biblical phrases in thoughts, conversation, and writings occurred spontaneously for the devout[4] and added weight and context to the material. The combination of dream and Scripture argued the validity of *Pilgrim's Progress*.

Restoration and eighteenth-century thinkers agreed, however, that most dreams result from the day's events and anxieties, unwise eating or drinking,[5] or somatic stimuli. Hobbes assumes that

> seeing dreams are caused by the distemper of some of the inward parts of the body; divers distempers must needs cause different dreams. And hence it is, that lying cold breedeth dreams of fear, and raiseth the thought and image of some fearful object (the motion of the brain to the inner parts to the brain being reciprocal). . . . In the same manner, as natural kindness, when we are awake, causeth desire, and desire makes heat in certain other parts of the body; so also too much heat in those parts, while we are asleep raiseth in the brain an imagination of some kindness shown. In sum, our dreams are the reverse of our waking imaginations; the motion when we are awake, beginning at one end; and when we dream, at another.[6]

His materialistic explanation was no more skeptical than that of many other thinkers, but few dismissed the significance of dreams entirely. Jeremy Taylor, whose opinion is quite similar to Hobbes's, included a skeptical passage allowing for the remote possibility of prophetic dreams:

> Dreams follow the temper of the body, and commonly proceed from trouble or disease, business or care, an active head and a restless mind, from fear or hope, from wine or passion, from fullness or emptiness, from fantastic remembrances, or from some common demon, good or bad: they are without rule and without reason, they are as contingent, as if a man should study to make a prophecy, and

by saying ten thousand things may hit upon one true, which was therefore not foreknown, though it was forespoken, and they have no certainty, because they have no natural causality nor proportion to those effects, which many times they are said to foresignify. . . .[7]

Here Taylor admits the remote possibility that there are demons and that some dreams may be significant. The difficulties for him are the large number of meaningless dreams occasioned by somatic stimuli and the lack of connection between dream and waking events.

Sir Thomas Browne addressed the latter problem directly in "On Dreams." He explains that "Virtuous thoughts of the daye laye up good treasors for the night. . . ."[8] for the "phantasmes of sleepe do commonly walk in the great roade of naturall and animal dreames; wherein the thoughts or actions of the day are acted over and ecchoed in the night."[9] He extends the cause–effect relationship from day to dream to future usefulness:

> However dreames may bee fallacious concerning outward events, yet may they bee truly significant at home, and whereby we may more sensibly understand ourselves. Men act in sleepe with some conformity unto their awaked sense, and consolations or discouragements may bee drawne from dreames, which ultimately tell us ourselves (232).

Dreams help people understand themselves, "tell us ourselves." The significance comes from the personal character of the dream; truths about the personality and nature of the dreamer cannot be repressed. By implication, dreams become another way for people to evaluate themselves. Contemporary thinkers such as Feltham argued the relationship between the state of mind and the dream; Plutarch's *Moralia* was a favorite reference for he had insisted that the noble soul acts honorably even in sleep and the dissolute soul expresses passion. Thomas Tryon's *A Treatise of Dreams and Visions* (1695) urged the analysis of dreams because they are self-generated and, therefore, a measure of redemption. These men, like Browne, admit that many dreams arise from natural causes such as foods eaten and the thoughts of the day. Even some "divine dreams" are but logical results of a pious life. But there are "demonicall dreams" and, therefore, why not angelical?[10]

While Browne admits that few dreams are *somnium coeleste*, he insists upon the possibility of such dreams and the importance of dreams in general. Reason simply could not deny the impact of certain dreams. Besides citing historical examples (Joseph and Plato are common), apologists for dream psychology ask as David Simpson did in *Discourse on Dreams and Night Visions* (1791), "And has not experience that many men have of significant dreams and night visions a more powerful effect on their minds than the most pure and refined concepts?"

Beyond its characteristics as dream vision,[11] *Pilgrim's Progress* uses what Fromm and Jung call symbolic language, a language which is highly visual, arresting, and drawn from myth, religion, art, literature, and the imagination. The story is egocentric and uses the dreamer in a variety of ways. Although dreams may have plots, many dreams are single, powerful pictures. Colors, the time of day, and objects may translate into a mood or an idea just as a literary metaphor does. Fromm defines symbolic language as

> the language in which inner experiences, feelings and thoughts are expressed as if they were sensory experiences, events in the outer world. Symbolic language is the language in which the world outside is a symbol of the world inside, a symbol of our souls and our minds.

> The picture you see in the dream is a *symbol* of something you felt.[12]

Perhaps no better expression of Bunyan's technique can be given. *Pilgrim's Progress* alternates just such scenes with interpretations. Objects of special significance play a great part. In the Palace Beautiful, Christian sees such things as Moses' rod and David's sling shot. The Valley of Humiliation includes vivid images, too. First Christian stands indecisively in the Valley, the dangers of hell balanced once again against the suffering of continuing the journey. Next the narrator describes Apollyon, the destroying angel of the bottomless pit, in detail.[13] Apollyon's clothing, like that of others whom Christian encounters, symbolizes his inner condition. Apollyon takes pride in his fishy monstrous scales, signs of his monstrous deformity. Next the fight, and finally, Christian resting and eating with his sword unsheathed in readiness appear to the mind's eye. The second part of the Valley of the Shadow of Death horrifies Christian because of the objects he must pass: snares, traps, deep holes, bones, mangled bodies, and Pope and Pagan's cave. Christian's gratitude at escaping the Valley increases his faith which he expresses in a song,

O world of wonders! (I can say no less)

That I should be preserved in that distress
That I have met with here! (68)

The recognition of grace makes his journey less frightening. The images
of light in the passage—the rising sun, the candle shining on his head—
help translate the image into feeling.

Bunyan's ability to transform the Bible's language and stories into
experienced events depends upon symbolic language also. He draws upon
the cultural symbols of giants, lions, valleys, flowers, darkness, and the
familiar phrasing of the Bible. In Beulah, for example, the description
depends upon phrases from the Bible and creates a mood as well as a
setting. "The flowers appear in the earth," "the voice of the turtle in the
land," and "the sun shineth day and night" illustrate phrases intended
to describe a state of being rather than a realistic season. Strictly speaking,
flowers do not appear and perpetual sunshine would be tiresome. As part
of a place of bliss and refreshment, however, they work together in the
way that dream pictures do. The symbolic renewal of the contract
between "bride and groom" takes place within sight of heaven. The
repetition of the sentence beginning "Here they . . ." underscores the
fulfillment of this place where they meet "with abundance of what they
had sought for in all their pilgrimage" (159). The city, however, is so
much more glorious than Beulah that they cannot look at it. The rooms
which Interpreter shows Christiana appear in the same way. In one room
is a chicken. When it drinks, it reminds the Christian to thank God by
turning its head up. When it clucks, it calls in the ways that Christ does
(210). Sights of sheep and flowers remind Christiana and the pilgrims
to accept the lessons of Christ's parables. Each picture re-creates a state
of mind, translates the visual into the emotional.

Because the images Bunyan uses are mythic and charged with associations, they give the narrative additional truth. The reader assents because
he recognizes. The images of places of rest, the stories of caves and giants
have always been the material of literature and folklore. Dreams, like
myth and metaphor, shorten the distance between the medium and
meaning. Freed of the demands for logical development, probability, and
plot, they draw their power from association. In their brevity may also
be special intensity. The collapse of ordinary notions of time and space
provides an imaginative solution to the writer's problem of creating a
construct of reality. In "this country of the soul," characters from the

Bible, folktales, and contemporary England walk a landscape somehow combining the Holy Land and England, yet the whole is dominated by the inner land of the dreamer.[14]

That Christian's journey takes a few days, a lifetime, a sleeper's (and a reader's) few hours simultaneously allows the fable to operate as imaginative literature and as heuristic moralizing. A similar merging of spaces occurs. Events take place in the dream, and both the dreamer and Christian think and reflect, adding other spaces for events. The dreamer is able to dream of resisting sleep, of sleep, and of dreaming.

The mechanism of the dream, far more powerful in Part I than in Part II, insists upon the involvement of the sleeper in his own dream. That he uses the phrase, "the wilderness of the world" suggests that he is in much the same state of mind as the man who asks, "What shall I do?" The den suggests not only a place but a sense of confinement reminiscent of the scores of Christian metaphors for the unredeemed spirit. The body as cage, the dungeon of the Castle—both come to mind immediately. The beginning clauses such as "Now I saw," "I beheld," and "Then I saw" remind the reader that we are not to be engrossed in the dream and lose sight of the dreamer. At one point, the dreamer asks Help a question and at another, he awakens only to fall asleep again. The dreamer is a part of the dream as the reader is a part of the story. Furthermore, the writer's relationship to the story adds yet another multidimensional relationship. Usually we think of story as the product of the writer, perhaps in the writer's head. Here the writer insists that the story was revealed to him and, therefore, he is in his own story opening a kind of chicken-egg paradox and allowing the reader entry into the story in the same way. Dreamer, reader, and writer observe, participate, and finally must bear the burden of interpretation.

The writers of many late seventeenth- and early eighteenth-century works take considerable pains to prevent suspense and uncritical immersion in plot and character. The attention is more commonly directed to process and implication. The intervention of the active dreamer serves much like the phrases in *Moll Flanders* directing the reader to follow her as she becomes first a "ruined" woman and then a thief. When Bunyan has the dreamer awaken, he reminds the reader insistently that he is seeing, not thinking. Bunyan reinforces the idea that events are not being consciously manipulated or ordered, and, in so doing, addresses the problem of truth in fiction. Furthermore, he leaves open the possibility that God sent the dream as revelation. Objectively, the outcome of Christian's journey is never in doubt after he is marked as one of the elect. The attention shifts to the path he must follow and the variations of the Way which other travelers experience.[15] Roger Sharrock explains the source of dramatic excitement as "the spectres of doubt and spiritual terror which still raise themselves in the confirmed professor" because the reader looks through his eyes and shares his uncertainty about the outcome.[16] The representation of man seeing through a glass darkly illuminates the working of Providence. Christian will defeat Apollyon, for example. Not only does the knowledgeable reader understand that the monster cannot harm those with the mark of salvation, but the narrative ends "as God would have it." Similarly, Robinson Crusoe gradually comes to understand his relationship to God through the ways God reveals, hides, or later discloses information about the world. For the writer who believes that the world and man's life have patterns and meaning, interest lies in the reaction to and implication of events rather than in incident.[17]

The dream structure allows Bunyan to conflate time. Christian's experience with Giant Despair illustrates the potential of the technique. He and Hopeful have fallen asleep after leaving the path. That they will be punished by delays at least for these two weaknesses can only be seen as inevitable. They are imprisoned and beaten from Wednesday until Saturday. On Friday, Christian despairs and cries out much as Job and Christ did. He feels forsaken. That night he faints. On Sunday morning, Christian remembers the key Promise and they escape. The story happens quickly in dream time, is measured in temporal days, and, furthermore, draws upon the time scheme of the resurrection. Likewise, their thoughts at times are locked into the dungeon and trapped by despair; at others, they manage to focus on natural means of escape and on the commands of God. The scenes of the book associate darkness and confinement with suffering; in the Slough of Despond, in the night on the Hill Difficulty, in the Valley of the Shadow of Death, in Doubting Castle, in the submersion in the River of Death, Christian struggles in a static and claustrophobic space. During his happiest intervals, he is often treated to open prospects, stretching before him like the promise of heaven. The sight of Immanuel's Land and the Delectable Mountains and of Beulah and the Celestial City open before him, reflect the beauty and joy of heaven while still reminding him of their incompleteness. Like the company of the good, such sights spur Christian on after they have encouraged and refreshed him. The dreamer and the reader, however, are aware of the deceptive nature of time and space. The River of Death is very much like the Slough of Despond, and dreamer and reader are left outside of the heavenly city. As Stanley Fish points out, the reader may not be able to escape temporal-spatial forms of thought, but he does learn their ultimate insufficiency.[18]

The collapse of time has both mantic and heuristic implications. Religious dreams have often been interpreted as prophetic, either in their communication of future events or in their function as warnings about the consequence of present behavior. The destiny of the damned is a familiar subject for mantic dreams. The ways to lose the path, the punishments for specific sins and weaknesses, and the signs and means of grace become the subject for heuristic moralizing. While Bunyan uses much that is traditional in sermons and religious writings, he also engages the reader more actively. Dreams must be interpreted, parables must be explored, and allegories deciphered. The subtle relationship between God's grace and man's constancy works itself out in time and space. The pilgrim can never do more than pause, never assume the self-confidence of Ignorance yet he is to trust utterly in God's grace whether that means a gruesome death and a ride to Heaven for Faithful or a long trip and a wait at the river for a summons. The sense of temporal pain and fatigue casts a small shadow on the conception of eternity. Christian can fight Apollyon for a day, nearly fall from weariness and yet see the event as part of an unbroken string stretching from the beginning to the end of the journey and also as a bitter sip compared to the perpetual refreshment of Heaven.

The egocentricity of dreams gives Bunyan considerable artistic freedom. He creates a dreamer who participates actively and can use the complexity of the self in dreams to project immediacy into Christian and characters like Ignorance. Characters like Interpreter come from the tradition of Biblical prophecy; characters like Sloth from Medieval drama, but a few others have the impact of the narrator's personality. One of the most fascinating characteristics of a dream is the occasional phenomenon when the dreamer becomes two or more characters in his own dream.[19] Not only does this produce the sense of watching the self act, but also there is the sense of seeing the self act in more than one actor in the dream. Like a play within a play, such an event provides another link to the reader. The reader is conscious of standing beside the narrator and feels as if he is participating in the society. Such a technique is the opposite of didactic sections such as those in *Colonel Jack* which specifically argue that the reader shares the condition of the characters. In the first few pages, Jack reminds the reader that both greatness and misery develop slowly and that ambition occurs universally in men. The conclusion urges men to lead a reflective life in order to understand events and God's design for his creatures (307–309). Colonel Jack often points out that his story is an analogy and, therefore, separate from the reader, but common humanity makes his story applicable to the reader.

The personality of the dreamer in *Pilgrim's Progress* projects itself to some extent in at least three characters: Christian, Faithful, and Ignorance. At the beginning, the dreamer and Christian are lost in the wilderness of the world. Both have the journey to make, and both are very ordinary men. In the concluding poem, the narrator both insists upon the value of his dream and admits the possibility of having missed some of the significance: "Now, Reader, I have told my dream to thee; / See if thou canst interpret it to me, / Or to thyself, or neighbour. . . ." [20] While interpreting it to the narrator would be like the happy conversations of the blessed, it might also be necessary for the dreamer who has been observer, not active pilgrim. Religious dreams ordinarily cannot be interpreted by the uninitiated. The ability to understand and appreciate *Pilgrim's Progress,* then, becomes a partial gauge to "know whether thou art blest or not." [21]

The difference between the conceptual systems accompanying waking and sleeping add a dimension to the egocentricity of dreams. While awake, people respond to challenge. They want to master and order their environment. While asleep, the self is the only system to which thoughts and feelings refer. [22] Because self-experience provides plot, character, and theme, the dreamer feels aspects of his personality and his longings translated into characters. The dream partakes of past experience, present condition, and has the potential for projection into the possibilities and threats of the future. Christian shares characteristics of the dreamer's past and personality while the dream has an element independent of both (Vanity Fair's wares are familiar and also charged with mantic symbolism). Faithful expresses noble, courageous ideals and dies heroically. The attraction of heroism and even Christian martyrdom flickers through both parts of *Pilgrim's Progress.* Especially in Part II, the narrator's pride in his book and his place in the series of tales of Christian heroes associates Faithful's personality with the narrator's. Hopeful encourages Christian with a review of heroic exploits:

> My brother, said he, rememberest thou not how valiant thou hast been heretofore? Apollyon could not crush thee, nor could all that thou didst hear, or see, or feel, in the Valley of the Shadow of Death. What hardship, terror, and amazement hast thou already gone through. . . ." (120)

The times of trial become a source of pride and hope in religious dreams.

Ignorance, also a sympathetic character, shares aspects of the dreamer's personality.[23] In neglecting to go through the wicket gate, he has omitted an essential condition of salvation. Ignorance appears at a very significant moment in the dream. The pilgrims have reached the Delectable Mountains and appear to have the Celestial City within their grasp. Two of the shepherds, Experience and Watchful, warn them against the Flatterer and sleeping. As if to underscore the need to be alert the dreamer awakes; he and the reader jarred into attention.[24] At this point, they meet the "brisk lad" Ignorance. Ignorance is confident and happy; he has been pious and honest but he admits that the gate is a long way from his country, Conceit. He tags along and fails to see the applicability of Christian's admonitions. The places and incidents they pass have no meaning; the talk of justification and joy of revelation make no impression (144, 146–147); he is obviously uninitiated. Other clues to his unredeemed nature are his preference for his own company, his being full of good "motions," and his reliance on his heart (148). Ignorance can never be saved; he has not repented by going through the gate, he does not understand "justifying righteousness," and he rejects revelation. Ignorance drops behind the pilgrims,[25] and finally the dreamer watches him cast through a door to hell at the very gates of heaven.

Ignorance represents the well-intentioned man who thinks about heaven and desires it. Bunyan finds it necessary to undercut Ignorance's arguments in notes, "He speaks reproachfully of what he knows not" (153) defends revelation, for example. Near the end of the dream, the narrator watches first Christian and then Hopeful cross into Heaven and then Ignorance destroyed. He describes all he sees and strains for more. Like a man behind bars, he cannot move enough to get a full view, and he cannot follow Christian into the Celestial City. He, Ignorance, and the reader have only vicarious pleasure and all are outside at the end.

Ignorance's death casts the ending of the book into a consistent warn
for watchfulness and humility.

The dreamer is cast back into his own situation. He must undertake
the journey himself, the dream is both encouragement and warning, but
could end with his identification with Ignorance as easily as with Christian. Ignorance demonstrates a commonplace of Puritan theology: "Most
sins of men in these daies of light are not for *want* of knowledge, but
against knowledge, admonition and conscience." [26] Ignorance chooses to
disregard warnings when he prefers to walk alone. Because of the availa-
bility of spiritual education, Ignorance's behavior is willful. He does not
hear, does not profit from his association with the blessed or from
revealed religion; the dreamer (and the reader) could make the same
choice. Again, the link between the writer and reader draws the reader
into the society of the fiction.

II

The satire of Swift's *A Tale of a Tub* shares many of the advantages of
dream narrative. Once again we enter a world in which ordinary expectations give way to an avowed private vision which may have prophetic
and certainly has heuristic implications. The voice of *A Tale of a Tub* is
Swift's most complex experiment with point of view and can be called
"narrator" only in a special sense. This "protagonist" plays a part more
like Bunyan's dreamer than like Christian, a central actor in the plot.
To treat him as narrator, however, draws attention to the extent to which
Swift uses him as a means of exploring the questions of identity, quest,
and experience addressed by Bunyan and Defoe. Through him, Swift can
manipulate time and space at will, and interpretations rest on the possibilities of the significance. The language of *A Tale of a Tub* is visual and
drawn from myth, religion, Western culture, literature, and the imagination. The bridge allowing the reader to enter the society depends upon
the materials of dream and, once in this new land, the reader encounters
another egocentric story, another landscape largely built with the materials of this complex narrator's inner topography.

Swift approaches the perception of the self as actor and as observer
through the conventional techniques of the satirist. Just as dreams provide a way to absorb the narrative, to make it distinctly egoistic, so does
the satirist's vision. "I see," "I see" is the satirist's refrain just as it is the

dreamer's.[27] He, too, can be aware that he is in the "story" and apart from it simultaneously, yet both are real, even equally real. The dreamer transforms experience into symbolic, highly visual terms and dictates the need for an interpreter. The satirist works with a similar language; in fact, Morton Kelsey appeals to political cartoonsand parable to explain dreams.[28] Furthermore, the satirist's material engages the reader in extraordinary ways. Truth, but not verisimilitude, a private vision offering human insights, multiple possibilities for interpretation, variously skilled interpreters—all are a part of satire as well as dream.

For the Dissenter, dreams could be valid experiences, influential and significant. They could be constructs of reality, synthesized simulations of complex impressions. The central problems of eighteenth-century fiction were the demands of form and "truth." [29] The dream frees the writer from both while insisting upon its own internal integrity. The reader comes with different expectations and participates in the discovery of the relationship between the construct and the experience. He tests and recognizes, and he establishes a relationship between the narrative and its influence, admits the satiric vision into valid experience and accepts its modifying powers.

In contrast to Bunyan who conflates time, Swift often cancels it. Despite references to dates and people, the reader, like the protagonists, becomes enmeshed in an experience in which ordinary measurements are meaningless. The narrative pattern of the *Tale* especially contributes to this feeling.[30] Not until *Tristram Shandy* will a narrator frustrate linear progress and plot so completely. The narrator interrupts his story of three brothers repeatedly and defies allegorical time by combining church history with the state of religion in England. Digressions rework themes and provide bewildering statements about the narrator. Is he a Bedlamite? tailor? fop? Where is he going, or more significantly, where is he taking us? The length of the book, like that of *Tristram*, purportedly depends at least as much upon whimsy, convention, and perversity as it does upon content and clarity. W. B. Carnochan points out that the narrator chooses to release the reader and himself from "hopeless" confinement.[31] Such a release, stated rather than developed, emphasizes the contrast between the author's acute awareness of a number of pages to be produced to make a tidy volume[32] and the customary demands for narrative form.

Similarly, once Gulliver is on the islands, his watch is useless. Like the prisoner with an indeterminate sentence or Crusoe on his island, the marks (workdays, Sundays, holidays) which give time a correlative disappear. Gulliver has no sense of the passage of events in England or the maturing of his children. Economic grumbling in Lilliput and deteriorating clothes have more meaning than a week. So powerfully has Swift replaced ordinary time, that the island narratives become the referrent for historical time rather than vice versa. Gulliver describes England during the last years of Queen Anne; this fact in 1730 or 1980 determines that the reader will scrutinize the island societies for parallels to the Harley-Bolingbroke years. The realities of Lilliput are not much more fanciful than those of Gulliver's description of England in Part IV. What becomes real is the effort to order, to control the environment.

In *A Tale of a Tub,* the narrator responds to the confident impulse to assert his understanding of his society and to the desire to climb out of it.[33] His ambition and self-praise mock his confidence, and, in the famous passage, happiness is "a perpetual Possession of being well Deceived," the reader recognizes the roots of the narrator's good cheer. Each chapter explains that the narrator will enlighten us, but as the section progresses, chaos overcomes image. The technique strips away the illusion of individual control, the concept of existing order to be discovered, and the result of group effort. Swift draws upon the conventions of fairy tales specifically.

The tale of the brothers begins traditionally enough. Everything is in order, "Once upon a Time, there was a Man who had Three Sons. . . ." Almost immediately, just as in a fairy tale, order breaks down; even the midwife does not know which brother is the eldest. They begin to rail and fight and participate in forms of social competition. Next they are at odds with their father's will and soon after with each other. Their births made them equal, but distinctions come quickly. In subverting the will, one brother excels, and the narrator explains "we shall hereafter find a name" for him. This brother takes over the house, now possessing the joint inheritance and wants his name glorified to "Father Peter" or "My Lord Peter." The other brothers become distinguishable, take names, and begin to restore their coats. The story ends with the excesses of Peter and Jack and the lost manuscript. The "accidents, turns, and adventures" were to explain recent Church history, but the contradictions in the headings that the narrator remembers suggest chaos. The tale begun so neatly with the built-in expectations of a moral and a conclusion ends in disorder.

The conclusion of *A Tale* begins with assertions of control: the author must be able to gauge the proper length; he must choose a subject appropriate to time, place, and temperament; he must know the "tricks"—hinting about authorship, pretending hidden meaning. Immediately, he admits that graceful endings to meals, lives, and books are rare. He admits his career, like many other people's, began because of a disappointment. He sees the issues not out of harmony with receipts and he simply stops writing. There can be no resolution; his control evaporates—he lost the manuscript, he will be at the mercy of "the World's Pulse" and his own for his next creation.

The book begins with the same contradictions. The dedication to Prince Posterity asserts ambition, the opening sentence denies it by describing *A Tale* as "the Fruits of a very few leisure Hours." [34] Posterity, now a child, suffers from a dim-witted "governor" who destroys modern works before Posterity can judge them; this governor wields the tools of time and death and commits infanticide. Books and men both "have no more than one Way of coming into the World," both come with great hopes, both can die in many ways, and are soon forgotten. *A Tale of a Tub* opens as a fragile vessel carrying the vain hopes of a modern writer, a toy sent out to divert an attack on a boat. The metaphor separates the book from the author yet affirms the connection. Section I introduces the theme of ambition and the metaphors of climbing and striving multiply. One must "press," "squeeze," "thrust," "climb" while gravity and weights pull down relentlessly. Posterity's guardian puts weights on the heels of works, words burden the age, which itself is heavy. Critics, madmen, modern authors scurry about while politicians, players, clergymen, and philosophers set up stages and race for the privilege of declaiming. Images of beating, gaping, flaying, sputtering, belching overwhelm the ascent, and ambition appears to be another form of masochism.

Not only the narrator but other types must sacrifice for their ambitions. The critic must give up "all the good Qualities of his Mind" and his existence resembles that of impulsive fowlers, rats, wasps, hangers-on, and dogs. The Aeolists go out to be blown up, tortured, and humiliated. Jack's religion sends him staggering down streets bumping into posts. In order to succeed in some professions, individuals must be willing to talk incessantly, think only of business, or analyze excrement. That the mad resemble the practitioners of professions underscores the violence to self that ambition requires.[35]

The work itself rather than the content assumes primary importance for the narrator and the book becomes nearly tangible, an object to be weighed and measured, its pages counted and its allusions admired. Jay Levine describes the narrator as a modern, sacred critic who cannot see the meaning for the text; commentary rather than parable arrests him.[36] At one point, the narrator chortles to think how his work will generate a series of glosses, each ingenious, each wrong, and each insignificant.

"Personality" in Swift's time referred to individual characteristics, that which made one person distinct from another. Nathan Bailey's dictionary defines personality as "the property of being a Distinct Person."[37] This distinct self is often threatened with extinction in Swift's works. Although Swift provides a central presence, the identity of this presence may shift, and the group to which he claims membership may absorb him entirely. Gulliver's ambition to be a Houyhnhnm, for example, leads him to exile in a stable. The struggling conductor of *A Tale of a Tub* finally sinks into the morass of his ceremonies. Having mastered the rules for his society, he finds himself devoured by them.

A series of poignant metaphors for man's struggling identity comes from the imagery of reflections. Gulliver turns away from his image in Houyhnhnmland. He can endure the sight of a Yahoo, and takes delight in seeing the horses, but he cannot reconcile his appearance and his ambition. His alienation from his own body represents the finality of his isolation. He sees himself first as being uncomfortably similar to the Yahoos, then as a reflection of them and finally as a Yahoo. The Houyhnhnm master speculates that man does not really possess reason but

... some Quality fitted to increase our natural Vices; as the Reflection from a troubled Stream returns the Image of an ill-shapen Body, not only *larger,* but more *distorted* (215).

"Troubled stream," "ill-shapen," "larger," "more distorted"—the phrases lament the perversion of reason and the despair over the picture of social institutions and status Gulliver has described. Man, created in the image of God, starts and turns away from his own image. When Gulliver spends hours before a mirror, he may not be expressing self-love but puzzling over his identity. He has rejected the Yahoos, his countrymen are different because they have not known the Houyhnhnms and he shuns them, and he can never be a Houyhnhnm. The mirror confirms his difference and

endlessly poses the questions, "What is man? What am I?" [38] In Brobdingnag, Gulliver had avoided mirrors because they confirmed his insignificance and worked against his retaining his identity. In Part IV he loses
his identity and seeks it in his mirror. He needs to "Habituate," to
"tolerate" and to accept.

The reader's relationship to the central presences of *A Tale of a Tub*
and *Gulliver's Travels* illustrates the potential power of bringing the
reader into a society in order to change his perceptions and his opinions.
A Tale of a Tub isolates a society, draws the reader in, and isolates him.
The reader finds himself captured ostensibly to listen to a pleasant fable
but actually to join the floundering of a series of groups who have lost
their way because they are convinced that they see clearly. The path is
without guideposts and the story without a beginning, middle, or end.
The reader experiences the disorder with the characters and with the
narrator. Gulliver is a more congenial guide. He does not purport to be
a guide, to be one qualified to initiate others until the very end. He seems
to be an ordinary fellow, one who could be seen as an everyman like
Christian or Robinson Crusoe. He records what he sees and tries to make
sense of it, just what the reader is doing. The reader follows him, joins
him and even identifies with him. The *Tale* maps the worlds of criticism,
religion, philosophy, and leadership as Gulliver explores the living spaces
of men. He looks at man, at what they do, how they work, and how they
relate to each other and to him. He tries to fit himself in and tells us
where the shoe fits or slips. What he wants seems quite reasonable: to
respect himself and to be respected.

Despite the major differences between the worlds of the *Tale* and
Gulliver's Travels, the effect of making reasonable men doubt reason is the
same. Both works describe the products of man's reason; whether man
turns to government, religion, or education, he botches the result. The
more systematic the philosophy, the more dubious its truth. The more
painstaking the critic, the more trivial and empty his insight. Part III
of *Gulliver's Travels* presents detailed pictures of the symbolic objects and
characters which represent reason run amok. The Laputans stand, heads
inclined, eyes rolling, with Flappers attending. They are as deaf to the
external world as the *Tale's* Goddess of criticism. Their clothing and
rooms are filled with astronomical and mathematical symbols and instruments. These sciences, whose purposes are to describe the real world, have
been appropriated by a people nearly oblivious to the external. Their

houses and the suit made for Gulliver demonstrate how far their methods differ from practical arts. Their study of music likewise produces cacophony. They insist that they are playing in tune to the music of the spheres, appropriately they reproduce the chaos of their own minds. Swift reminds us of the connection between the music of the spheres, harmony, and order, and the desirable productions of mankind by staging a Laputan concert. Each one plays his instrument to what he hears. The singularity of each perception and performance contrasts with the ideal of order. Their conversation, their state of mind, and their domestic lives expand the image of unrest and disorder. The family, politics, science, and society bear the stamp of the character of the Laputan. The kind of insensibility shown in the Laputan exists in the external world making the Laputan a caricature and a reflection of man's misguided attempt to free himself from distractions in order to exercise his intellect.

In Part IV, Swift gives the reader another representation of reasonable creatures. Here Gulliver and the reader share the same dilemma. What are we to make of reasonable creatures whose shape is so different from man's? What are we to think of creatures who can handle such natural events as childbearing and death so calmly? Swift presents choices in terms of societies: the Yahoos, the British in the years of war and domestic turmoil, and the Houyhnhnms. Gulliver cannot join any of these groups without doing violence to his own self-image. What, then, is the reasonable man to do? Debate the choices and retreat to the stable to regroup? It is tempting to draw parallels between Gulliver and the critics; after all, the continuing dialogue between the "soft" and "hard" schools raises many of the same considerations and dissatisfactions which Gulliver feels.

Weston La Barre in "The Dream, Charisma, and the Culture Hero" explains that the culture hero does the dream work of his society and fulfills a need to cope with unresolved problems and anxieties from the phylogenetic past of the society.[39] *Pilgrim's Progress* and Christian address the Puritan anxieties directly. *Gulliver's Travels* and *A Tale of a Tub* address the problems of the new man. Coming at a time of great change in ideas about science, religion, government, and the nature of man, Swift and Bunyan express many of the anxieties of their time and present portraits of men asking and then acting upon the question, "What shall I do?" The commonplace that both *Pilgrim's Progress* and the *Tale* participated in outdated debates over issues alive decades earlier breaks down in the face of the unresolved problems they raise about identity, experience, and quest. *Gulliver's Travels* is the most complete integration of the modern strains of thought in narrative.

III

Lukács insists that the novel affirms the dissonance between the immanence of being and empirical life.[40] Defoe, the master of verisimilitude, gives his best characters an intense and often bizarre inner life. He, like Swift and Bunyan, constructs a point of view which he leads the reader into accepting as a valid representation of the external world. In Defoe's works, however, the moralizing and didactic urges blend into storytelling in a different way. The narrator is more than an individual; he becomes a psyche whose perceptions and struggles operate not on a single psychological plane but between what Erich Kahler calls "strata of the psyche."[41] The narrative, thus, becomes more internalized and more confessional, and the description of the world more subjective. This world is ambiguous and complex, open to various reactions and interpretations.

Consider Roxana. Examined in the gallery of Defoe protagonists, her end might be the least expected. She is the well-brought-up daughter of a middle-class family, and her marriage to a brewer has every chance of maintaining her position. Her downfall and increasing depravity, however, suggest that her first fall is *the* fall; from that time on she is a whore in her own eyes, marked by the first sin. Motive in Defoe's novels is seldom simple; rather it is cumulative. Roxana goes beyond poverty and gratitude to vanity, and her actions spring from her nature as much as from the lessons life has taught her. Roxana is almost always more the woman than Moll. She is young and pretty and naturally longs to be "courted, caress'd and embrac'd." Even as a child she "lov'd a Crowd, and to see a great many fine Folks" (I,1). She has sold things and dressed in rags for a long time—the affectionate tenderness that the jeweler-landlord accords her is thus more difficult to resist. Finally fear motivates her; should she refuse the gentleman, she would "fall back into the same Misery."

Roxana's speech advocating the single life illustrates the extent to which her early motives have crystallized.[42] Had she accepted the Dutchman's offer of marriage, she might have found settled retirement. Her refusal, variously interpreted as advocating the economic capability of women, as an "exemplum on the evil consequences of avarice," and as a casuistical debate,[43] actually is consistent with her deepest impulses and conception of herself—and of others and society. She ponders the situation at length, recognizes that the Dutchman has discovered and met her primary objection, and, yet, from her tangled, vexed thoughts, she refuses to marry him. She says,

> He had indeed, remov'd my principal Objection, nay, all my Objections, and it was not possible for me to give any Answer; for if upon so generous an Offer I shou'd agree with him, I then did as good as confess, that it was upon the Account of my Money that I refus'd him; and that tho' I could give up my Virtue, and expose myself, yet I would not give up my Money, which, though it was true, yet was really too gross for me to acknowledge, and I cou'd not pretend to marry him upon that Principle neither; then as to having him, and make over all my Estate out of his Hands, so as not to give him the Management of what I had, I thought it would be not only a little Gothick and Inhumane, but would be always a Foundation of Unkindness between us, and render us suspected one to another; so that, upon the whole, I was oblig'd to give a new Turn to it, and talk upon a kind of an elevated Strain, which really was not in my Thoughts at first, at-all; for I own, *as above,* the divesting myself of my Estate, and putting my Money out of my Hand, was the Sum of the Matter, that made me refuse to marry. . . . (I,171)

By repeating "all my Objection" and "The Sum of the Matter," Defoe emphasizes the fact that Roxana has a single motive. Her refusal, however, is couched in terms designed to fulfill her characteristic desire to appear respectable and moral. She finds herself trapped; she cannot accept because the Dutchman will see her reason, one "too gross . . . to acknowledge" and, like the knowledge of an illicit love affair, it will be a source of resentment and suspicion between them. Roxana feels she has no choice but to "talk upon a kind of an elevated Strain, which really was not in my Thoughts at first, at-all. . . ."

Roxana's "gross" reason is based on avarice and ambition. Three aspects of it emerge. First, she has been mistreated as a mistress; her husband took all she had, ignored all of her good advice, and finally left her a pauper, while both the jeweler and the Prince made much of her and left her a great deal richer. Roxana has learned that freedom to leave is a powerful weapon, and has no desire to be in another's power. The arguments against being a mistress which follow do not answer this objection; they do list many difficulties and even consider the likelihood of being left, but although she might be abused, she is free and can make new alliances without the encumbrance of a legal husband. Later she is still afraid to surrender her autonomy:

> ... while I was a Mistress, it is customary for the Person kept, to receive from them that keep; but if I shou'd be a Wife, all I had then, was given up to the Husband, and I was thenceforth to be under his Authority only; and as I had Money enough, and needed not fear being what they call a cast-off Mistress, so I had no need to give him twenty Thousand Pound to marry me, which had been buying my Lodging too dear a great deal (144).

Her first husband had made her distrust men, and she must learn the limitations of her independence before she believes that she is risking less to cast her lot with the Dutchman than to try to profit by her freedom.

Her second motive is her desire for money. She knows that her past life cannot be examined too closely and even fears the Dutchman will upbraid her for their adultery. Again, the problem has roots in the past when her husband and even the Prince blamed her at times for their dissatisfactions. Finally, she is motivated by ambition. She has risen a great way since she had to give up her children in England—how far could she go? In retrospect, she sees she was "blinded by my own Vanity" and had "a thousand wild Notions in my Head, that I was yet gay enough, and young, and handsome enough to please a Man of Quality; and I would try my Fortune in London, come of it what wou'd." In having Roxana dream of being nothing less than mistress to the King, Defoe brings about the turning point in the reader's opinion of Roxana. Up to this point, she, like Moll, has been able to separate both conscience and self from her actions, or at worst, make her life appealing and her lamentations engaging; after her debate with the Dutchman she has shown herself to be disingenuous and to be pretentiously, immorally, and unnaturally ambitious, unwise and headstrong.

Indeed, Roxana's refusal to marry the merchant marks the book's crisis. After this point, Roxana is locked into a life of deception. She must bear his child in secrecy, and her life in the Pall-mall is one of disguise and scandal. She disappears for three years during which she doubles her "Substance," resumes her riotous life, but finally wants to live so as not to be "scandalous to my own Family." Ironically, her need for disguise and secrecy increases. Her speech to the merchant had insisted upon her independence, but she is never free again. She acts out what she says she wants, and the distance between her actions and her longing for a respectable, good life increases. The tone of the narrative changes after her speech. It becomes more objective, and richness and detail of dialogue and of descriptions of Roxana's thoughts decrease. The narrative reflects Roxana's growing stupefaction; she discusses and debates later, she describes with less energy, feeling, and detail.

Her alienation can be measured in countless ways. She loved her first children and surrendering them hurt her deeply; she attempts to use the Prince's child to bind him to her, but she refuses to marry the father of her last child. Finally she is willing to kill a child to preserve her façade of respectability. Perhaps it is Defoe's most masterful fictional stroke when he leaves us to wonder if Susan has been murdered. Were she dead, we would weigh Roxana's guilt. Because we do not know, we see that Roxana wished her dead, has detailed images of how she might die, and experiences a degree of guilt appropriate only for a murderer. Because we do not know if Susan is dead, we see Roxana's state of mind, and our sight is undistracted by the effort to affix responsibility for the deed.

In spite of her faults, Roxana may be the most Calvinistic of all of Defoe's protagonists. She is certainly the most aware of her warring nature. She knows that she is sinful and yet has another ambition continually before her. If she cannot wrench goodness from within, perhaps she can put it on and eventually it will suffuse her being. She dresses like the sober Quakeress and, in an even more futile ploy, hopes that the Dutchman is right when he says "Titles sometimes assist to elevate the soul."

She, Jack, and Moll are also the most conscious of the possibility of being forced to give up their self-concepts.[44] Jack and Moll are rudely reminded of the distance between their perceptions of themselves and the perceptions of those around them; Roxana, however, reminds herself. All are somewhat ridiculous in their lack of foresight. They cannot fully know what they want to be nor can they live up to what they feel they should be. Defoe manages to convey the sense of their straining to become in a way that signals that more than financial security is at issue. Financial security becomes a metaphor for security of identity.[45]

The most skillful sections of Defoe's novels allow glimpses of the passion beneath the process of the revelation of motive. Passion, often passion of considerable force, springs from the violence of the conflict caused by the demands of the temporal and eternal worlds and from the sense that the character is on the brink of internal chaos. In the increasing grasp of the complexity of motive and personality, Defoe's developing skill as a novelist is most apparent. Moll confronts the loss of self in Newgate; Jack risks it in the center section of the book in his entanglements with women. Roxana is never far from it:

> My new Spouse and I, liv'd a very regular contemplative Life, and in itself certainly a Life fill'd with all humane Felicity. But if I look'd upon my present Situation with Satisfaction, as I certainly did, so in Proportion I on all Occasions look'd back on former things with Detestation, and with the utmost Afflection; and now indeed, and not till now, those Reflections began to prey upon my Comforts, and lessen the Sweets of my other Enjoyments: They might be said to have gnaw'd a Hole in my Heart before; but now they made a Hole quite thro' it; now they eat into all my pleasant things; made bitter every Sweet, and mix'd my Sighs with every Smile.
>
> Not all the Affluence of a plentiful Fortune; not a hundred Thousand Pounds Estate; (for between us we had little less) not Honour and Titles, Attendants and Equipages; in a word, not all the things we call Pleasure, cou'd give me any relish, or sweeten the Taste of things to me; at least, not so much, but I grew sad, heavy, pensive, and melancholly; slept little, and eat little; dream'd continually of the most frightful and terrible Monsters; falling into Gulphs, and off from steep and high Precipices, *and the like*; so that in the Morning . . . I was *Hag-ridden* with Frights (264).

She goes on to lament that she is not Catholic and that no one can grant her absolution. The metaphors of acid, fantasies of falling and being pursued by witches and fiends, and descriptions of her haggard appearance and inability to be good company show her devastated by inner chaos. She is powerless and, worse, she knows she is at the mercy of these nightmares. When Amy does away with Susan, Roxana is driven very near madness. She sees Susan "ever before [her] Eyes" and is haunted by her. She imagines her in scene after scene in the posture of a victim of a gory murder. She seems on the verge of screaming and running mad. The descriptions of emotions are rich and full. Connotations and metaphors convey motive and psychological tension accompanying the recognition of responsibility. Defoe's argument that this is the way the world is moves him into the company of the psychological novelists.

Defoe, like Bunyan and Swift, wants the reader's attention on process. Moll changes from a romantic, dreaming girl to a woman who puts common sense and security first; Jack realizes the vague instincts and propensities he has for being a gentleman. Defoe recognizes the reader as observer and transforms him into a participant with one of his most effective and habitual narrative devices: the character's directions to watch "x" come about. Many of these alerting sentences ("What valuable Pains were here thrown away upon One, who he was sure, at last to abandon with Regret!" [46]) give direction in the novels. The warnings often occur as the protagonist enters one of the isolated societies.

Robinson Crusoe depends upon the technique heavily. One of the funniest examples concerns his building a canoe. He admits

> I pleas'd my self with the design, without determining whether I was ever able to undertake it; not but that the difficulty of launching my boat came often into my head; but I put a stop to my own enquiries into it by this foolish answer which I gave my self, Let's first make it, I'll warrant I'll find some way or other to get it along when 'tis done (146).

The next five paragraphs tell the actual story of the building and his attempts to launch the canoe. Quite a bit of Crusoe's character (and human nature) emerge in this bright episode. Building a canoe is an appealing idea to a marooned man. Crusoe has frequently taken the initiative in running away to sea, in Brazil, and how much more in keeping with this schematic characterization is Crusoe's attempt to seize the rudder of his destiny than to sit submissive, waiting. Crusoe is also used to "coming through" bad situations by one means or another. How like him to assume "I'll find some way or other." Finally, as Coleridge and numerous others have pointed out, Crusoe is no supernatural hero. He can be average, extremely unskillful, downright stupid, and occasionally just lucky enough to get out of a bad spot. Crusoe was admirable in his self-control and methodical settling in, but he made crooked baskets, accidentally found corn growing, blundered into the cannibals, got put off a ship in India, and built that canoe.[47]

On a larger scale, the technique is often used to introduce a major portion of a book:

> At about Fifteen Years of Age, my Father gave me, as he call'd it in French, 25000 Livres, that is to say, two Thousand Pounds Portion, and married me to an Eminent Brewer in the City; pardon me if I conceal his Name, for 'tho he was the Foundation of my Ruin, I cannot take so severe a Revenge upon him (*Roxana*, 7).

Here the reader is jarred from a hurried and generally advantageous life story by "pardon me if I conceal his Name, for 'tho he was the Foundation of my Ruin. . . ." Roxana has had all the advantages—wit, beauty, and money—and had every reason to expect a happy life. But a scant three pages into the book, she is about to be ruined at fifteen. The brewer's extravagance, their bad feelings (bickering over the carriage, for instance), and her moral descent are foreshadowed. The reader is not surprised but waits for the ruin, pays more careful attention to the characters' actions, looks for signs of the impending trouble, and even begins to sympathize with a rather shocking character. First, Roxana is young—fifteen—and was given, was married to the brewer although she admits his handsome face pleased her. She did not choose to marry; her obedience began her trouble. Second, she will not name the brewer; no matter how dishonorable he was, she will act honorably. With this suspense-robbing paragraph, the narrative slows down. What follows is a leisurely description of the brewer, advice to ladies ("Never, Ladies, marry a Fool") and a catalog of her husband's offenses. Roxana is superior in every way; she is an eighteenth-century entrepreneur who knows how the business should have been conducted. But at the end, she is in rags, has had to take her children to her husband's family, and is selling everything piece by piece. Now she says, "Hitherto I had not only preserv'd the Virtue itself, but the virtuous Inclination and Resolution; and had I kept myself there, I had been happy. . . ." Another sentence has been provided to tell the reader to watch how Roxana will lose her virtue along with everything else.

The beginning of *Moll Flanders* is an even more sweeping overview. The plan for her life is

> . . . I was not only expos'd to very great Distresses, even before I was capable, either of Understanding my Case, or how to Amend it, but brought into a Course of Life, which was not only scandalous in itself, but which, in its ordinary Course, tended to the swift Destruction both of Soul and Body (2).

Throughout *Moll Flanders,* Defoe uses this technique to instruct the reader. It might have been more dramatic to learn that Jemmy was a penniless fraud on the wedding night, but Moll's explanation,

> the glittering show of a great Estate, and of fine Things, which the deceived Creature that was now my Deceiver represented every Hour to my Imagination,

hurried me away, and gave me no time to think of London, or of any thing there, much less of the Obligation I had to a Person of infinitely more real Merit than what was now before me (152).

the reader not only enjoys seeing two clever cheats get what they deserve, but also learns how both Moll and Jemmy deceived each other. A code of "don't fall for this" as clear as the code for foiling pickpockets emerges. Another important step in Moll's hardening results from Jemmy's trick. Again she has been "dazzl'd," "hurried," followed her heart, and been burned. This is especially ironic because she has just helped another widow marry wisely. Never again does she marry without sound knowledge of her husband's circumstances. For this reason, her marriage to Jemmy after Newgate is more convincingly a kind of love match. She knows Jemmy has nothing but "good nature," weighs what her resources will buy, and buys Jemmy for herself.

In Defoe's novels, dreams occasionally take over when the inner condition of a character needs expression.[48] Defoe realized the complex relationship between external events and the life of the mind which included self-concept, past experiences, and the possibilities of dreams and visions as more than mere products of somatic stimuli. Roxana's frightening dreams and visions multiply as her state of mind deteriorates. She imagines the landlord-jeweler first as Death's-Head, then with a bloody head, and finally in bloody clothing. Appalled by her foresight as well as the murder, she stands amazed. She had feared his going, and her premonitions[49] prove true. The vision symbolizes the relationship between her life and her liaison with him. The Death's-Head marks her soul at the time she gives in to their relationship. The bloody clothes which prefigure Susan's death begin the imagery of her dreams about Susan's body. Because the dream comes in three parts, it represents more than the death of the jeweler. Later Roxana suffers from a morbid imagination and nightmares. Most of her fears are visual and symbolic. Houses crumble and destroy her, lightning melts the "Sword (Soul) in this Scabbord of Flesh" (260). The imagery of soul housed in a destructible shell, threatened by God's justice gives way to sensations of falling and visions of monsters, both suggesting Hell. Once she comments that such dreams and horror often lead to repentance, and such dreams do occur frequently in repentance narratives. Bunyan feared that the steeple would fall on him,[50] others describe Satan as a red bull aiming his horns at the sinner's heart, frogs tearing their flesh, and serpents blocking the door leading to Jesus, the Healer.[51] Roxana's dreams never go beyond the emblems of her evil nature. When she thinks that Amy has killed Susan, she repeatedly envisions gory death scenes. Each scene presents a mangled corpse: beheaded, bludgeoned, hanged, drowned, bloated. Roxana has always thought the worst of herself and acted to bring self-image and behavior together.

The pattern of developing fiction shows Defoe growing confident in his ability to express ideas without repetition and his virtuosity in employing techniques for more complex purposes. In many ways, *Robinson Crusoe* is an exploratory work. Defoe suggests a number of different cause-effect relationships and, consequently, a variety of motives. Although he undoubtedly wanted to take advantage of a profitable venture, to defuse Gildon's attack, and to tie up loose ends in *Strange and Surprizing Adventures,* his sequels to the first book also indicate his desire to explain the character of Robinson Crusoe. Defoe wanted his characters to be believable enough that readers could imagine them in other situations and project their actions; the first book alone does not allow that although the ending provides a glimpse of Crusoe in the larger world. Crusoe copes with situations parallel to those on the island, fearing the lack of food, clothing, and shelter. And once again he experiences the fear of being devoured. The threats to his body match the recurring threat to his faith which seems perilously close to being swallowed up by apprehensions. Fights in the wilderness affirm a personality developed on the island. His leadership comes easily, and he acts with certainty. In an ordinary European setting, he demonstrates his capacity to deal with the real world: animals, men, economic need, insecurity, and self-doubt. *Farther Adventures* and *Serious Reflections* develop this tenuously established character.

Crusoe's ambivalent attitudes toward companionship on his island provide a paradigm for the repetition in the three parts of *Robinson Crusoe.*[52] Crusoe fears men; he remarks to Xury that animals *or* men might devour them, imagines fierce natives on the island, and rejoices in his own solitude. His reaction to the human footprint and his immediate surmise that the Englishmen landing on his island cannot be honest reveal his deepest feelings about mankind. Yet he longs for conversation and can be thrown into despair by his parrot's voice or by evidence that other men were nearly cast on his island. *Farther Adventures* shows more troubled relationships with men; at one point, he is even forced off a ship. At another his interference with pagan rites seems to be a complete contradiction of the wisdom he exhibits when he concludes he has no right to kill the cannibals. *Serious Reflections* picks up the theme in "Of the Immorality of Conversation, and the Vulgar Errors of Behavior." Crusoe explains the dangers of conversation with evil men, kinds of undesirable conversation, and the ways parable and allegory differ. He makes distinctions between fables, on one side, and the misrepresentation of real episodes and talk extended to impress and divert on the other. The distinction rests on the author's intention, and these stories designed to deceive, delude, betray, or advance he condemns. Significantly, the section ends with a passage insisting that the first two volumes of *Robinson Crusoe* justify themselves when regarded in the tradition of the Bible and of *Pilgrim's Progress*.[53] At this point, Defoe reaches beyond an attempt at explaining Crusoe's relationships with men and argues a unity of narration for all three books. *Serious Reflections,* purportedly written by Crusoe,[54] imposes consistent and ultimate meaning on Crusoe's experiences and his book.[55] Defoe concludes his exploration of companionship very close to Bunyan's position: "immoral" conversation is worse than solitude, but the dialogue of the serious, often shaped by allegory and catechism, has an important place in man's life.

The distrust for language which Everett Zimmerman feels that Defoe expresses through Crusoe indicates a deeper confusion about the power of language.[56] Defoe seems to be insecure with dialogue, description, or chronicle of gesture. He repeats Crusoe's experiences in a variety of ways, and in the repetition conveys motive and personality. In *Moll Flanders, Colonel Jack,* and *Roxana* especially, Defoe explores motive more freely and seems more comfortable with its ambiguity. Jack and Captain Singleton have a common childhood. Rather than being made over, Jack intends to make himself over. His concept of himself is substituted for William Walter's directions. His motives spring from his knowledge that he must be both a moral man and an economic success while his prudence and education make him inadequate for the task. The cumulative motive of the Defoe hero fits him especially well. He must reason out what the right thing is, what the efficacious thing is, and then hope that he has the prudence to have judged correctly and that he will not be overwhelmed by the self he cannot control.

Motivation is not a central concern in *The General History of the Pirates,* but Defoe's experience in presenting motive pays dividends here. Some of the most interesting parts of the book depend on unusual or satiric motivation. Anne Bonny and Mary Read, the female pirates, were both dressed and reared as boys. Both grew up stronger and more courageous than many men. Here, as in *An Essay upon Projects,* Defoe suggests that education and culture account for many differences between the sexes.[57] Defoe uses the schematic method to suggest motive to good purpose here. Both win in hand-to-hand combat at some point and remain on deck fighting when all but one man hides. Mary Read has several "masculine" speeches. Of hanging she says "she thought it no great hardship, for were it not for that, every cowardly fellow would turn Pirate, and so infest the seas that men of courage must starve . . . [and] that many of those who are now cheating the widows and orphans, and oppressing their poor neighbours who have no money to obtain justice, would then rob at sea, and the ocean would be crowded with rogues like the land, and no merchant would venture out . . . (135–136)." The assignment of satiric motivation enlivens other passages. Captain Bartholomew Roberts is said to have been able to change his principles "And what he did not like as a private man he could reconcile to his conscience as a commander." The stroller's comparison between the motives of pirates and kings in the life of Bellamy is swift and incisive. Such wry, biting remarks save *The General History* from the limitations of criminal biographies by deft observations on the similarities in human natures and societies. By ignoring the clichés or exaggerating the euphemisms ordinarily used to mask actions, Defoe uncovers hypocrisy and virulence.

At times didactic purposes compete with artistic success. In his desire to explain and teach, Defoe allows his characters to preach. In Defoe's best books, expository material is integrated smoothly. *Colonel Jack,* often described as an uneven book at best, fairly jerks and stumbles while *Moll Flanders* moves continuously, the protagonist's eyes glinting with life. In *Colonel Jack,* the expository material is inartistically presented; it breaks the movement and works against sustained impact. The interest and sense of immediacy die when the narrative pauses and catechistic dialogue intervenes. Despite the serious and comic potential of Jack's succession of marriages, the theme never develops much power. Jack's six-year marriage to the widow exemplifies the major problem. The lengthy courtship and sober conjugal life augur well, but the marriage fails, and the reflections upon the failure occupy nearly as many words as the courtship and marriage together. The wife begins to drink while recovering from disease and childbirth. Jack describes the effects of intemperance in lurid and distracting terms:

> In this Life of Hellish Excess, as I have said, She lost all that was before so Valuable in her: and a Villain, if it be proper to call a Man, that was really a Gentleman, by such a Name, who was an intimate Acquaintance coming to pretend a Visit to her, made her and her Maid so Drunk together, that he lay with them both, with the Mistress, the Maid being in the Room, and with the Maid, the Mistress being in the Room (242).

Such exaggerated and sensational examples are used to emphasize the bad effects, but the unity of the incident and the lesson are badly overshadowed. The wife's behavior is nearly as extravagant as the fictitious examples also given.

A similar incident occurs in *Roxana*. After her husband deserts her and Amy disposes of the children, Roxana becomes a mistress to the landlord. She and Amy joke about the landlord possessing Amy, and there are hints that Amy finds the man more attractive than Roxana does. He has been a tyrant to Roxana by seizing her furniture, but Amy blushes and thinks of sex immediately. She tells Roxana that she is sure he will ask a "favor" and urges her to comply,

> "Why look you, Madam, if he would but give you enough to live easie upon, he should lye with me for it with all my heart" (28).

As she serves dinner, Amy is merry and hurries away to put on her best clothes. Roxana naively comments that Amy did all of these things because she loved her mistress to excess. Neither can sleep, and Amy gets up several times to dance around the room, "a Testimony still of her violent Affection for her Mistress." On his next visit, Amy works in his room as Roxana and he tour it:

> Well, *Amy*, says he, I intend to Lye with you to Morrow Night; *To Night, if you please Sir*, says Amy, very innocently, *your Room is quite ready*: Well Amy, says he, I am glad you are so willing. . . .

Embarrassed, Amy runs away. He kisses Roxana, and she is stirred by gratitude and desire to what she calls love. She "courts" him to stay the night, and he agrees and asks her to prepare a wedding supper. After he leaves, Roxana admits that he "fires" her blood. Amy knows what the outcome will be in spite of Roxana's futile "I hope he won't's."

> ... he will ask you, and you will grant it too; I'm sure my Mistress is no Fool; come, pray Madam, let me go air you a clean Shift; don't let him find you in foul Linnen the Wedding-Night (37).

Her suggestive language and casuistical arguments both frighten and titillate Roxana. Her imagination seizes on the confrontation and the surrender. Here she associates Amy with the Devil in two ways. Amy reminds her of their poverty, and poverty is a devil, to them. Like the devil, Amy argues Roxana into the jaws of Hell under the guises of friendship and practical advice:

> Look ye, Madam, said she, if you won't consent, tell him you'll do as Rachel did to Jacob, when she could get no Children, put her Maid to Bed to him; tell him you cannot comply with him, but there's Amy, he may ask her the Question, she has promis'd me she won't deny you (39).

Roxana relents, swayed by gratitude, a contract, and a purse of guineas. Before the consummation, however, he dances with Amy and they joke about putting Amy to bed with him: "And the Girl wou'd no more have refus'd him, than I intended to do. . . ."

A year and a half later, Amy brings the subject up again. She brags that she would have been pregnant twice in that length of time. Roxana says, "Let him try," and Amy's only objection is that he now belongs to Roxana (45). Amy continues to tease, " . . . if you put me to Bed to him, that's another Case, I believe I shall not rise again very soon." They joke at supper, and the behavior of the landlord and Amy seems designed to bring the jest to conclusion. He waits in bed, and Amy comes in to undress Roxana. Instead Roxana undresses Amy (who is wearing very little). Amy makes little resistance. This incident confirms Roxana's opinion that she is no wife. She sits by the copulating couple and reflects on what it means about her morality and the quality of this union. At this time, she expresses hostility toward Amy. She admits that she cannot tolerate the idea that her maid is better than she. Later Amy and the landlord regret the incident, but Roxana encourages them until Amy bears a daughter. Spleen, Swift's favorite motive, pushes Roxana on "to make others as wicked as myself. . . ." Roxana records that she bears a daughter and notes "as well as Amy" and the next year a "charming," healthy son.

The Rachel/Bilhah story is finally acted out in Roxana's relationship with Amy. Contemporary commentators on Genesis 30 dwell upon the unnatural relationships and Rachel's discontented and envious personality.[58] Matthew Henry, for instance, writes, "We have here the ill Consequences of that odd Marriage which Jacob made with the two Sisters," a sister's child should be closer than a maid's, and "Rachel had done that absurd and preposterous Thing of putting her Maid into her Husband's Bed." He compares Rachel unfavorably to Isaac's wife Rebekah and to Hannah, calls her "importunate and peremptory," and concludes, "See the Power of Jealousy and Rivalship." Defoe's allusion to the Rachel/Bilhah story underscores the peculiar relationship which develops between Roxana and Amy, in addition to the faults in Roxana's personality, yet reminds the reader that a mistress has put her maid to bed with her husband before, thereby making the incident more acceptable and credible. Unlike the incident in *Colonel Jack,* the episode in *Roxana* is prepared for by the earlier allusion to the Bible story and by the complexity of the relationship between maid and mistress.

Everett Zimmerman has pointed out that Amy serves as a surrogate and alter-ego for Roxana. Amy, in fact, often does what Roxana has decided is immoral but desirable.[59] Roxana might be able to suppress her desire or even think of other alternatives, but Amy argues the price so vividly that Roxana sees only the negative consequences. The potential for action puts Amy in competition with Roxana. If Roxana will not have the landlord, Amy will. If Roxana cannot manage Susan, Amy can. Amy's temperament precipitates Roxana's decisions, and her ability to link her welfare with Roxana's doubles the burden. "They" starve, "they" are in dire straits, "they" are threatened, and the normal master/servant relationship is perverted until corruption replaces care, and Roxana's child like Rachel's Joseph, is threatened. The destruction of natural barriers and normal obligations results in chaos and misery. Roxana's feelings and motives become as complex as modern psychologists allow, and the collective reasons, mixing the commendable and the despicable, determine actions about which Roxana is ambivalent. On the one hand, she feels she had little real choice, on the other she knows she is less than she hoped. Her successive costumes and addresses testify to her warring personality.[60] She would like to be exotic and outside sober English society: she puts on a Turkish costume or becomes the mistress of a prince under an assumed title. She would like to be a pious married woman: she dresses as a Quaker and troubles herself about her children.

What Defoe does in *Roxana* is to let motive and situation interact and stand alone. Responsibility, obligation, desire for approval, jealousy, personality—all of these complicate decision-making, and the longer the association, the more charged the atmosphere. Defoe takes pains to develop the trauma of Roxana's final break with Amy and to spin out the nuances of relationships with others. She knows several characters for extended periods of time and renews contact with the Prince, the Dutch merchant, and Susan.

The contrast to Defoe's technique in *Colonel Jack* illustrates the more skillful integration of incident in the later novel. In *Colonel Jack,* the scene in which his wife and maid share the same man adds another disappointment to Jack's life, sets him adrift again, and makes a statement about the consequences of alcoholism. The same incident in *Roxana* has far more significance for the novel as a whole. The relationship between Roxana and Amy, Roxana's complex personality, and the degradation of her character hastened by circumstances and self-destructive urges work together for the first time in this episode. The relatively shallow use of such a powerful scene in *Colonel Jack* distracts in its discrepancy between meaning in the book and impact in experience. In *Roxana,* the scene and its meaning match. This scene more than Roxana's liaison with the landlord serves as the pivotal point in her final judgment on her self. Her opinion of herself solidifies, and what she is willing to do expands. The central theme of responsibility takes shape.

Before the incident, Roxana sees her responsibilities in an entirely traditional way. First, she must be an obedient daughter. Then she must be a loyal wife, and the loyalty extends into her narrative. Simultaneously desiring to justify herself and remain dutiful, she refuses to tell the husband's name and admits she consented to the match. She does not blame her father or her brother for leaving her without independent wealth. The children worry her considerably and she weeps over the food, clothing, and future of her five children. After Amy has placed the children with the wealthy relative, Roxana's obligations shift. Amy has claims on her now because Roxana owes her money and gratitude. Amy has refused to desert her and has solved her greatest problem.

Gratitude is also a prime motive for Roxana's first adulterous relationship. The landlord has helped her and after a while she admits that she is "mortgaging Faith, Religion, Conscience, and Modesty" and is giving herself "over to the Devil to show myself grateful to my Benefactor." Later she will discharge her obligation to the Dutchman in bed. Amy becomes Roxana's family, and they make a strange marriage. Much is made of the number of times they sleep together. Responsibilities divide: Roxana earns the money, Amy makes the arrangements; Roxana cautions, Amy persuades. Roxana calls Amy her agent and assumes responsibility for some of her actions.[61] Her confused values in expressing gratitude toward the landlord and Amy contrast to the legitimate kinds of responsibility she expresses toward the Quaker, her children,[62] and the Dutchman once they are married. She decides to reform partly because she does not want to be "scandalous" to her children and takes considerable pains to have them provided for. The Dutchman's happiness, generosity, and well-being concern her, and she is afraid she will be responsible for unhappiness for him. She broods about adding the profits of "whoredom" to his honest fortune and bringing the blast of heaven down on him, too. Caught at the end between her guilty association with Amy's deed and her loyalty to her children, she finds both ties have been false. Neither relationship was what she hoped for and believed in.

The discussion of *Roxana* is the beneficiary of the simulated societies of the other novels in three ways. First, the societies isolate the protagonist and the forces working on him. Roxana exists separate from the exterior world. Her nightmares, thoughts, and fancies recall Robinson Crusoe's on the island. Like the haunted modern character, she lives in fear that she will betray herself. Roxana is as lonely as H. F. or Crusoe or Moll when she knows she has married her brother. Exile translates from the mental reflected in physical setting to exile in the midst of concerned friends. Second, the societies provide opportunities for repetition and authorial intrusions. Roxana's tortured thoughts circle in similar ways, and Defoe allows events to speak for themselves. Finally, the simulated societies often compel the character to evaluate himself. Such is the case for Moll Flanders (and Crusoe):

> Then I repented heartily of all my Life past, but that Repentance yielded me no Satisfaction, no Peace, no not in the least, because as I said to myself, it was repenting after the Power of farther Sinning was taken away; I seem'd not to Mourn that I had committed such Crimes, and for the Fact . . . but I mourn'd that I was to be punish'd for it (99).

Moll reflects when she is thrown into Newgate and adds when she is condemned to die:

> It was now that for the first time I felt any real signs of Repentance; I now began to look back upon my past Life with abhorrence, and having a kind of view into the other Side of time, the things of Life as I believe they do with every Body at such a time, began to look with a different Aspect ... (113).

Similarly Robinson Crusoe after settling on the island has time to think, and eventually records in his journal:

> Even after I was afterwards, on due consideration, made sensible of my condi-tion, how I was cast on this dreadful place, out of humane kind, out of all hope of relief, or prospect of redemption, as soon as I saw but a prospect of living ... and was far enough from being afflicted at my condition, as a judgment from Heaven, or as the hand of God against me; these were thoughts which very seldom enter'd my head (74).

Both Moll and Crusoe prepare the reader for these thoughts. In the prefaces to these books the purported writer's story is recommended, in a large part, by their exemplary repentances. With the retrospective viewpoint, Moll and Robinson Crusoe keep up a running commentary on the state of their souls. Moll has gauged her indifference to religion, her rationalizations, her hardening throughout the book; when she writes of her reform in these terms and stages, the reader expects this emphasis and recurring thread in the narrative. Robinson Crusoe illustrates the "wisdom of Providence." Phrases typical of Puritan writers such as Bunyan and Bradford ("it pleased God that ... ") as well as sentences echoing the Scriptures or confessions of the church abound ("What is this earth and sea which I have seen so much, whence is it produc'd, and what am I, and all the other creatures, wild and tame, humane and brutal, whence are we?") His description of this reform is even more gradual and smooth than Moll's. He says that at first his only thoughts about God were expressed in the ejaculation, "Lord ha' mercy upon me." Crusoe has come from a solid middle-class family; he would be expected, then, to have some religious education. His reaction to his great fear and misery follow the pattern of the nominal Christian in such a situation. He prays because he thinks he ought to, and knows nothing else that might get him out of his predicament (even though he probably doesn't believe this will really help): "Pray'd to God for the first time since the storm off the Hull, but scarce knew what I said, or why: my thought being all confused" (99). He has been eight years in a condition he calls "stupidity of soul," by which he means insensibility. The evolving thoughts about God in his enforced solitude begin with anger at God and include musing about the nature of a God who could "utterly ruin" one of his creatures and create all with some "secret power." His confusion finds rest in superstition more often than in insight until it culminates in his understanding of the dream he had in the midst of a violent fever. He begins to study the Bible and sees his life as controlled by Providence.

Psychologists are aware of the comfort of seeing trouble as the will of God. It both makes the experience bearable and throws a cloak of piety over the suffering which strengthens the ego. Crusoe is in a situation which few could endure for twenty-eight years and in obviously unsound mental and physical health. His spiritual condition, like that of Moll, has been an ongoing concern, and the reader knows it is an important part of the narrative. When Crusoe comes to understand and have faith in the ultimate wisdom and benevolence of God, he meets the reader's expectations for the narrative pattern and mythic elements of the book.

Jack's observation in Virginia, in contrast, jars:

> During this Scene of Life, I had time to reflect on my past Hours, and upon what I had done in the World, and 'tho I had no great Capacity of making clear Judgment, and very little reflections from Conscience, yet it made some impressions upon me; and particularly that I was brought into this miserable Condition of a Slave by some strange directing Power, as a Punishment for the Wickedness of my younger years . . . (119).

His protest, "and 'tho I had no great Capacity of making a clear Judgment, and very little reflections from Conscience" makes whatever he says sound unconvincing and too sophisticated for this disavowal. Jack's religious education is non-existent. Furthermore, while his "instincts" toward gentlemanly behavior may be believed because he has ample models around him, his sudden instinct for the Puritan ethic is hardly credible as an example of natural religion. "Some strange directing Power" punishing him for a wicked childhood sounds superstitious. Moreover, Jack knows that he was wicked primarily because his experiences with the old woman showed him he was hurting others and with Will showed him that thieves were brutish. It would be more believable had Jack said, "Perhaps there is a God"—surely he had heard of God even if primarily in curses. But to say "some strange directing Power" carries the "instinctive" belief too far. What is an integral part of the "histories" of Moll and Crusoe is awkwardly introduced and hurried in Jack's story. Where expository material comes out of the character's own voice, and is interjected as a fleeting reminiscence rather than sustained remonstrances, it serves Defoe's instructional purposes as well as the artistic ones of developing, motivating, and revealing character.

The inner lives and landscapes of Robinson Crusoe, Moll Flanders, and Roxana become as compelling as the external situations. Their vision and narration consume the society as surely as Bunyan's dream or Swift's satire. All three writers convey the truths of dream which have to do with fears, anxieties, hopes, and the feelings of living in society. Defoe moves closer to the technique of the modern novel because he fully intends to place his characters in a recognizable, contemporary world and to use that world to reflect the inner lives of his characters. In Defoe we have a less overt illustration of a philosophical or religious position than we have in the narratives of Bunyan and Swift. Defoe shows an organic process of growth coming from the individual's confrontation with external reality and his own reflections and interior experience. Dreams in his novels continue to be possible signs from Heaven and re-creations of daytime thoughts; because they partake of the kind of dream-visions of Bunyan and surrealism of Swift's most complex and creative satires even as they are signs of troubled thoughts and passions, they must be considered as another form of experience. They must be evaluated by the character and the reader almost on the same terms as event and dialogue are. When we compare the wild dreams of the Portuguese nun (*Five Love-Letters from a Nun to a Cavalier*, 1678), Aphra Behn's *The Fair Jilt* (1688), and Eliza Haywood's Alovisa in *Love in Excess* (1719) we can see the difference. Defoe has gone beyond his contemporary novel writers to infuse the dreams of his characters with symbolic and emblematic meaning. Roxana may have the same gory dreams, and they may come at similar times. She may be tossed by desires for revenge and haunted by guilt, but her dreams have dimensions beyond those of Alovisa; hers are full of Biblical language and are the means of providing checkpoints and benchmarks for the progress of her soul.

The great contribution to fiction that Bunyan, Swift, and Defoe made was the egocentric narrator. Before *Robinson Crusoe* in 1719, secret histories, fantastic tales of erotic nuns, and courtship tales made original by exotic turns of plot were the stuff of fiction. We may forget that hundreds of French and Spanish tales much like the novellas of Behn, Gildon, and Manley dominated bookstalls. Jane Barker was still leaving her wayward heroines in the hands of fish (*Exilius*, 1715), Charles Gildon was putting together tales of adultery, blackmail, avarice, and mayhem (*The Golden Spy*, 1709), and Delarivière Manley jumbled political slander with erotic scenes of beautiful women discovered in perfumed beds in her secret histories. Most of these same writers would turn to writing books more like the domestic conduct books, and novelists like Penelope Aubin and Mary Griffith would join their ranks. For example, Barker would turn to stories of English country life and families finding financial success by selling boiled wheat in her Patch-Work Screen books, Davys abandoned the form of *The Amours of Alcippus and Leucippe* for *The Reform'd Coquet*, and Haywood would write novels like *Betsy Thoughtless*. In all of these minor novelists' work, however, the plot was of foremost consideration, and heroes and heroines existed to have things happen to them, to endure, and to offer lessons about the implications of different courses of action.

In the work of Bunyan, Swift, and Defoe the egocentric narrator's personality and vision give form to the work.[63] The structure of the novel becomes the form the character uses to explain himself and his experience as a human being to himself and others. Even in Bunyan's work the narrator absorbs the narrative as none of the fictional protagonists of turn-of-the-century novels do. Mansoul is character and city, Christian's journey absorbs his whole attention and his personality. For him, as for Swift and Defoe later, the metaphors and shape of narrative become analogy to the consciousness. He, like they, felt existence and attempted to communicate the simultaneous awareness of event and mind's activity. As the narrator interprets experience, he goes beyond even the most vivid contemporary novel characters to unify the work and give force to its themes. In imposing pattern and meaning, the narrator asserts his personality and also offers himself as a kind of supra-individual whose experiences irradiate the external world. Paradoxically, the concentration on the life of the mind makes external events more significant and more powerful.

CHAPTER V

LIMITS AND FULFILLMENT

OPPOSING the concept of social harmony and personal well-being, the Western mind imagines strife, disorder, isolation, and diminishing sense of purpose. In troubling times, the artist addresses this vision specifically as Aristophanes, Juvenal, Orwell, and Eliot did. He sees the always endangered image of the good society immediately threatened and must bring others to the same conclusion. The problem posed for the artist is that of constructing a world which can be apprehended as real while bearing heuristic and mantic themes. Furthermore, to carry the author's vision, the construct must forbid both mere recognition by the reader and, conversely, rejection. In fascinating ways, the artist who perceives his world in these terms deals with control and helplessness on two fronts. He himself seeks to control a world in which he feels more than a moderate amount of helplessness. He must select from and order what he perceives as a fragmenting world. Secondly, he must control an image depicting increasing impotence. His efforts, then, may deny his vision.

The artist's characters bear much of the burden for his themes of harmony and well-being and, in contrast, of strife and dissatisfaction. Bunyan's choice of form and the man's cry, "What shall I do?"—Swift's societies with their anthropological detail, and Gulliver's obsessive questioning, "How is man perverting the image of God?"—Defoe's striving characters who carve out middle-class lives—all demonstrate the artists' selection and isolation of character and setting. And all draw their enduring appeal from the characters' alternating feelings of control and helplessness. Christian sinks physically when he mentally mires down. A comparison of his feelings when he rejects Talkative and Ignorance or when he fights Apollyon with his thoughts in the dungeon or in the frantic climb back to get his roll make the power of control tangible. Similarly Gulliver does tricks and searches for opportunities to bring himself to the Brobdingnag king's attention in contrast to the times he decides without apology to disobey the Lilliputian king's orders. When the Houyhnhnms banish him, Gulliver feels humiliated and impotent. His shame increases his desire to hide and to reject the men his master calls Yahoos and with whom he insists Gulliver belongs. His rejection of his family becomes an exertion of control of his environment and self-respect. Robinson Crusoe's greatest triumphs come in moments on the island when he feels powerful rather than helpless. He feels success when he controls time by keeping a record on a stake, ientifies seed time and charts currents, completes his fortifications, makes boards and a grindstone, and explores his island completely. His assertion that he is master and king applies to his environment as much as to his government of the colony: " . . . I was made Master of my Business, and knew exactly when the proper Season was to sow; and that I might expect two Seed Times, and two Harvests every Year." [1] His greatest triumphs are over his mental state. He strives for composure and most often achieves it in the times when he feels most confident of God's care.[2]

A Tale of a Tub dramatizes the anxiety over control and fulfillment. The compulsive joining, persuading, and proselytizing in Swift's works express the insecurity of his satiric targets. The *Tale's* brothers justify their actions with each other, then separate and persuade others. They cannot stand up to the fashionable world, to Peter, or to their own mutilated coats. The Tailors' deity in Section II consumes men and watches others swallowed up by their clothes. Their faith and the brothers' opinion summed up in the slightly revised passage "in Them we Live, and Move, and have our Being" demonstrate the substitution of belief and freedom for dependence upon artificial appearance. Regardless of character and capability, a man dressed in a certain way is called a "judge." The same substitution of disguise and symbol for essential truth occurs in language. Wit, conversation, humor, and raillery match fashionable ornaments. The desire to conform leads to all kinds of false pleading, locking up the will, and finally to such pressing debts that Peter takes over the house. Peter wears three hats, a bunch of keys, and an angling rod as signs of his pretensions, then runs mad with spleen, and his inability to tolerate dissent bespeaks his insecurity.

Similarly, the narrator's elaborate *apologia* for modern writers overargues. He admits that criticism motivates him and, like Tristram Shandy, that his material slithers out of control. His consciousness of the act of writing creates a narrator creating himself. The contradiction between the urbane master of the prefatorical and digressive form reveals the self-justifying hack. Rather than being creative, he is parasitic. Rather than being learned, he is an allusion-dropper. Rather than being incisive, he is muddled. Examine his arguments and we find the food he himself describes—worm-infested, maggot-ridden, dangerous to the teeth. He cannot even control his analogies. In the act of demonstrating mastery, he exposes an unbridled pen. The subject consumes the narrator and his language. He announces that he has lost his manuscript and must release the reader; again, he insists upon his power (to release the reader and, incidentally, himself) while admitting he has no choice, no means to maintain influence.

Gulliver operates in the same way at times. He falls in with the projectors and offers his own schemes, he accepts Houyhnhnm interpretations yet he insists that he is a perceptive, reliable narrator. His explanations of his behavior plead control but his behavior argues his immersion and loss of self. Like the narrator of *A Tale of a Tub*, he finally washes his hands of his book. The publisher, his cousin, and his readers have betrayed him. He and the modern present themselves as misunderstood and unappreciated. The discrepancy between intention and product provides humor along with the familiar satiric picture of the diminutive narrator proclaiming his truth solemnly. The effort to control and order becomes finally the evidence of impotence.

For Bunyan, anxiety and assurance alternate in the Christian life. At first everything is a threat—the self, the family, acquaintances, places, any of these can be the door to Hell. Again the image of being swallowed up and lost appears. Christian spends a great part of his journey feeling anxious, wary, and fearful. He fears the River at the end more than almost any part of the trip, and he nearly sinks in it. Christiana has more assurance in beginning her trip and more knowledge of her destination, but she, too, experiences considerable anxiety. Her nightmares wake her, she trembles, and sweats. Not until the Valley of the Shadow of Death does she understand the kinds of darkness that Christian had gone through. Secret, Reliever, Great-heart, and others guide or accompany her and the pilgrims, and Christiana's sense of assurance is always greater than Christian's. She expresses surprise and outrage when Ill-favoured accosts them, and Mercy feels comfortable in the Valley of Humiliation.

Christian's and Christiana's anxiety exists in proportion to their knowledge and faith. Christian begins by saying, "What shall I do?" and undertakes the journey blindly. He rarely knows what lies ahead, feels only intermittent signs of grace. Christiana wants to be saved, she knows her goal far earlier. Her dream and Secret invite her to God, and she freely puts her trust and safety in guides. Christian is alone; Christiana accompanied. The paradox of individual responsibility within a Providential world works itself out in both pilgrimages. Both realize that they must undertake the journey and, furthermore, must travel a defined path adhering to a strict code of conduct. What they can control is limited by their own internal experiences as well as by external forces. In spite of these attacks, a center of being must be inviolable and unwavering. At times this core shrinks drastically. Their helplessness is most apparent in their relationship to God whose grace and periodic intervention finally controls their destinies. As in *A Tale,* yet for different reasons and in completely different ways, the assertion of the self defines the limits and testifies to ultimate helplessness. The common narrative patterns of man the solitary adventurer and woman the virtuous mother, man finding his way and woman being led, work themselves out in Bunyan's two narratives and teach the same lessons.

Defoe, like Bunyan, re-creates the tension felt by the adventurer. Crusoe, Singleton, and Jack feel considerable anxiety because they do not know what lies before them. Both their desire and their fancies race before the present moment and create an approach-avoidance conflict. They have a goal and realize the need to persevere, but they fear the unknown. Crusoe wants to find the source of the footprint yet he wants to hide; he wants to see the cannibals, yet he dreads the discovery.[3]

All three writers realize the sources of loss of control. Men make foolish mistakes; they lose control of themselves and lose sight of their interests. Swift creates deluded, crazed, and pathetic characters. Bunyan shows men sleeping, being led astray, and giving in to lust, avarice, and drink. Defoe understands the irrational obsessions that send Crusoe to sea, lead Moll to steal the bundle, and awaken Roxana's fear of Susan. Most consistently and most movingly, all three writers portray man's gullibility and intellectual limits. Time after time, their characters simply are not intelligent enough to steer the best course.

To many readers, Bunyan studies God, Swift man, and Defoe society, yet all three relentlessly anatomize the human drive for self-realization set against the threat of loss of self. For all three, the need to explain the ways of God becomes inseparable from the description of the temporal experience of man. The same limitations bemuse them all. First, all see men experiencing a battle within; conflict, ambivalence, fear, anxiety, all of the labels that psychology has put at the tip of our tongues become the reality for their protagonists at some time. Mansoul is the metaphor; Roxana and Defoe's other protagonists stand poised, torn, as G. A. Starr describes, by social, moral, and psychological imperatives;[4] Gulliver's retrospective descriptions of the decisions he made about what to tell and how to tell it on the islands and in his *Travels* allude to the divisions within the ambiguity of choice. Second, all believe in the horror of the "lethargy of soul" which can debilitate a man without warning or remedy. Mr. Badman is often described as lying down, slumping, sitting, slouching, all metaphors for his hopeless condition. Defoe's characters fight the desire to sit down and weep, and Swift's Irishmen slip into bestiality.

For all three writers naiveté is not innocence but limitation, potential gullibility, imperceptiveness, threat. Furthermore, all realize the limits of human reason and wisdom. The thoughts of Defoe's characters scurry down paths like rats in a maze, Swift's men turn projector in hopes of overcoming limits, and Bunyan's forge ahead hoping God will take over when sight fails. None can escape the vision of man as the jest of the universe, continually insisting upon his dignity and importance, yet frequently tripping, falling in manure, admiring the wrong people, puzzling over the ways by which they make their fellowmen laugh. In fact, man's mind seems to assure his stumbles and embarrassment because his imagination knows no limits and aspires to becoming what he can only imagine.

Gulliver's Travels presents this theme in several ways. Gulliver discovers his limitations on every island and in increasingly painful ways. Book III has tragic dimensions. These distorted and wrongheaded creatures know what they want to create, can communicate their vision to Gulliver, and yet accomplish nothing except to make themselves ridiculous. The projectors on one side of the street in the Academy of Lagado, for example, want sunny summers, more food, fruits out of season, cures for diseases, silk, increased knowledge and improved communication. On the other side of the street, the political projectors intend to find a way to teach ministers to consult the public good and to know their true interests, that of their people. These goals are necessarily thwarted, on the one side by the nature of the physical world and, on the other, by human nature which other projectors strive to use rather than fight.[5] The metaphors of disease and the extreme remedies damn the visionary hopes of the first set of projectors. The violence of the *Modest Proposal* is of a piece with the sixth chapter of Part III; that wisdom and good cannot triumph calls forth a stream of ingenious and wrongheaded schemes from supposedly well-intentioned people. Trapped by his understanding of limits, the projector can only create debased schemes.[6]

Betrayed and ultimately unaided by his reason, the good man strives not only to realize his potential but to understand his experience. Bunyan's and Defoe's religion inclined them to seek the meaning of mundane events; Swift's view of history led him to search for symbols in historical events. The possibilities and results hidden in apparently trivial matters fascinated them all, and a recurrent theme in their works is the attempt to locate the design and separate out accident. *Robinson Crusoe* and *Pilgrim's Progress* exist to a considerable degree to describe God's relationship to man and the natural world. When Defoe presents incidents such as the forgotten seeds, the discovery of the footprint, and the coming of Friday and insists upon the possibility that God acts through accident to effect design, his technique approaches the level of allegory. Crusoe's extended reflections on the events dramatize the limits of reason even as they explore forms of reality. Likewise, Swift was fascinated by the influence that petty actions have on the course of history. Whether it be a king's sexual appetite, a general's preference for land battles, or a palace fire,[7] Swift insists upon the power of the apparently irrelevant. The protagonist for Bunyan, Swift, and Defoe pits his limited and beseiged reason against a chaotic barrage of experience and impressions.

Peter's brothers, the Aeolists, the Irish, the readers of Partridge's prophecies, and the romantic young men of the scatological poems seem to possess a limitless capacity to be wrong. The danger of being misled is especially threatening. In his nonfiction writings, Swift often addresses his readers as if they belong in the work itself and as if they had been taken advantage of. *The Conduct of the Allies* depends heavily upon this stance.[8] "What Arts have been used to possess the People with a *strong Delusion,* that *Britain* must infallibly be ruined, without the Recovery of *Spain* to the House of *Austria?*" he marvels and contrasts the rational judgment of the past and future to the insanity of the present. He never misses a chance to set up a sentence as he does this one; the fact that England's labors will benefit another nation (Austria) is repeated often.

The reader, as the past's posterity, has inherited a glorious England while the reader's posterity will inherit the difficulties created by the madness of present action. He notes that in the past "our Victories were then of some Use as well as Glory; for we were so prudent to Fight, and so happy to Conquer, only for our selves." The grandchildren of the author of this "detestable project" will not see an end to the consequences of a war begun "to make France acknowledge the late King, and to recover *Hudson's Bay*," Swift laments. Repeating the ideas that "Posterity will be at a loss to conceive what kind of Spirit could possess their Ancestors...," "Posterity will marvel...," "Posterity will think that those who first advised the War, had either not the Sense or the Honesty to consider...," Swift contrasts the rational judgment of the past and future with the insanity of the present.

Swift presents the folly of the English people in a variety of ways until they become both auditors and participants. He describes the people in irrational scenes: those beggared by the war waste fuel by lighting a bonfire to celebrate the conquering of a new town for the Dutch to garrison; the fruits of war are reduced to rags hanging in Westminster Hall. He itemizes the delusions the English have been under, carefully playing their gullibility against the guile of their deceivers. Certain phrases become a refrain: "It was pretended that the war could not possibly last above one or two campaigns"; "Some would pretend to lessen the merit of this"; " 'tis wonderful." A staggering list of examples of imbecility juxtaposes the abuse and the "reasonable" perspective:

Abuse	*Perspective*
The desire to force people to recognize the British monarch.	Englishmen should have too much pride to stoop so low.
Conducting the war primarily on the northern border of France.	"We have now for Ten Years together turned the whole Force and Expence of the War, where the Enemy was best able to hold us at Bay...."
Conducting the war primarily on land.	England is a "Maritime Power."

Bearing the greatest share of the burden of the war.	They have the least to gain of all the major participants.
What they have conquered.	They have gained a town a year for the Dutch, and the French king probably sits down with his advisors and agrees on the date to surrender the town.

Swift's descriptions begin by creating a tone of wonder: "*We* have been deluded, how could this happen?" They begin to play on the prejudices of ordinary Englishmen and, finally, provide scapegoats and a solution, both much desired by a people in economically troubled times. Ending the war becomes the sensible and courageous thing to do rather than the sign of giving up "all they have fought for." The end is accomplished through the specious picture of the Allies and the past ministry scheming, conniving, and passing money from hand to hand in the background of a portrait of a benevolent and all too honorable Queen surrounded by her noble but gullible subjects, now exhibiting visible signs in their dress of the straits the war has brought them to. At this point, the reader and the actor in the work are indistinguishable, and gullibility explains the misery of the English people.

I

Christian, Mercy, Attentive, and numerous other characters in Bunyan's works share the human myopia. They can be taken in as Christian is by Mr. Worldly Wiseman, they can make the wrong choices as Christian does when he leaves the path to cross the meadow, and they can be unable to conceive the future and the consequences of actions. As the character realizes his limits, he becomes more anxious and cautious. *Grace Abounding to the Chief of Sinners* describes a number of phenomena which Bunyan could not control. Unbidden, curses and blasphemies came to his mind to his "great confusion and astonishment." He chooses the image of a child

whom some gipsy hath by force took up under her apron, and is carrying from
friends and country; kick sometimes I did, and also scream and cry; but yet I was
bound in the wings of temptation, and the wind would carry me away.[9]

Each phrase builds upon the image of powerlessness. He is a child, small
enough to be bundled under an apron, he is "bound." He cannot see:
under the apron, he is hurried by wings and wind. The images draw upon
senses other than sight: he feels movement, suffocation, is blown and
hurried; he kicks, screams, cries. The situation and his thoughts are
outside his control; his mind betrays him. Bunyan's fictional characters
fight such moments with physical movement, prayer, and the "weapons"
of faith. Grace, which comes like the wind or spirit leading Bunyan to
curse, appropriately sweeps such tendencies away.

Coleridge admired Defoe's making Crusoe an ordinary man who
could make crooked pots, unwieldy rafts, and a boat which he could not
launch. Such intellectual lapses appear in all of Defoe's protagonists. The
characters express the frustration of feeling their internal limits by
sitting down, cradling their heads, wringing their hands, moving in a
tangled pattern. Roxana sits among rags and weeps, then scurries from
room to room while she considers her first adultery. Jack and Moll
endlessly "reason," sometimes analogously wandering through mazes of
streets.

Increasing the characters' powerlessness is the frequency of accidents.
Uncertainty about the future provides much of the suspense in Defoe's
novels. In Roxana, Farther Adventures of Robinson Crusoe, Memoirs of a
Cavalier, and Colonel Jack, the reader becomes convinced that each peaceful interlude will end with a disaster. The tension in the novel is
sustained by the threatened event which will once more put the main
character in danger. Even when the character is not in the midst of a
crime or in other danger, he lives under the threat of accidents.

Colonel Jack's fortunes rise and fall many times. His early years are
so poverty-stricken and his naiveté so convincingly portrayed that he
seems continually on the brink of starvation or arrest. Several times in
criminal situations, Jack's silence saves him, but incidents such as the
night he kept awakening "frighted to the last degree" every hour when
he heard the watch sustain the mood. Certain calamity again threatens
when he deserts the army. Once Jack has the minimum education and
a secure financial basis, the pattern of the book changes subtly. Up to this

point, Jack has been nearly continually on the edge of misfortune; now he will have periods of prosperity and well-being which will be suddenly terminated. This pattern is established and reinforced to the point that suspense comes from the expected change of fortune rather than from the desperation of the present situation. A typical turning point comes after he has lived contentedly in London for two years:

> In the Private *Condition* I continued about two Years more, when the Devil owing me a Spleen, even since I refus'd being a Thief, paid me home, with my Interest, by laying a Snare in my way, which had almost ruin'd me.[10]

With this as the only transition, a woman lays siege for him, marries him, cuckolds him and demands exorbitant separate maintenance which nearly ruins him. Another time he announces abruptly, "But I, that was to be the most unhappy Fellow alive in the Article of Matrimony, had at last a Disappointment of the worst sort. . . ." This pattern continues through two more marriages, his unwise look at the Preston rebels, and his final economic ventures in the Gulf of Mexico in which he nearly loses his wife, his money, and his freedom.

Colonel Jack, then, is a book in which the main character repeatedly feels his "Fortunes were settled for this World, and I had nothing before me, but to finish a Life of infinite Variety," but who discovers that "Man is a short sighted Creature at Best, and in nothing more than in that of fixing his own Felicity." The first half of the book in which Jack is more continually on the brink of disaster is so compelling that the second half seems slow by comparison. The pattern seems episodic or even strung out until it is established, and then it is so firmly set, that we cannot believe that Jack finally lived a settled life.

Bunyan includes natural obstacles—sloughs, darkness, the threat of rock slides—and sickness as unexpected problems, but, undoubtedly, the greatest source of anxiety is society. The examples, the values, the threats of the human environment engender the greatest sense of helplessness and inspire the strongest efforts to control. "Example" teaches individual faults such as gambling, corrupt practices such as cheating in business, and demeaning values such as emphasis on luxury and show. Attentive comments on Mr. Badman's character:

> This was a bad beginning indeed, and did demonstrate that he was, as you say, polluted, very much polluted with original corruption. . . . Not but that they

[children] learn to sin by example too, but example is not the root, but rather the temptation into wickedness (p. 153).

At the time when Swift's ambitions were high, his opportunities seemingly at their most promising, and the danger of the collapse of the Harley-Bolingbroke coalition still before him, he described man's situation in pessimistic terms:

> It was, that Persons of transcendent Merit forced their Way in Spight of all Obstacles; but those whose Merit was of second, third, or fourth Rate, were seldom able to do any Thing; because the Knaves and Dunces of the World, had all the Impudence, Assiduity, Flattery, and servile Compliance divided among them, which kept them perpetually in the Way, and engaged every Body to be their Sollicitors.[11]

He insists that the great promote the useful rather than the deserving, and his image of the competition conjures up striving, clamoring crowds. The disorder threatens social harmony and, in turn, the individual. About this time, Swift cries out against Archbishop King's badgering letters, pointing out that he cannot assure his future with the ministry. Swift's prose satires often show the same progression. First, a busy, teeming crowd mills about. Lilliput seems overpopulated. Crowds gather around Gulliver's sleeping body, they shoot hundreds of arrows at him, they climb on him, peep at him, suspend their work to stare. He fights the desire to crush forty or fifty of them at a time, 900 men participate in moving him, and he feels "great Numbers of people" around him. Next, those who might lead honorably are thwarted and assigned meaningless chores and finally must devote considerable energy to staying in power. The last step is the individual's realization that he is alone; at this point, he begins to feel a loss of purpose. For example, Gulliver becomes melancholy and longs to leave when his efforts to impose meaning and find a place for himself fail; he cannot believe in the Lilliputian government or his life as a freak in Brobdingnag for very long, and his unhappiness increases as his sense of alienation grows.

The isolated societies define the forces on the individual and expose the relationship between the development of the society or institution and the development of the individual. John's little society in *Journal of the Plague Year* parallels the development of John as leader with the evolution of the society. The former biscuit baker assumes the position of leader as he deals with the problems of hostile villages for his people and keeps them supplied with food. At each town, men fearing plague or theft question the emigrants. Without directly lying, John evades telling the villagers that the group is from London and persuades village after village to supply them with "certificates of passing," food, and tents. In a fairly typical incident, John has the men carry poles camouflaged with clay and mud to look like guns. They intimidate the constable with cleverly placed fires and a pacing "army" of men in order to get supplies and passage around a town. Defoe details John's elaborate deceptions and his dialogue with the constable in order to remove any doubt in the reader's mind that John is the leader. His army training stands him in good stead, but his slippery tongue and resourcefulness justify his leadership. Like John, the other protagonists demonstrate their qualifications early—natural parts: common sense, "capacity," resourcefulness, industry, courage.[12] As the leader develops, so does his society just as John's becomes well-disciplined, prosperous, and secure.

The London John left also illustrates the symbiotic development of individual and society. As order and authority collapse, personalities cave in. Repeated descriptions of theft and callousness make situation and character inseparable. Only a few can resist the effects of the plague as the waterman does; even nurses begin to smother patients.

The conjunctive development in many cases repeats the process of maturation or civilization. For instance, the individual and the society explore the situation, define perimeters, set limits, and proceed to develop their potential and to produce. Christian is an infant when he begins his journey. He recognizes that he is lost, begins the journey on which he learns his relationship to God and the truths (or rules) of salvation. He assumes the responsibilities of a mature Christian by fighting Apollyon and beginning to catechize and guide other pilgrims. Finally, his example inspires others and leaves a trail rich in signposts. His journey augments the number of Christians. The movement in the societies from the acquisition of basic necessities to the establishment of a comfortable environment to the codification of laws and punishments to the beginning of economic expansion is another way to explain the process. Crusoe on the island dramatizes the movement from fortification to colonization at the same time he moves from isolated fear into the society of men. Finally, he assumes leadership easily as he does when the group crosses France.

Bunyan's protagonists learn they have no place in societies alien to their moral nature. Mr. Badman finds his inclinations acted out in society. Just as Swift's madmen epitomize elements of English professions, so do succeeding groups express Mr. Badman's moral propensities. Mr. Wiseman lists Badman's childhood sins as lying, stealing, breaking the Lord's day, idleness, swearing, cursing, and refusing to be instructed. As an apprentice, he makes friends as bad as himself and begins to drink and steal from his master. As an adult, he uses his father's money to start a business, mistreats a good woman, cheats his friends and customers, learns to make a profit by breaking, and dies surrounded by profane men. The relationship between childhood and adult behavior illustrates the sinful nature encouraged and developed by example. In his mature, dishonest business practices, his lying, stealing, and idleness appear. His lack of respect for God, himself, and others, Wiseman believes, appears in his cursing and refusal to be improved or instructed. The man who curses, for example, feels "scorn and contempt of others" and shows pride and desperate wickedness of heart. His disregard for others makes him unfeeling when he abuses his wife or business associates.

What Mr. Badman wants to do he finds in society. Drinking, adultery, and swearing go largely unpunished and uncensured in society. The ability to trick and cheat others sometimes passes for cleverness. Attentive calls the method of profiting by declaring bankruptcy "as common as four eggs a penny" and reminds Mr. Wiseman that false reckoning and dishonest scales are not considered "so great an evil by some." The legal system allows the bankruptcy practice, and the gathering of drinking, gambling friends is taken for camaraderie and happiness.

From the beginning, Mr. Wiseman insists upon Mr. Badman's blindness and stupefication of soul. Mr. Badman cannot respond to knowledge of the eternal consequences of his actions, and he cannot even recognize the ways others exploit him. Even when his companions flatter him and borrow from him and set him up to pay for drinks, he cannot see that he is being exploited. His relationships become frivolous and predatory. The pride which Mr. Wiseman explains in such detail[13] hardens his heart and closes his senses. By the time of his death, he and his society are indistinguishable.

In contrast, Bunyan's sympathetic characters seek and find others inclined toward good. Although they must often look more diligently, they, too, find a society which shares their qualities. As they experience such a society, their propensities are nurtured and developed, too. They begin to love and trust themselves and others and become more charitable. Christian, for example, trusts his own judgment and begins to guide others toward Heaven. Rather than exploiting others and feeling anxious and avaricious, Christiana's abilities seem to expand. She encourages others, gives food and water to others, and takes care of people as she does Mercy when she asks the Shepherd for the mirror.

When man and society develop well, love and trust result; when they develop negatively, the outcome is misanthropic. Rather than the protagonist changing,[14] the development usually involves new understanding of experience and reality. The change has to do with perception and judgment, not personality itself. When the insights are good, benevolence and security result; when wrong, pride, contempt, and exploitation follow. The crucial formative influence on the character may be what he learns about society and his place in it.

Initiation into the practices and realities of society occupies a central place in Swift's work.[15] He seems to enjoy taking the reader (and his protagonists) on a tour, pointing out unpleasant details as he goes. *Gulliver's Travels,* for example, tours English institutions and professions over and over, each time discovering new abuses. The profession of law sustains repeated and increasingly specific attacks. In Lilliput, the laws associated with politics primarily bind people to tasks. They are identified with contortion; the ministers do acrobatic tricks, people swear by arranging the arms and legs in awkward positions, and Gulliver is assigned unusual duties. Civil laws, contrasting to England's, protect citizens more effectively. The Lilliputians punish deceit more harshly than violence and reward those who obey the law. The assignment of the hierarchy of crimes and the belief in positive reinforcement contrast to the English emphasis on punishment and lack of insight. The Lilliputians, unlike the English and the Brobdingnagians, do not execute criminals publicly or carelessly. In Lilliput and England, however, service to the state is often rewarded with envy, suspicion, and plotting.[16]

The middle books of *Gulliver's Travels* develop the idea of law as tyranny designed to frighten subjects rather than teach them. In Book III descending islands, poison, ostracism, and rules to control the Struldbruggs have analogues in English society. Part IV has three developed sections on the legal system: the description of the suit over the cow, the analogy the Houyhnhnm draws between lawyers and the Yahoo trick of a third robbing two other Yahoos who are arguing over a stone, and the incident of Gulliver's desire for a law swearing travelers to tell the truth. The entanglement of law with political power exists in each society, but only in Lilliput does law reward. The images of distortion associated with the legal system appear in every part. While Gulliver may swear twisted like a pretzel in Lilliput, he describes the warping of truth through convention and language in Part IV. The movement from imaginative parallel to specific, though exaggerated, case criticizes a number of aspects of the eighteenth-century legal system including the determination of the seriousness of crimes, the power of rulers to impose pointless behavior legally, and the existence of machinery which not only excludes the criminal but makes the process which robs or condemns him all but incomprehensible.

Defoe creates a character, then places him in a situation and describes the character's reactions and discoveries, and finally restores the character to his original place in the narrative. Nothing in the rhetoric or the events of the first few pages of Defoe's novels suggests that the character is chosen or unique. The tone is matter of fact and the exposition direct and plain. The bodies of the novels, however, immerse the character in society after society, and he learns the nature of reality in some of the same ways that Swift's and Bunyan's characters do. Moll Flanders almost becomes a casualty of society. She learns that money alone assures a husband and security. She learns to sell her body as well as the illusion of wealth and makes the two indistinguishable. She learns to be a master thief, picking up the knowledge of how to be a fence, and how to turn a near-arrest into profit. Moll, however, meets good people in each situation: Robin, the banker, Jemmy, even Mother Midnight make sacrifices for her. Time after time, Moll almost becomes indistinguishable from her milieu. Her wit and a few scruples keep her above those around her, and the intervention of people like the banker rescue her when she most needs it. At the lowest points in her life, help comes from outside. Moll herself feels that she has become nothing but a Newgate bird; then Mother Midnight rescues her.

The human factor in society and the possibility for a certain amount of independent action in a group make Moll's experiences heartening rather than embittering. She, like Christian, looks for helpful people, and the direction she steers is toward security and love rather than toward alienation and misanthropy. In moving in this direction, Moll seeks more than her rightful place in society, economic gain, and security. She seeks to set up normal family relationships including finding a mother. In this quest, she often casts unlikely women in the role. She moves from mother figure to mother figure as she moves from society to society:

Her nurse, a woman undoubtedly paid for keeping Moll, but
   whom Moll insists she should call "Mother."
The Colchester matriarch. Here Moll insinuates herself into
   the family and becomes a vicarious daughter.
The vivacious lady in London who brings her out in com-
   pany before she marries the linen draper.
The widow of the sea captain whom she helps marry to a
   good suitor.
Her mother in Virginia.
The Bath landlady who reduces Moll's rent and encourages
   her relationship with the gentleman.
The Governess, "Mother Midnight."

Moll remains with the Governess for the greatest portion of the book. Significantly, it is only after she has "grown up"—been a thief, repented, found her only living, legal husband, and became a settled wife that she claims her son and assumes the role of mother herself. While she learns criminal ways from most of the women, she does find a measure of security and care with each. That she does little or nothing for any of them and that she seldom remarks on their unmotivated generosity emphasizes her child's role. Ironically, each one has succeeded in the masculine world of the eighteenth century better than Moll, and none but the Colchester woman has a husband.

II

The dynamic relationship between individual and society and the coex- isting threat of loss of self and the possibility of growth of self work themselves out in *Robinson Crusoe*.[17] Defoe, like Swift, has good reason to ponder how the same event could break one personality but benefit another. Peerage or the pillory, inspiration or stupefaction—what shifts the balance? Long before *Crusoe,* Defoe had shown an interest in the individual under pressure. He had written about the Duke of

Marlborough and Robert Harley as their fortunes changed after 1710, Charles XII of Sweden (1715), James Butler's apparently surprising treason (1715), and most significantly perhaps, himself as a Newgate prisoner and then as an alien counter-agent in Scotland. He, like Swift, probably believed that "Persons of transcendent Merit forced their way Way in Spight of all Obstacles," but he and Swift were of different temperaments. Swift once wrote about himself,

> I remember, when I was a little boy, I felt a great fish at the end of my line wh. I drew up almost on the ground, but it dropped in, and the disappointment vexes me to this very day, and I believe it was the type of all my future disappointments.

Swift expected frustration, and his category of "transcendent Merit" seems quite small. Defoe found life more problematical and had more interest in heroes and types of heroism. In the years he wrote fiction, he created one protagonist after another who was remarkably resilient, ingenious, and ambitious and whose dreams and aspirations were misunderstood or ridiculed by those around him.

Generations of scholars have speculated about the genesis of *Robinson Crusoe,* but surely Defoe's fascination with man under pressure is one of the primary reasons Defoe created Crusoe. In the dawn of Defoe criticism, scholars linked Crusoe with Selkirk, Dampier, and the travel books, looking little further.[18] Later scholars explained that the book was "allusive allegorick history" and similar to *Pilgrim's Progress,* found the book closely related to the period's interest in the nature of man and economic individualism, or interpreted Crusoe's physical isolation as parallel to his spiritual alienation. It seems to me that what caught Defoe's imagination was not types of books or theories, although he was interested in them, but a personality, an extraordinary man. Even the failure of Crusoe's colony emphasizes the concentration on the individual. The colony fails at the end of the book because it fails to take the next step in civilized development: active, growing trade with the rest of the world, and it never develops artistically. Crusoe loses interest, and the quality of the settlers is unpromising. Only in the most minimal ways is the colony out of the stone age. Insufficient capital has been invested and no new enterprising settlers come. A quick comparison with the constant influx of men and developers in the American colonies or in the West Indian colonies reveals the problem; even Misson's colony immediately sets up trade with other colonies. Defoe's *General History of Discoveries and Improvements* (1725–27) criticizes the Romans for this same failure to develop trade. This suggests that Defoe was primarily interested in the man in an isolated society and the development of leadership and law rather than in creating a theory and directive for colonization or civilization. Had Defoe wanted to do that, he probably would have approached it in a more realistic manner—the colonists would have planned what was needed, considered what could be exported profitably, and brought in the manpower and resources necessary. After all, Crusoe had made a considerable fortune in Brazil just this way and such endeavors do exist in the other books (*cf.* Madagascar in *The General History* and Colonel Jack's plantation). Defoe's writings in the *Review* and in pamphlets in the interest of credit and the South Sea Company indicate he was well able to create an economic model.

Defoe's lifelong admiration for King William and King Gustavus Adolphus of Sweden, his fascination with Raleigh, the Duke of Marlborough, and even Jonathan Wild are well known. In *The General History of the Pirates,* he wrote, "It is bravery and stratagem in war which make actions worthy of record; in which sense the adventures here related will be thought deserving that name" [history]. In *A Short Narrative of the Life of Marlborough,* Defoe defines the hero as "Temperate, Sober, Careful, Couragious, Politick, Skilful, so he is Courteous, Mild, Affable, Humble, and Condescending to People of the meanest Condition" and "Watchful, Alert, Thoughtful, Foreseeing, being all qualities necessary for so great a Charge." The early novels and "lives" group around this type of leader; in 1719 there were *Robinson Crusoe, Farther Adventures,* and *The King of Pirates* which considers Gow primarily as leader and colonist; in 1720, a life of Sir Walter Raleigh, another of Charles XII of Sweden, *Memoirs of a Cavalier, Captain Singleton,* and *Serious Reflections*; in 1721, the life of Sedley. All of these men carry on some military activities and are basically resourceful, vigorous men who act outside ordinary society. Pirates occur in two books and soldiers in three. Seventeen twenty-two finds Defoe turning to London as the primary setting for the first time.

After 1722, a second group of novels may have been influenced by attacks such as Charles Gildon's. Gildon was a hack writer, the butt of two Defoe poems, "Mere Reformation" and "Pacificator," and author of *The Life and Strange Surprizing Adventures of Mr. D . . . De F . . . , Of London, Hosier.* This pamphlet was published soon after *Farther Adventures,* and *Serious Reflections* answers many of its objections.[19] The pamphlet parodies the title page and preface and ridicules Defoe's political affiliations and the more fantastic events in *Robinson Crusoe*. Gildon's attack calls attention to the fact that some of Defoe's contemporaries considered Crusoe a scoundrel and objected to his "whimsical" religion:

> Why, that you have made me a strange whimsical, inconsistent Being, in three Weeks losing all the Religion of a Pious Education . . . you make me a Protestant in London, a Papist in Brasil; and then again, a Protestant in my own Island, and when I get thence, the only Thing that deters me from returning to Brasil, is meerly, because I did not like to die a Papist. . . .[20]

Seizing on Defoe's rather offhand statement that Robinson Crusoe is parable or allegory, Gildon has Defoe say that Crusoe is "the true Allegorick Image of thy tender Father D . . . l; I have been all my life that Rambling, Inconsistent Creature, which I have made thee." Turning from an *ad hominem* attack on Defoe's political apostasy and trips to Scotland in order to hide from creditors,[21] Gildon attacks the book specifically in "An Epistle to D . . . De F . . . e, The Reputed Author of *Robinson Crusoe*:"

> I Have perus'd your pleasant Story of Robinson Crusoe; and if the Faults of it had extended no farther than the frequent Solecisms, Looseness and Incorrectness of Stile, Improbabilities, and sometimes Impossibilities, I had not given you the Trouble of this Epistle. But when I found that you were not content with the many Absurdities of your Tale, but seem'd to discover a Design, which proves you as bad an Englishman as a Christian, I could not but take Notice in this publick Manner of what you had written; especially when I perceiv'd that you threaten'd us with more of the same Nature. . . .

Gildon accuses Defoe of quoting Scripture to "make the lie go down," having religious reflections that are neither just nor even truly religious, defending Popery with falsehoods, deterring people from going to sea, of multiplying inconsistencies and weaknesses in reasoning.[22]

In *Serious Reflections,* Defoe draws on the publicity this and similar attacks generated and answers most of their charges. *Serious Reflections,* however, is but part of Defoe's response to the stinging attacks on the veracity and value of his earlier books. In 1721, Defoe wrote no fiction and only one life. Always one to defend himself, Defoe wrote books in 1722 "with a religious application of events to the uses to which wise men always apply them, viz, to the instruction of others by this example, and to justify and honour the wisdom of providence in all the variety of our circumstances, let them happen how they will." *Moll Flanders, Due Preparations for the Plague, Religious Courtship, Journal of the Plague Year, Peter Alexowitz,* and *Colonel Jack* all might contain models for the serious reader. All of them adhere more closely to the theory that a fable makes the moral memorable and persuasive and can be seen as "allegorick histories" made of composites as Defoe implied *Robinson Crusoe* is. Defoe seems careful to avoid the pitfalls of his earlier books; it is almost as if he were clarifying his stances and elaborating on themes which had been misunderstood and attacked earlier. For instance, *Colonel Jack* includes a specific attack on a Catholic priest, shows people and especially women prospering after going to sea, quotes Scripture less frequently, and modifies the religious reflections and conversions.

Defoe's last novels may be more representative of his interests than those of the first two groups. In *Colonel Jack,* Defoe had examined marriage rather carefully, and the five women come off badly. Roxana is very similar to two of these wives but differs in exemplary ways. Amy and Susan are both more fully developed feminine figures than usual and such themes as that of servants' behavior and retribution are reworked. *The General History,* three lives of Wild, and two of Gow seem to bring Defoe full circle: back to pirates and extraordinary men, back to doing lives over and over to examine different angles, to make money, to expand on a theme. His fiction including *Roxana* shows a definite movement from notable leaders to criminal leaders with an increasing concentration on influences and motives. After 1724, Defoe abandoned the novel form. Political and social issues engaged him anew, and he found other types of writing more suitable means of reaching his audience. In 1725, the year after *Roxana* appeared, Mary Davys's *Works* and Eliza Haywood's collection, *Secret Histories,* led an undistinguished publication list. Defoe returned to writing standard conduct books such as *Conjugal Lewdness* and *A New Family Instructor* and combined adventure stories with his renewed interest in history and geography [*The Four Years Voyages of Capt. George Robert* (1726), *The General History of Discoveries and Improvements* (1726), *Robert Drury's Journal* (1729), and *Memoirs of an English Officer* (1728)]. All of these, like the numerous lives of Wild and Sheppard which he did, are based on real or ordinary people and are largely composed of rather ordinary events.

A second way of locating the purposes and genesis of Crusoe's island is to look at Robinson Crusoe's immediate precursor, Defoe's *The Memoirs of Majr. Alexander Ramkins,* later titled *The life and strange Surprizing Adventures of Majr. Ramkins, a Highland Officer, Now in Prison at Avignon.* While Major Ramkins is primarily concerned with explaining the perfidy of the French nation concerning King James II, the seeds of *Robinson Crusoe* may be found. Ramkins, a loyal Jacobite, serves James for twenty-eight years (Crusoe is on the island twenty-eight years) in England, Ireland, and the continent. In this retrospective memoir, Ramkins is able to see how well James served France's political purposes. His anecdotes range from the rather personal and subjective impression of the lack of anxiety on the Queen's face at one of the sham invasions to a cold analysis of how fear of a French-supported restoration of James tied England's hands in conquering Ireland, led to the growth of the policy of preventing what Queen Anne would call "the exorbitant power of France," and allowed the Bourbons to succeed to the Spanish throne.

In this memoir, however, is a mishmash of incidents seemingly arranged in no progressive order but structured to break the propaganda aimed at Jacobites and particularly Scottish Jacobites. The advertisement promises "a very agreeable and instructive Lesson of Human Life, both in a Publick and Private Capacity, in several pleasant Instances of his Armours, Gallantry, Oeconomy, etc." The lesson for a man's "public capacity" can hardly be missed: Britons should "not imbark themselves in a foreign Interest for the future." Ramkins has lost his inheritance and twenty-eight years of his life, and is now in prison because of his foolish trust in James. As the memoirs draw to a close he repeats, "Did not king James both Ruin himself and Thousands of Families merely by going into French Measures" and "It was not Secret to me and several others above Twenty-eight Years ago, that *France* was never sincere in this affair; but as their projects came nearer to a Conclusion, they took less care to conceal the Secret." Defoe sees France as a nation unwilling to keep treaties and trusts and Ramkins as an example of man's shortsightedness.

The lessons for a "private capacity" are less clear. Ideas which Defoe later developed to present for the reader's edification are scrambled here; short, illustrative incidents are numerous. As Crusoe, Singleton, Jack, and the Cavalier do, Ramkins says his "Design" was "to make the whole earth the Theatre of his Life." He comes nowhere near the later heroes in doing this, however. Like Crusoe, his intention was "to Travel and gain Experience in the World," and find "something worthy my Curiosity." His and Crusoe's parents oppose their plans and both are exiled from home and suffer because they leave. In both cases, they appear to be willful young men rather than serious sinners. They are mistaken, even deluded, but not wicked. Furthermore, in books from *The Family Instructor* (1715) to *Conjugal Lewdness* (1727), Defoe characterized young men as rash, impetuous, and often at the mercy of their curiosity.[23] Just as we have seen impetuous action punished in the novels, so it is here. The punishment seems to be the result of action rather than of God's avenging fury.

Another revealing absence in *Majr. Ramkins* is that of economic interest. The reader is cautioned against losing his money in foreign interests as the Jacobites did, but that is about as far as an interest in economics goes. Money does appear twice in *Majr. Ramkins,* however, as it will be used in later books: as necessary for respect and as an object to motivate an adventure. As the Major makes his plans for going abroad, he converts his inheritance into cash; his old Captain assured him "it would prove my best Friend upon all Occasions, for that the World had but a very mean Opinion of Merit when strip'd of other Advantages to recommend it." [24] Ramkins has little patience with finances; what money buys—the world's good opinion—is important. In the way that money is important to Moll or Jack, it is important to Ramkins. This is made clear when his wife spends all he has. He is mortified at the change in the opinion that others have of him, but he still loves his wife dearly, finds her an "inseparable" companion, and remarks that they amended their way of life, forgetting for a time the vexation with the Jacobites. This incident is much like one in *Colonel Jack* and the comments are good descriptions of Jack's experiences with his five marriages. Ramkins blames himself much as Defoe implies that the reader should fault Jack:

In conclusion, I put on the Trummels, and never question'd, but I had made the most prudential Choice that any Person could do; but there is some thing in Womankind which can never be found out by Study or Reflection.

and

There is a secret Devil in every Woman, which is often Conjur'd down by a Husband's Temper; and though many Men may pass for bad Husbands by their

Morose Carriage, 'tis less prejudicial, than that Indulgence which few Women have Discretion to make use of.

. . . I could not so much blame her as my self for if Children, Servants, etc. make a loose from their Duty, who are chiefly to be blam'd, but such gentle and restraining Methods did not curb 'em, but let 'em feel they had Reins in their Hands.[25]

The second incident involving money comes when a fellow sergeant tries to get Ramkins's money while he is recuperating from a wound. Ramkins confronts him and both go off drinking, laughing about the sergeant's pious excuses. While money is at stake, it is just the object for a diverting story and seems no more emotionally charged than the snuff box which caused even greater confusion.

One of the best comic episodes in *Ramkins* is that of his religious conversion. Ramkins says, "In this Retirement it was that I began to be very Serious: A Soldiers Life has many Occurrences which are not very reconcileable to strict Morality." He is in pain, has a high fever, and drinks beer and begins to hallucinate. He admits he "was then in a very improper State to settle Accounts in Relation to the next World" as he entertains his brother and other "nurses" by besieging towns, crossing seas without ships, and rebuking snuff boxes and Spanish ladies. He curses the priest, imagines himself a prisoner, and thinks the priest and his brother have come to strangle him. "This was a terrible Attack, and the Enemy had made such a Breach, that I desired to wisper [sic] a Word with the Priests, telling him I wou'd Capitulate next Morning about Eight a Clock." Thus is Ramkins "saved." Crusoe also hallucinates, but in keeping with his anxious state on the island, his dreams are not so humorous. Defoe had a lifelong belief that the religious side of a man was as indispensable to complete characterization as modern novelists consider the sexual, and in both books, he includes diverting conversions. The ludicrous one produces a Catholic; the other helps Crusoe order his world. Moll and Jack represent less "enthusiastic" and, for Defoe's contemporaries, more realistic ones.

The theme of the threat of loss of self versus the possibility for self-realization occurs in the novels written throughout Defoe's career. Each protagonist's strong personality resists becoming part of amorphous groups. Something extraordinary makes Jack question the life of a gentleman thief, Moll of a master shop thief, and Crusoe of an abandoned wretch. Each finds meaning, explains to his own satisfaction the reason for his situation and the impact on his life. "Nature," that heartbeat revealing right and wrong, asserts itself, and the character refuses to be overwhelmed by the sense of isolation and chaos. Crusoe asks why he must spend twenty-eight years on the island and what the purpose of his existence is, but he concludes that he has learned the secret of happiness and come to understand the nature of God. Moll and Jack wonder why they are repeatedly cast out of their secure states, but they conclude that every event has been part of a movement toward understanding. In striving and exploring, each character defines and redefines Defoe's conception of happiness. The middle station of life, so vividly described in the first pages of *Robinson Crusoe,* free from hardship and misery on the one hand and from avarice, envy, and ambition on the other, establishes the golden mean for characters in Defoe's novels. At the end of some of the novels, the characters are not as rich or influential as they have been, but they are satisfied. Moll's and Jack's lives in Virginia are simple. They do not "cut a figure in the world" or ride in a coach. Crusoe never builds a country home in England; Captain Singleton retires with a good woman. Contact with society confirms their apprehension of reality: happiness comes from a moderate position and inner composure. Jack can never be happy as long as he impetuously leaves home and takes a voyage to the Caribbean—he repeats Crusoe's mistake and is destined to learn the same lesson. Society for Defoe is as real, as forceful, and as complex as it is for Swift, and the pilgrimage of the spirit is as important as it is for Bunyan.

III

Bunyan's dreams, Swift's satires, and Defoe's governments all allow their creators to select a small number of factors and isolate them for examination. These writers manage to detail steps in a process so that the reader can observe sequence and assign cause-effect. Just as a slow-motion film can show how an athlete was injured, so do these processes work. At times, process is compressed, again isolating only pertinent influences and determining cause and effect. For example, *Pilgrim's Progress* not only compresses Christian's adult life, but also separates the process of points from step to step in Christian's journey. Similarly, *A Tale of a Tub,* outlines the history of criticism while it shows how criticism reached its present state and dissects the ways it is carried out. *Gulliver's Travels* is set between the years 1699 and 1716, the years in which Swift and many other intellectual Englishmen were disillusioned with the "Augustan" dream.[26] Gulliver's disillusionment and critical appraisal of England parallel Swift's, while the isolation of institutions and human characteristics contributes to both the process of disillusionment and the process of understanding the follies of society.

Defoe's societies combine the concern with institution and mores with the influence of the ways the protagonist interprets his life. Robinson Crusoe brings as much of his civilization to the island as he can. Just how much he has internalized becomes clear when other men come to his island. First, he is king and master to Friday. He is emperor when he rescues Friday's father and the Spaniard, and he stratifies the colony by making the Spaniard overseer. When he works to win the English ship from the mutineers, he is "generalissimo," a title more prestigious than "general" in that it means commander of all the armies in a country (OED). The Englishmen think of him as a colonial governor, but he thinks of himself as king and remains unseen until he believes his prisoners to be suitably awed. When his island has settlers, he assumes the absolute powers of colonial governors in the most primitive states. At times, there is a hint of irony or humor in his titles. His description of himself as king of cats, goats, and a parrot and the comedy of being "generalissimo" reduce his claim to miniature. In his behavior, Crusoe acts out the rules and explains the reasons for England's practices. He threatens the sailors with English penalties—hanging in chains for mutiny—and leaves them with rules for treating other settlers fairly. The institutions of society have served him well and he combines their lessons with revealed religion in the government of himself and his island.

While he admits the negative aspects of the nature of man, his book is the most optimistic view of society produced by the three writers. Crusoe has a number of faults throughout his life including presumption and arrogance. He can also be angry, violent, and despairing. The men who come to his island display such evils as cannibalism, murder, and theft. Despite the faults of men, the effect is optimistic. Crusoe can maintain his sanity and prosper. The men can form a society with mixed nationalities and races and thrive for a time.

The great achievement of these three writers is the creation of extraordinarily gripping imaginative constructs. In a time when readers increasingly insisted upon probability, Bunyan, Swift, and Defoe modified old forms and created new. Although *Pilgrim's Progress, A Tale of a Tub, Gulliver's Travels,* and *Robinson Crusoe* were criticized for their form and content, they were immediately popular. The settings for the stories freed the writers to some extent and allowed them to change the forces working on the characters, the kinds of people met, and the types of work and behavior the characters would be expected to perform. The characters escape their place in society and move into situations lacking structure. The reader becomes more willing to accept the unexpected; he submits himself to the fictional more readily and suspends not only his demand for realism but also his ethical judgments. Yet the reader demands a certain amount of probability, and, therefore, the writer must satisfy this need for an apparently verifiable, recognizable "truth."

These writers manage to communicate a version of reality within their imaginative constructs primarily because of their belief in the universality of human experience. History, religion, philosophy, and literature supported this opinion, and, while Bunyan and Defoe's heritage differed from Swift's, the results on their thought and art are similar. To speak of this opinion is not to deny differences but to point out the implications of the considerable uniformity that does exist. Both rationalism and the idea of a community of believers condemned the individual perspective and emphasized mutual edification as the purpose of literature. All saw man as an isolated being, a seeking soul, yet sharing the experience of all men on earth. Man can never lose himself entirely in nature, with other men, or in God although he experiences moments of belonging which increase his sense of alienation while affirming the peculiar optimism inherent in such loneliness. An unbroken line derived from the idea expressed by Augustine, "*Inquietum est cor nostrum, donec requiescat in te,*" exists within the belief in the common essence and experience of man. Christian, Gulliver, and Crusoe feel compelled to leave home so they can explore the most important questions about their natures only when cut off from their communities.

Man as a seeking soul, a being longing for rest within a destiny worthy of him provides the sources of optimism and despair. The quest for "something worthy of my Curiosity" invigorates each narrative. R. S. Crane has argued that Gulliver's Utopia is his native England,[27] and certainly most of Gulliver's highest ideals have distinctively English roots, but so do his most egregious errors. For example, Gulliver describes England, the English Parliament, legal system, population, and history to the Brobdingnag king. The Courts of Justice exist to determine "the disputed Rights and Properties of Men, as well as for the Punishment of Vice, and Protection of Innocence." The King, unfortunately, asks questions which expose the practice of Parliament, the courts, and the professions. Men conceived the English ideals, and Gulliver admires them, but in the hands of men like Gulliver they become blurred and blotted Corruptions of the original conceptions. Gulliver is hurt by the king's conclusions, and he describes himself as a patriot at some length. Then, acting as many another Englishman might do, he offers the king a great invention which will allow the king to realize his potential as ruler of the world. At this point, both Gulliver and the king behave naively. The king doubts men's destructive power, and Gulliver proves this power in the act of defending his people. Gulliver's admiration for gunpowder and the King's refusal of it are faces of the same coin, the result of a "confined Education."

Similarly, Colonel Jack experiences some of his greatest disillusionments when he examines his ideals. His education brings him into contact with English law, with gentlemen, with social rituals, and with middle-class women. None is what he imagined and none rescues him. At several points, Jack seems to be firmly established in the middle class yet he is on the point of despair. In Virginia he is quite secure, yet he feels buried alive. After the death of his alcoholic wife, he feels despondent and vaporish for a full year. Again he has security in Virginia only to be cast into a state of apprehension by the transportation of the Preston rebels. Jack's wandering temper and a series of accidents prevent him from reconciling his state of mind with his economic condition.

The peculiar nature of man determines that he will be able to imagine a good society and to apprehend a version of himself which is fulfilled, and yet he cannot fully realize this self nor can he mold society into the image he has created. Swift's correspondence describes his envy of Pope's and Bolingbroke's more graceful acceptance of the human condition; Defoe's endless projects and willingness to forgive slights and accept whoever was in power, and Bunyan's vivid descriptions of the alternation of faith and despair find expression in their imaginative writings. All of them manage to make what man can imagine as vital and as "real" as what man can see around him.

Because they believe in the unity of the conceived and the external worlds, the imagery and symbolism found in their works is peculiarly graphic and dynamic. U. Milo Kaufman, Paul Hunter, G. A. Starr, Martin Kallich, and other critics have identified the archetypal and mythic images present in their works,[28] and learned and ordinary readers have always recognized the power of their rhetoric. Whole scenes (Christian's burden falling, Colonel Jack dancing by the tree where he has lost his money, Gulliver jounced on the giantess's nipple) and individual objects (Christian's roll, Roxana's Turkish costume, the brothers' coats) assume unforgettable visual detail and special significance. When Moll writes on the glass with the diamond, she describes the conflict between money (necessity) and love (desire). In *Moll Flanders,* the dungeon, one of the traditional symbols for despair in Puritan writing, is described as the "emblem of hell"; in *The Fortunate Mistress,* the storm at sea threatens Roxana and works as floods do in spiritual narratives. The inextricable linking of images associated with religious concepts with secular ambitions of the characters suggests the way allegory could be transformed for the new century. *A Tale of a Tub* becomes an object and religion is a coat. Swift's personal writings show how reflexive such thinking was to him. He saw the loss of the fish he believed safely hooked as a type for his life and, at another time, paused at the sight of a tree which was dead at the top even as its trunk and lower branches flourished and said, "I shall be like that tree." Bunyan intentionally blends the landscapes, idioms, and events of contemporary England and the Bible in order to create man's situation as a citizen of the world and of eternity. Roxana's and Moll's is a layered narration, one level devoted to a catalogue of more or less sequential events, one level recording movement toward the goal of economic security, and one level a barometric reading of spiritual worth. In a single moment, Roxana can be performing a dance, gauging the reaction of those who watch, and aware of the hypocrisy and manipulation she is engaged in. Swift can create a land of tiny men leaping, creeping, and climbing, another of men with flying islands and sorcerers, and his vision of the ignoble side of politics is so accurate that men can debate the specific historical objects intended for over 250 years.[29] Because possibility is so inextricably bound to reality, some ambiguity inevitably results, and this ambiguity begins to capture the essence of humanity.

One of the most characteristic qualities of the novel begins in these works, the internalization of theme. As the novel develops, plot becomes less important and the narrator gradually fades; the novel is consumed by the individual, the protagonist. This individual absorbs his culture, its conflicts, its aspirations, and its day-to-day experiences. This internalization of theme has a number of crucial implications. First, it creates a supraindividual who is more individual, unique even, more than an Everyman, yet who is more than an individual case.[30] His highly individual experiences illumine the human condition and approach the epic in their cultural description. The genius of Bunyan in describing Vanity Fair, of Swift in having Gulliver confront the Yahoos, and Defoe in setting characters on islands depends on the violation of Aristotelian probability while arguing truth.

Second, this supraindividual extends reality. He insists upon the validity of his experiences and his interpretation of his experiences, at the same time that his experiences become part of a shared culture and part of a collective consciousness with which all of us can identify. When reality can be individual, can be a dream or a life, the reader must turn to his own life and experiences and recognize the inseparable nature of his internal and external worlds. The universal structures of warfare, voyage, shipwreck, journey, vision provide means of joining the types of reality, but these writers go a step farther in that they create symbols that are individual and based in fictional events. These symbols assume no divine or mythic origin, no reference outside the material world. The words that become idioms, "Vanity Fair," "Lilliputian," "Yahoo," and "man Friday" (recently "girl Friday"), describe a reality that the artist created and yet whose truth is immediately apparent and timeless.

Third, the internalization of theme encourages the creation of compelling, if not heroic, personalities. The didactic, moral, and mantic purposes of Bunyan, Defoe, and Swift determine a consciousness of the relationship between fable and moral. That commentary and explication occupy so much of their works and sustain considerable power hints at the vigor of early devotional literature and foreshadows the novel's introspective cast. Long sections of Bunyan's works and Defoe's conduct books move by catechism and exegesis. Passages describing characters' considerations of options and evaluations of behavior are variations on this technique.[31] The narrator of *A Tale of a Tub* obsessively explains his behavior and Defoe's characters reason endlessly; Christian explains why he cannot turn and run away from Apollyon. The significance of event begins to have double implications. While events had always been seen as having potentially great influence in the course of a life and, perhaps, importance for the spiritual understanding of that life, event becomes the impetus for secular themes. Events occur for the mind to work upon, and the revelation of character depends on the process. The individual grapples with conventional obstacles and traditional goals, but personal contradictions and ambiguous imperatives now create additional tension, and the intensity of the experience rises. The outcome becomes more problematic and the levels of consciousness divide. The levels are apparent in *Moll Flanders*. She simultaneously leads a life full of incident while an image of herself exists separate from some of her actions. Furthermore, a social judgment of her conflicts both with her self-concept and the reader's understanding of her at crucial points in the narrative.[32] Similarly, Gulliver and Christian exist in their actions, in their minds, and in a broader frame of reference which judges them by external standards and yet allows another, separate judgment to be made by the reader.[33] The result of the simultaneous generation of perspectives is the release of powerful tension and conflict.

Out of the conflict and complexity, the great central characters of the novel develop. Defoe's Roxana provokes strong and often subjective responses.[34] She has been defended and damned as a demon, but no one disputes the way her personality dominates the novel and bears the theme. Figurative or connotative language, event, and reaction to event bear the burden earlier placed on prison, island, or New World. Her isolation is mental rather than physical; the symbol of the "special society" has been internalized. She moves from confinement to confinement. As a young wife her foolish husband keeps the horses, and she stays grudgingly at home. When he leaves her, she sits among her rags, letting only a few people in. With the landlord and the Prince she hides away. Even the Prince calls her state "confinement." The episode in England when she gives masked balls finds her mysterious and unknown. She retires with the Quakeress and ends as an exile, alienated even from her husband by her past. Her actions cut her off more effectively from God and men than Crusoe's marooning or Jack's indenture did them. She longs for a respectable identity, but no new situation occurs to allow her to escape her past. Roxana experiences the anxiety, the loss of role and proscribed behavior, the recognition of an undefined situation, and the conflicting feelings of isolation-centrality and control-helplessness of the isolated societies but the opportunity for advancement without her earlier crimes never appears. The pessimism of Roxana comes from the repeated *huis clos* of the protagonist's life, so much a contrast to the "new dition" allowed Crusoe, Moll, Jack, and John the biscuit baker. She, like Gulliver, is finally confronted with the awful awareness of her own image.

Outside of English society, Moll and Jack encounter fewer world obstacles and can deal with internal obstacles more directly. Class, wealth, occupation, and expectations no longer determine most behavior. The narrator's dream of the pilgrimage, Gulliver's voyages, and various Defoe colonies free the protagonists from the demands and perceptions of others. On an island with giants, Gulliver could not be expected to behave like a middle-class seaman. His class and occupation mean very little to those around him. He, like Christian and Crusoe, is simply Man. He borrows from England, from his past, and draws upon his personality, his present, to create what advantages (his future) he can. He internalizes the lessons, values, and realities of his society and, when successful, demonstrates that he is a better creature than the members of the amorphous society just as Jack is a better plantation overseer, Christiana is a better mother, and the Drapier is a better tradesman. Roxana can never escape. Her life completes the pattern of Defoe's examination of the relationship between ability and opportunity. Roxana does not lack ability, but she cannot bring her image of her fulfilled self into harmony with her situation. Her titles and her marriage are based on the manipulation of social reward systems rather than on the gradual attainment of the virtues as well as the trappings of social position. In some ways, Roxana's life has been easier than Jack's or Moll's, but she has never been put in the "perfectly new Condition in which [she has] no Temptation to the Crimes [she] formerly committed, and [with] a prospect of Advantage for the future" which Jack describes.[35]

Finally, the internalization of theme intensifies the protagonist's drive for fulfillment. The burden of defining his calling and of understanding what form or pattern his life has shifts from Providence's determination to his own shoulders.[36] Swift, Fielding, Sterne, and even Charles Gildon perceptively recognized and mocked the certainty with which Bunyan and Defoe imposed form on life, yet all of them convey the separation between event and self. Every event, regardless of its apparent triviality, has meaning in psychological and secular ways, and the characters must resist the threat of event while striving to bring action and self-image into harmony. Arrival at the Celestial City with Christian is not enough; Christian must be as steadfast as he demands of himself, and the dreamer must undertake the trip himself, a reminder of the continuous army of seeking souls.[37] The awareness of the space between actuality and what Weber called *Beruf* becomes the great theme of the novel.[38] Gulliver, the *Tale's* hack, Jack, and Roxana fail to resolve the conflict and come to stand for a tragic aspect of the human condition. Regardless of a pre-existent order, the human experience is one of conflict and limits, and to conclude a life is to falsify it.

Those who wrote prose fiction recognized the unsatisfying nature of a conclusion leaving the dreamer outside, the hack with a lost manuscript, Gulliver in a stable, and Roxana describing the "blast" of Heaven. In the development of the form of the novel, they did as Richardson and Fielding did in their greatest works and supplied a conclusion which resolved conflicts and "settled the characters for life." Aware of the dual nature of experience, they also concluded their works so that the protagonists' actions corresponded closely to their moral natures. The action of their works takes place in the foreground of an engraving with the church, the society, the economy, and the family in the background. The characters, and the novel form itself, comprehend the external world and internalize it in a way that is almost eccentrically individual and yet communicates a recognizable, illuminating version of reality. The internalization of theme moves the reader across the bridge between the external world and the novelist's conception and, in so doing, expands reality,[39] breaks down limits, and unifies the private and public worlds. In the work of a great writer, the result is an intense experience generated by a character of extraordinary energy who imposes pattern and meaning on his own life and his society, and recognizes (to some extent) that he is imposing meaning. He is creating himself and the context of his existence and as such offers himself as interpreter while paradoxically insisting upon his unique will and the illusion of his mastery of himself and his world. That all three of these writers can simultaneously reveal the irony and the failure of the protagonists and also create reliable interpreters lays a provocative foundation for the novel.

NOTES

INTRODUCTION

1. Among the early studies which increased interest in the novel are E. M. W. Tillyard, *The Epic Strain in the English Novel* (London: Chatto and Windus, 1954); Alan D. McKillop, *The Early Masters of English Fiction* (Lawrence: University of Kansas Press, 1956); Ian Watt, *The Rise of the Novel* (London: Chatto and Windus, 1957); Martin Battestin, *The Moral Basis of Fielding's Art* (Middletown, Connecticut: Wesleyan University Press, 1959); Wayne C. Booth, *The Rhetoric of Fiction* (Chicago: University of Chicago Press, 1961); Maximillian E. Novak, *Defoe and the Nature of Man* (London: Oxford University Press, 1963); Sheldon Sacks, *Fiction and the Shape of Belief* (Berkeley: University of California Press, 1964); and Ronald Paulson, *Satire and the Novel in Eighteenth-Century England* (New Haven: Yale University Press, 1967).

2. Even earlier was Charles Sorel's *Le berger extravagant* which was also published under the title *L'anti-roman ov L'histoire du berger Lysis* (1627) and appeared in England as *The Extravagant Shepherd. The anti-romance; or, The History of the Shepherd Lysis* as early as 1653.

3. The conference was held at Brown University in April 1977, and *Novel*, 11 (1978), 197–217, includes an edited version of the panel discussion, "Character as a Lost Cause." Mark Spilka's opening statement is "Character has not been a viable critical concept for some time in novel study" (p. 197). The panel does, however, demonstrate that the critical study of character is in good health.

4. Among the well-known studies contrasting Swift and Defoe are Paul Dottin, *Daniel Defoe et ses Romans* (Paris: Les presses universitaires de France, 1924), I, 159; 192–193; John F. Ross, *Swift and Defoe: A Study in Relationship* (Berkeley: University of California Press, 1941); R. I. Cook, " 'Mr. Examiner' and 'Mr. Review': The Tory Apologetics of Swift and Defoe," *HLQ*, 29 (1966), 127–146; J. Paul Hunter, *The Reluctant Pilgrim* (Baltimore: Johns Hopkins University Press, 1966), p. 210.

5. Jonathan Swift, "A Letter to a Young Gentleman, Lately Enter'd into Holy Orders," in *The Prose Works of Jonathan Swift,* ed. Herbert Davis (Oxford: Blackwell, 1948), IX, 166. All quotations from Swift's prose are from this edition.

6. A few discussions of Swift's fictional techniques are Ricardo Quintana, "Situational Satire: A Commentary on the Method of Swift," *UTQ,* 17 (1947), 130-136; William B. Ewald, *The Masks of Jonathan Swift* (Cambridge, Mass.: Harvard University Press, 1954), pp. 124-157; Henry W. Sams, "Swift's Satire of the Second Person," *ELH,* 26 (1959), 36-44; Jon S. Lawry, "Dr. Lemuel Gulliver and 'The Thing Which Was Not,' " *JEGP,* 67 (1968), 214; Steven Cohan, "Gulliver's Fiction," *SN,* 6 (1974), 7-16. For Bunyan, see Wolfgang Iser, *The Implied Reader* (Baltimore: Johns Hopkins University Press, 1974); John L. Lowes, "The Pilgrim's Progress" in *Essays in Appreciation* (Boston: Houghton Mifflin, 1936), pp. 62-67; Roger Sharrock, *John Bunyan* (London: Macmillan, 1968), pp. 116-117.

7. *Cf.* G. A. Starr's discussion of Roxana's dialogue in *Defoe and Casuistry* (Princeton: Princeton University Press, 1971), p. 181. Wayne C. Booth in *The Rhetoric of Fiction* points out that the narrator of *A Tale of a Tub* "is a dull and foolish man, but the book he 'writes' is a great one partly because of the contrast between his role and that of the implied author," p. 235.

8. Jonathan Swift, "On the Trinity," IX, 166.

CHAPTER I / Initiation and Integration

1. John Bunyan, *The Strait Gate* in *The Works of John Bunyan,* ed. George Offor (Glasgow: Blackie and Son, 1853), I, 370.

2. Roger Sharrock calls Interpreter's House an "emblem theatre" in "Bunyan and the English Emblem Writers," *RES,* 21 (1945), 107; U. Milo Kaufman argues that the visit gives Christian "brief training in hermeneutical procedure" in *The Pilgrim's Progress and Traditions in Puritan Meditation* (New Haven: Yale University Press, 1966), pp. 61-62.

3. Robert Shenk interprets this as a sign of an act of will rather than election in "John Bunyan: Puritan or Pilgrim?" *Cithara,* 14 (1974), 79.

4. See Mark 2:5; this is a sign of healing.

5. Shenk also describes Christian as a member of a "spiritual community," p. 91.

6. Bunyan characterizes hypocrites in *The Life and Death of Mr. Badman* (London: Dent, 1928; rpt. 1969), 212, 217, *et passim.*

7. Bunyan, *Badman,* p. 191; Proverbs 29:27.

8. Kaufman compares Bunyan's descriptions of Hell to those of Bayley, Ambrose, and others, pp. 159–163.

9. John Bunyan, *The Pilgrim's Progress*, ed. Roger Sharrock (London: Oxford University Press, 1966), pp. 167–168.

10. The journey metaphor is extensively treated by Hunter, *Pilgrim*, pp. 23–50, 86, 103–108, 113, and 199–200.

11. *Cf.* Benjamin Boyce, "The Question of Emotion in Defoe," *SP*, 50 (1953), 47–58.

12. *Cf.* Maximillian E. Novak, "Robinson Crusoe's Fear and the Search for Natural Man," *MP*, 58 (1961), 238–245; Hunter, *Pilgrim*, pp. 171–173; Everett Zimmerman, *Defoe and the Novel* (Berkeley: University of California Press, 1975), pp. 31–33.

13. Daniel Defoe, *The Farther Adventures of Robinson Crusoe* (Oxford: Blackwell, 1927), pp. 127–129.

14. The belief in the necessity for physical release of emotion was common in the eighteenth century. *Cf.* such divergent examples as Charles Gildon, *The Life of Mr. Thomas Betterton* (London, 1710), "It is impossible to have any great Emotion or Gesture of the Body, without the Action of the Hands . . . ," p. 76; see also pp. 41–79; and Henry Fielding, ". . . Sophia sunk trembling into her Chair, and had not a Flood of Tears come immediately to her Relief, perhaps worse had followed," *Tom Jones*, XVI, ii.

15. Maximillian E. Novak devotes a chapter of *Defoe and the Nature of Man* to Defoe's idea of the hero, pp. 129–161.

16. Daniel Defoe, *The Life and Strange Surprizing Adventures of Robinson Crusoe* (Oxford: Blackwell, 1927), I, 70–71.

17. *Cf.* Boyce, pp. 50–51; Novak, *Nature of Man*, pp. 11–12 *et passim*; A. W. Secord, *Studies in the Narrative Method of Defoe* (New York: Russell and Russell, 1963), p. 238; Everett Zimmerman, "Defoe and Crusoe," *ELH*, 38 (1971), 377–396.

18. Paul K. Alkon explicates the "brilliant adventure of the single footprint" in "The Odds Against Friday: Defoe, Bayes, and Inverse Probability" in *Probability, Time, and Space in Eighteenth-Century Literature*, ed. Paula R. Backscheider (New York: AMS Press, 1978), pp. 29–37.

19. Defoe explains that the book shows the mischief and danger pirates cause; introduction, *A General History of the Robberies and Murders of the Most Notorious Pirates*, ed. A. L. Haywood (London: Routledge & Kegan Paul, 1955).

20. Defoe, *General History*, p. 451.

21. Daniel Defoe, *Moll Flanders* (Oxford: Blackwell, 1927), II, 103.

22. Defoe, II, 98.

23. Boyce, pp. 53 and 57–58.

24. For a discussion of Moll's being forced to face the "real eighteenth-century *huis clos*," see Arnold Kettle, "In Defence of Moll Flanders" in *Of Books and Humankind,* ed. John Butt (London: Routledge and Kegan Paul, 1964), pp. 55–67.

25. Daniel Defoe, *Roxana: The Fortunate Mistress,* ed. Jane Jack (London: Oxford University Press, 1964), p. 208. Modern critics have explored Roxana's identity and dissatisfaction in detail. See Zimmerman, *Defoe,* pp. 180–187; David L. Higdon, "The Critical Fortunes and Misfortunes of Defoe's *Roxana,*" *Bucknell Review,* 20 (1972), 79–82; C. R. Kropf, "Theme and Structure in Defoe's *Roxana,*" *SEL,* 12 (1972), 477; John J. Richetti, *Defoe's Narratives: Situation and Structure* (Oxford: Clarendon Press, 1975), pp. 192–225; Spiro T. Peterson, "The Matrimonial Theme of Defoe's *Roxana,*" *PMLA,* 70 (1955), 166–191; G. A. Starr, *Casuistry,* pp. 165–189.

26. Ezra K. Maxfield finds the Quakeress a rogue and hypocrite in "Daniel Defoe and the Quakers," *PMLA,* 47 (1932), 179–190; Homer O. Brown argues that Roxana's disguise as a Quaker indicates the "self she would like to be" in "The Displaced Self in the Novels of Daniel Defoe," *ELH,* 38 (1971), 581.

27. Defoe, *General History,* p. 370.

28. Michael Shinagel, *Daniel Defoe and Middle-Class Gentility* (Cambridge, Mass.: Harvard University Press, 1967), pp. 246–266; James Sutherland, *Defoe* (London: Longmans, Green & Co., 1954), p. 13; J. R. Moore, *Daniel Defoe: Citizen of the Modern World* (Chicago: University of Chicago Press, 1958), pp. 328–339.

29. Defoe, *Farther Adventures,* II, 117–118.

30. Jonathan Swift, *A Tale of a Tub* in *The Prose Writings of Jonathan Swift,* ed. Herbert Davis (Oxford: Blackwell, 1939–1968), I, 106.

31. Swift, "Of Public Absurdityes in England," V, 80; see also "Predictions for the Year 1708," II, 144–145.

32. Gulliver, as C. J. Rawson, Sheldon Sacks, and others remind us, is not a character in a novel; yet he has fictional characteristics. While I intend to treat Gulliver as satiric instrument, I shall often discuss his fictional elements as well. See C. J. Rawson, *Gulliver and the Gentle Reader* (London: Routledge & Kegan Paul, 1973), p. 27; Sacks, pp. 31–35.

33. Arthur E. Case points out this progression briefly in *Four Essays on Gulliver's Travels* (Princeton: Princeton University Press, 1945), 121: see also Larry S. Champion, "Gulliver's Voyages: The Framing Events as Guide to Interpretation," *TSLL,* 10 (1969), 531–533; W. B. Carnochan, "Some Roles of Lemuel Gulliver," *TSLL,* 5 (1964), 520; Sacks, p. 41.

34. On Gulliver's fragility and the relationships between Books I and II, see Carnochan, "Roles," pp. 524–526; Paul Fussell, "The Frailty of Lemuel

Gulliver" in *Essays in Literary History*, eds. Rudolf Kirk and C. F. Main (New Brunswick, N. J.: Rutgers University Press, 1960), pp. 114–116.

35. Jonathan Swift, *Gulliver's Travels*, XI, 222–223.

36. R. S. Crane suggests that Swift gives us no reason to set man apart as a third species in "The Houyhnhnms, the Yahoos, and the History of Ideas" in *Reason and the Imagination*, ed. J. A. Mazzeo (New York: Columbia University Press, 1962), p. 244; A. O. Lovejoy points out that the idea of species had begun to break down in the eighteenth century, *The Great Chain of Being* (New York: Harper & Row, 1936; rpt. 1965).

37. On the Hobbesian elements in *Gulliver's Travels* see T. O. Wedel, "On the Philosophical Background of *Gulliver's Travels*," *SP*, 23 (1926), 442–443; David P. French, "Swift and Hobbes—A Neglected Parallel," *Boston University Studies in English*, 3 (1957), 243–255; Robert H. Hopkins, "The Personation of Hobbism in Swift's *Tale of a Tub* and Mechanical Operation of the Spirit," *PQ*, 45 (1966), 373–378; Basil Hall, " 'An Inverted Hypocrite': Swift the Churchman" in *The World of Swift*, ed. Brian Vickers (Cambridge, Mass.: Harvard University Press, 1968), pp. 51–53; W. A. Speck, "From Principles to Practice: Swift and Party Politics" in *The World of Swift*, pp. 76–77.

38. Some of the studies of biblical themes include Roland M. Frye, "Swift's Yahoo and the Christian Symbols for Sin," *JHI*, 15 (1954), 203, 217; John B. Radner, "The Struldbruggs, the Houyhnhnms, and the Good Life," *SEL*, 17 (1977), 427–433; and J. Leeds Barroll, "Gulliver and the Struldbruggs," *PMLA*, 73 (1958), 45–50.

39. I do not wish to enter the controversy concerning the extent to which the horses are exemplary. The point here is that Swift has Gulliver perceive the Houyhnhnms as good.

40. Swift, *Gulliver's Travels*, XI, 262.

41. Swift, XI, 264.

42. W. B. Carnochan, "The Complexity of Swift: Gulliver's Fourth Voyage," *SP*, 60 (1963), 41–42, suggests that the last lines of *Gulliver's Travels* show the pain of his isolation.

43. See Calhoun Winton, "Conversion on the Road to Houyhnhnmland," *Sewanee Review*, 68 (1960), 21, 30; George Falle, "Divinity and Wit: Swift's Attempted Reconciliation," *UTQ*, 46 (1976), 25–27; Philip Pinkus, *Swift's Vision of Evil* (Victoria: English Studies of the University of Victoria, 1975), II, 92; Ricardo Quintana explains that myths are extended metaphors in Swift's works and all make the point that "the only myth genuinely embraced by Swift is the myth that there are no myths. . . ." "Situational Satire," pp. 135–136.

44. Leland D. Peterson summarizes the controversy in relation to Swift's

Project for the Advancement of Religion in "Swift's *Project*: A Religious and
Political Satire," *PMLA*, 82 (1967), 54-63.

45. Opponents of this interpretation will say that Swift deliberately excluded
religion, but I believe that the moral considerations are too important in
Gulliver's Travels and religious convictions too intrinsic to Swift's thought
to allow complete neglect of this theme.

The quotation is Hebrews 11:1. Swift's sermon "On the Trinity," in
which he quotes this passage, refers to the importance of revealed religion
and mysteries. *Cf.* Phillip Harth, *Swift and Anglican Rationalism* (Chicago:
University of Chicago Press, 1961), pp. 21-38; and Ricardo Quintana, *The
Mind and Art of Jonathan Swift* (London: Methuen, 1936: rpt. 1953), p. 150.

46. Harth, p. 32. See also James E. Gill, "Beast Over Man: Theriophilic
Paradox in Gulliver's 'Voyage to the Country of the Houyhnhnms'," *SP*,
67 (1970), 547; Quintana, *Mind*, 150.

47. Swift, "On the Trinity," VII, 424.

48. Swift's respect for history and historians is indisputable. The office he
sought most actively was historiographer and, as J. W. Johnson points out,
Swift often wrote from the point of view of an historian; "Swift's Histori-
cal Outlook," *JBS*, 4 (1965), 52-77. See also R. I Cook, "Swift's Polemical
Characters," *Discourse*, 6 (1963), 30-48; J. R. Moore, however, insists that
Swift's personality and writing style forbade his success as an historian,
"Swift as Historian," *SP*, 49 (1952), 583ff.

49. Herbert Davis's introduction to *The Drapier's Letters*, X, xi; Oliver Ferguson, *Jonathan Swift and the Irish* (Urbana: University of Illinois Press, 1962),
pp. 31-32.

50. Entire books have been written on Swift's relationship to his narrative
voices. The best known is probably Ewald's *The Masks of Jonathan Swift*. See
also Charles Beaumont, *Swift's Classical Rhetoric* (Athens: University of
Georgia Press, 1961) and Kathleen Williams, *Jonathan Swift and the Age of
Compromise* (Lawrence: University of Kansas Press, 1958), p. 11 *et passim*.

51. The effect is similar to that described by Robert C. Elliott in "Swift's
Satire: Rules of the Game," *ELH*, 41 (1974), 421-426, and by C. J. Rawson:

> The flayed woman (and stripped beau), on the other hand, are momentary
> intensities which do not merely serve the argument they are meant to illus-
> trate, but actually spill over it. They take us suddenly and with devastating
> brevity, outside the expectations of the immediate logic, into a surprising and
> 'cruel' domain of fantasy, (p. 34).

See also David P. French, "Swift, Temple, and 'A Digression on Madness,' " *TSLL*, 5 (1963), 53; and F. R. Leavis, "The Irony of Swift" in *Swift:
Modern Judgments* (New York: Macmillan, 1968), p. 125.

52. Swift, *Drapier's Letters*, X, 53.

53. For discussions of Restoration and eighteenth-century demands for realism see J. Paul Hunter, "The Loneliness of the Long-Distance Reader," *Genre*, 10 (1977), 464–469; Erich Kahler, *The Inward Turn of Narrative*, trans. Richard and Clara Winston (Princeton: Princeton University Press, 1973), pp. 98–99; Vivienne Mylne, *The Eighteenth-Century French Novel* (New York: Barnes and Noble, 1965), pp. 13–26, 263–268 *et passim;* Morroe Berger, *Real and Imagined Worlds* (Cambridge, Mass.: Harvard University Press, 1977), pp. 172–174, 176–180, 182–185.

CHAPTER II / Organization and Government

1. Daniel Defoe, *The Validity of the Renunciations of Former Powers, Enquired into, And The Present Renunciation Of The Duke of Anjou, Impartially Considered* (London, 1712), p. 2.
2. Swift frequently condemned the idea of a standing army. See the *Examiner*, III, 164; he says that keeping a standing army in times of peace "hath in all Ages been the first and great Step to the Ruin of Liberty," p. 146. Defoe wrote about the issue also and supported a regulated, limited militia; see *Some Reflections on a Pamphlet* (1697), *An Argument Shewing, that a Standing Army* (1698), and *A Brief Reply to the History of Standing Armies in England* (1698); *Review*, V, 5–6.
3. Jonathan Swift, "The Sentiments of a Church-of-England Man," II, 5–8, 13–14; "A Project for the Advancement of Religion," II, 44–63; the *Examiner*, III, 111, 125, and 161; Peterson, 54–63.
4. Swift, "A Discourse of the Contests and Dissentions in Athens and Rome," I, 227.
5. Swift, I, 226; see also "The Sentiments of a Church-of-England Man," II, 1–2.
6. See the *Examiner*, III, 31, 9, and 123; political lies are "born out of a discarded Statesman's Head, and thence delivered to be nursed and dandled by the Rabble." See also "Sentiments of a Church-of-England Man," II, 1–2.
7. Swift, "A Sermon upon the Martyrdom of King Charles I," IX, 220–223, and 225.
8. Swift, *Examiner*, III, 113–114, 146, and 196; II, 23–24. Robert C. Elliott, *The Shape of Utopia* (Chicago: University of Chicago Press, 1970), p. 55; Z. S. Fink, "Political Theory in *Gulliver's Travels*," *ELH*, 14 (1947), 151–156; Edwin B. Benjamin, "The King of Brobdingnag and *Secrets of State*," *JHI*, 18 (1957), 576 discusses Swift's opinion of mixed governments.

9. Swift, "A Project for the Advancement of Religion," II, 47.
10. Cf. Irvin Ehrenpreis, The Personality of Jonathan Swift (Cambridge, Mass.: Harvard University Press, 1958), p. 63; Angus Ross, "The Social Circumstances of Several Remote Nations of the World" in The World of Jonathan Swift, ed. Brian Vickers (Cambridge, Mass.: Harvard University Press, 1968), p. 221; Swift, "Doing Good," IX, 234–235.
11. Swift, Contests and Dissentions, I, 232.
12. Swift, "A Project for the Advancement of Religion," II, 47.
13. See Examiner papers #33 and #39 for Swift's description of the legitimate power of monarchs.
14. Swift, Tale of a Tub, I, 108–110.
15. Oliver Ferguson concludes that "in Swift's eyes, the guilt for the country's lamentable condition was shared by the English and the Irish alike. Swift certainly assigned the greater portion of blame to the English, and he was aware that Ireland's guilt was somewhat mitigated by the fact of generations of oppression," p. 167. See also Charles Firth, "The Political Significance of Gulliver's Travels" in Essays: Historical and Literary (Oxford: Clarendon Press, 1938), pp. 224–225, 228–234, 236–241; Donald T. Torchiana, "Jonathan Swift, the Irish and the Yahoos: The Case Reconsidered," PQ, 54 (1975), 195–212, details the similarities between descriptions of contemporary Irishmen and Swift's of the Yahoos; Anne Cline Kelly, "Swift's Explorations of Slavery in Houyhnhnmland and Ireland," PMLA, 91 (1976), 847–848.
16. Swift, Gulliver's Travels, XI, 278.
17. Defoe, General History, p. 485.
18. Swift, "Sentiments of a Church-of-England Man," II, 18.
19. Swift, A Tale of a Tub, I, 105.
20. Leonard W. Labaree, Royal Government in America (New Haven: Yale University Press, 1930), pp. 102–106, 115–118, 131–133, 147–149, and 269. I am grateful to my colleague Frank Shuffelton for information about colonial America. Swift speaks of the American colonies with ease; see XII, 58–60, 76–81, 136; XIV, 10, 27; III, 262; Corr. V, 19, 58.
21. Labaree, pp. 374, 383, 393, and 401; Kelly, p. 847. Swift had a low opinion of the ways colonists were treated; see "A Proposal for the Universal Use of Irish Manufacture," IX, 21; Drapier's Letters, X, 81–94.
22. Labaree, pp. 115–118; H. Shelton Smith, R. T. Handy, L. A. Loetscher, American Christianity (New York: Scribner's, 1960), pp. 191–192; Swift, Examiner, III, 161.
23. Labaree, pp. 37–44, 74–75, and 104.
24. In "Sentiments of a Church-of-England Man" Swift wrote, "few States are ruined by any Defect in their Institution, but generally by the Corruption

of Manners; against which the best Institution is no long Security, and without which, a very ill one may subsist and flourish . . . ," II, 14. *Cf.* Elliott, *Utopia,* pp. 58 and 60; Paulson, *The Fictions of Satire* (Baltimore: Johns Hopkins University Press, 1967), pp. 9-10; Jeffrey Hart, "The Idealogue as Artist: Some Notes on *Gulliver's Travels,*" *Criticism,* 2 (1960), 125-127.

25. Swift, *Gulliver's Travels,* XI, 278-279.

26. Swift, *A Tale of a Tub,* I, 102.

27. Swift, *The Conduct of the Allies,* VI, 7. Compare Defoe's *Reasons against a War with France* (London, 1701), p. 12.

28. Ehrenpreis, *Swift: The Man,* p. 500.

29. George M. Trevelyan, *England Under Queen Anne: The Peace and the Protestant Succession* (London: Longmans, Green, 1934), pp. 192-193.

30. Swift, *Gulliver's Travels,* XI, 230 and 231 respectively.

31. Swift, *Gulliver's Travels,* XI, 175.

32. Charles Beaumont, p. 139.

33. Hugo Reichard argues that Gulliver is the Houyhnhnms' man among us in "Gulliver the Pretender," *PLL,* 1 (1965), 316-318.

34. Defoe, *The Validity of the Renunciations of Former Powers,* p. 1.

35. Martin Kallich puzzles over the meaning of "lie" in "Swift and the Archetypes of Hate: *A Tale of a Tub*" in *Studies in Eighteenth-Century Culture,* ed. Harold E. Pagliaro, IV (Madison: University of Wisconsin Press, 1975), pp. 47-52. Gulliver's lies are famous and well-catalogued. See, for example, Frank Brady's introduction to *Twentieth-Century Interpretations of Gulliver's Travels* (Englewood Cliffs: Prentice-Hall, 1963), pp. 6-7; W. B. Carnochan's *Lemuel Gulliver's Mirror for Man* (Berkeley: University of California Press, 1968), p. 118; Reichard, pp. 316-326; Robert C. Elliott, "Swift's *Tale of a Tub*: An Essay in Problems of Structure," *PMLA,* 66 (1951), 452-454.

36. Swift, *A Tale of a Tub,* I, 77.

37. Swift, I, 45.

38. Henry Fielding, *Tom Thumb,* ed. L. J. Morrissey (Berkeley: University of California Press, 1970), preface, pp. 17-18.

39. Kathleen Williams, *Jonathan Swift and the Age of Compromise* (Lawrence: University of Kansas Press, 1958), traces the sources, pp. 142-143.

40. Swift, *Gulliver's Travels,* XI, 171.

41. Daniel Defoe, *Giving Alms No Charity* (London, 1704); Peter Earle, *The World of Defoe* (New York: Atheneum, 1977), p. 183.

42. Novak, *Nature of Man,* 29-36, and "Robinson Crusoe's Fear and the Search for the Natural Man," *MP,* 58 (1961), 238-240.

43. Daniel Defoe, *Jure Divino,* Book II, p. 10, (London, 1706).

44. *Cf.* studies of the island "society" in John J. Richetti, *Defoe's Narratives*

(Oxford: Clarendon Press, 1975), pp. 46–47 and 57–58; and W. B. Carnochan, *Confinement and Flight* (Berkeley: University of California Press, 1977), pp. 34–35; Hans W. Hausermann, "Aspects of Life and Thought in *Robinson Crusoe*," *RES*, 11 (1935), 447–450; James Egan, "Crusoe's Monarchy and the Puritan Concept of the Self," *SEL*, 13 (1973), 453–454; Schonhorn, "Politics," p. 31.

45. Daniel Defoe, *Robinson Crusoe*, II, 38–39.

46. Defoe, II, 47.

47. Novak, "Crusoe the King," p. 337; Frank H. Ellis, "Introduction" to *Twentieth-Century Interpretations of Robinson Crusoe* (Englewood Cliffs: Prentice-Hall, 1969), pp. 12–13.

48. Daniel Defoe, *Advice to the People of Great Britain* (London, 1714), p. 4. See also his *A Secret History of One Year* (London, 1714), p. 29.

49. Novak, *Nature,* p. 11, 16, 22–24, 37, and 63–64.

50. Daniel Defoe, *Captain Singleton*; page numbers refer to the Shakespeare Head Edition, pp. 27–28.

51. Defoe seems to have thought that the best form of government would be a modified democracy; one in which men participated in decision making and, more significantly, in the selection of a leader who would rule with great power. In his works, this form of government seems to exist only in special circumstances and for brief periods. *Cf.* Novak, "Crusoe the King," p. 347; Schonhorn, pp. 42–48.

52. Singleton forbids gambling because arguments result. Many of his speeches insist upon the necessity for unity; see, *Singleton*, p. 116 for an example.

53. John's colony at Epping has many similarities to the societies in *Colonel Jack* and *Captain Singleton;* work is divided and the group is highly unified.

54. Maximillian E. Novak discusses Misson and his colony in his introduction to *Of Captain Misson,* Augustan Reprint Society #87 (Los Angeles: Clark Library, 1962); and in *Economics and the Fiction of Daniel Defoe* (Berkeley: University of Califronia Press, 1962), pp. 109–112; 145–146; see Schonhorn, pp. 44–48.

55. Defoe, *General History*, p. 371.

56. *Cf.* Brown, pp. 564–567.

57. Novak, *Misson*, pp. i–ii.

58. Both Swift and Defoe build this requirement that governing assemblies meet regularly into their most idealistic governments.

59. Bunyan, *Works,*, II, 488.

60. William York Tindall, *John Bunyan: Mechanick Preacher* (New York: Columbia University Press, 1934), pp. 137–143.

61. Roger Sharrock says, "Bunyan's fiction is much more developed as a medium for describing common life than is usual in allegory" in *Bunyan:*

The Pilgrim's Progress (London: Arnold, 1966), p. 11; Herbert E. Green suggests that much of Bunyan's allegory is not allegory at all in "The Allegory as employed by Spenser, Bunyan, and Swift," *PMLA*, 4 (1888–1889), 159–163.

62. Bunyan does not describe government in the City of Destruction, Carnal Policy, Morality, or Conceit.

63. Bunyan, *Pilgrim's Progress,* pp. 210–211.

64. Barbara K. Lewalski explores the uses of such symbols in literature in "Typological Symbolism and the 'Progress of the Soul,' " in *Literary Uses of Typology,* ed. Earl Miner (Princeton: Princeton University Press, 1977), pp. 80–81.

65. Diabolus in *The Holy War* provides a contrast to Faithful; Diabolus wins followers by employing various deceits.

66. Tindall, pp. 136–140.

67. Bunyan, "Seasonable Counsel," II, 694, 709; 714; "The Water of Life," III, 547.

68. *Summa Theologiae,* Part I, "Treatise on Man," 94.

69. *Cf.* Sacvan Bercovitch, *The Puritan Origins of the American Self* (New Haven: Yale University Press, 1975), pp. 8–11; Thomas Hooker summarizes the common opinion,

> As they see more and can therefore judge better of the worth of persons and things, so their conscience now hath more scope, and the light of reason hath more liberty, and allowance to express that they know, and nothing now can withstand and hinder. For while men are held captive under the power of their lusts and corruptions of their hearts, in which they live and which for the while they are resolved to follow—though their reason happily do yield it, and their own hearts and consciences cannot but inwardly confess it, the persons are holy, the sins are vile which they condemn and dangers dreadful which they forewarn—yet to profess so much openly to others and to the world were to judge themselves while they would acquit others. . . . When the truth that is by their judgments assented unto and by their hearts yielded, and therefore should break out and give in testimony to the good ways of God, their corrupt and unrighteous and rebellious hearts hold it prisoner, will not suffer it either to appear unto others or prevail with themselves.

"Repentant Sinners and their Ministers" in *The American Puritans: Their Prose and Poetry,*" ed. Perry Miller (Garden City: Doubleday, 1956), pp. 167–168.

70. Bunyan, *Mr. Badman,* p. 253.

71. Daniel Defoe, *The Livery Man's Reasons, Why he did not give his Vote for a Certain Gentleman* (London, 1701), p. 12.

72. Then, as now, many interpreted "Thou shalt not kill" strictly. Compare Defoe, *Robinson Crusoe,* I, 197–201, and *General History,* pp. 365–374.

73. Hobbes described the state of nature thus:

    In such condition, there is no place for Industry; because the fruit thereof is uncertain: and consequently no Culture of the Earth . . . no Arts, no Letters; no Society; and which is worst of all, continual feare, and danger of violent death; and the life of man, solitary, poore, nasty, brutish, and short.

    Leviathan, Part I, chapter 13.

74. Douglas Hay, *Albion's Fatal Tree: Crime and Society in Eighteenth-Century England* (New York: Pantheon, 1975), pp. 17–63.

75. Hay, p. 29.

76. As late as the nineteenth century, a French judge sent to study the English legal system noticed the tendency toward abbreviated investigation; detailed in Hay, p. 37.

77. Hay, pp. 32–33.

78. Daniel Defoe, *An Account of the Late Horrid Conspiracy to Depose their Present Majesties* (London, 1691), p. 28.

79. Daniel Defoe, *Impeachment, Or No Impeachment* (London, 1714), pp. 5–6.

80. William Blackstone in *Commentaries on the Laws of England* describes the psychological factor in trial proceedings; the judges "whose learning and dignity secure their jurisdiction from contempt, and the novelty and very parade of whose appearance have no small influence upon the multitude . . . ," 4th ed. (Oxford, 1770), III, 355–356.

81. Defoe, *General History,* p. 260.

82. Defoe, *Colonel Jack,* I, 12.

83. Novak, *Economics,* pp. 20, 104 *et passim.*

84. Novak, *Nature of Man,* pp. 52–53 and 113–128; and McBurney, pp. 331–335, discuss the centrality of the theme of gratitude.

85. Kelly, pp. 846–855.

86. Torchiana, pp. 195–212.

87. Kelly's study elaborates on this point, pp. 848ff.

88. Kelly carries this argument to the extreme by applying it to Gulliver, pp. 852–854.

89. Swift, *Drapier's Letters,* X, 53.

90. Swift, X, 63.

91. Daniel Defoe, *Caledonia* (Edinburgh, 1706), p. 24.

CHAPTER III / Piety, Commerce, and Freedom

1. Georg Lukács, *The Theory of the Novel,* trans. Anna Bostock (Cambridge, Mass.: M. I. T. Press, 1971), pp. 60–61.

2. Techniques present to some extent in the picaresque, comedy of manners, the romance, satire, biography, the epic, sermons, and conduct books. Ronald Paulson in *Satire and the Novel* describes English realistic fiction as the mixing of genres and intentions, the secularizing of the tradition of spiritual biography, pp. 9-10, 43.

3. Sacks, pp. 26 and 267-270; Ian Watt also discusses the ways Defoe's works differ from novels, pp. 130-131.

4. Richetti, p. 18.

5. Charles De Secondat, Baron de Montesquieu, *Esprit des lois*, XX, 7.

6. Harold Golder finds Christian re-enacting a series of conventional situations common to chivalric heroes in "Bunyan's Valley of the Shadow," *MP*, 27 (1929), 59-64. Charles H. Firth discusses Bunyan's familiarity with romances in his introduction to *The Pilgrim's Progress* (London: Methuen, 1898).

7. Compare the list of those who fail to get into Heaven in Bunyan's *The Strait Gate*.

8. Bunyan, *Pilgrim's Progress*, p. 174. C. N. Manlove discusses the forward movement of the narrative in "The Image of the Journey in *Pilgrim's Progress*," *Journal of Narrative Technique*, 10 (1980), 23-26. This study was published after this book was completed.

9. Harold Golder identifies the metaphors of the pit, the dungeon, and flood as conventional for despair in "Bunyan's Giant Despair," *JEGP*, 30 (1931), 366.

10. Starr in *Autobiography* describes despair as an habitual stage in salvation, pp. 44, 63, 108-109.

11. Monica Furlong classifies the characters in *Pilgrim's Progress* and points out that a number of them such as Apollyon and Pope embody sin in other ways. *Puritan's Progress* (New York: Coward, McCann, and Geoghegan, 1975), pp. 107-108.

12. While Bunyan incorporates biblical language better than most, generations of Protestant writers did the same. *The Lives of the Methodist Ministers*, ed. Thomas Jackson (London: Wesleyan Conference Office, 1865), include many examples of imaginative combinations of idiomatic and biblical metaphors; John Pawson describes his conversion by saying, "The things of this world were made bitter to me, and my lawful business became a burden. The love of this world, and all desire of making a figure in life ... got their death's wound in my mind at that time. ..." IV, 17. *Cf.* Starr, *Spiritual Autobiography*, pp. 17-18, and Watkins, *Puritan Experience*, pp. 209-212. This is not to say that Bunyan's language is primarily biblical; rather, he uses words and phrases from the Bible effectively; *cf.* Sharrock (Arnold), p. 60, and Tillyard, p. 388.

13. Lukács, *Theory*, p. 71.
14. Bunyan, *Pilgrim's Progress*, p. 185.
15. *Cf.* G. R. Cragg, *The Church and the Age of Reason* (Grand Rapids: Eerdmans, 1960), pp. 65–72 *et passim;* Martin J. Greif, "The Conversion of Robinson Crusoe," *SEL*, 6 (1966), 551–574; "A Sermon of the Salvation of Mankind" in *Creeds of the Churches*, ed. John H. Leith, (Garden City: Doubleday, 1963), pp. 239–251; see especially p. 246; and The Westminster Confession of Faith (1646), especially "Of Saving Faith" and "Of Repentance unto Life."
16. Sharrock (Macmillan), p. 80; Hunter, *Pilgrim*, p. 86; Starr, *Autobiography*, pp. 42–43, 45–46, 115; Watkins, pp. 40–41 and 47–49. Watkins and Hunter agree that the conversion experience is not the dominant one in spiritual autobiography.
17. From the Westminster Confession, "Of Free-Will":
    When God converts a sinner and translates him into the state of grace, he freeth him from his natural bondage under sin, and by his grace alone enables him freely to will and do that which is spiritually good. . . .
18. Westminster Confession, "Of Providence."
19. This experience is most evident in Mansoul in *The Holy War*.
20. For discussions of *The Holy War*, see Tindall, pp. 118–165, and Sharrock (Macmillan), pp. 118–138.
21. John Bunyan, *The Holy War*, ed. James F. Forrest (New York: New York University Press, 1967), p. 8.
22. Richetti describes Crusoe's change as his converting God from an antagonist into an ally, p. 42.
23. Sharrock notes the "extraordinary loneliness" which transforms objects around him into menaces, all "projection of inner conflict" and representative of "the dramatic excitement of the struggle with evil" in "Personal Vision and Puritan Tradition in Bunyan," *The Hibbert Journal*, 56 (1957), 55, and "Spiritual Autobiography in *The Pilgrim's Progress*, *RES*, 24 (1948), 106.
24. Bunyan, *Holy War*, p. 63.
25. Bunyan, p. 9.
26. Elizabeth W. Bruss discusses the linguistic nuances in *Autobiographical Acts* (Baltimore: John Hopkins University Press, 1976), pp. 44–56.
27. Bercovitch, pp. 8–11.
28. Watkins, pp. 10, 63–66; Bercovitch, p. 31.
29. Hunter, *Pilgrim*, pp. 126–147; Starr, *Autobiography*, pp. 74–105, 185–197.
30. Watt, pp. 114–115. *Cf.* David Blewett, *Defoe's Art of Fiction* which was published after this study was complete (Toronto: University of Toronto Press, 1979).

31. Richetti, p. 18.

32. See Brown, pp. 566–568 and 571; Singleton's fear has been neglected by critics.

33. Defoe, *Crusoe*, I, 34.

34. Novak compares her to a successful hospital administrator in *Economics*, p. 99.

35. Defoe, *Colonel Jack*, II, 133.

36. Defoe, *Jack*, II, 97.

37. Defoe, *Moll*, II, 99–100.

38. Defoe, II, 37.

39. Defoe, *Jack*, I, 189. Defoe seems to have this conception of honor in mind throughout *Colonel Jack*. A summary statement is Guillaume du Vair's.

> True Honour is the report of good and vertuous Action, issuing from the Conscience into the Discovery of the People with whom we live; and which (by a reflection in our selves) gives us a testimony of what others believe of us, and to the mind becomes a great satisfaction

from *The Morall Philosophy of the Stoicks*, trans. Charles Cotton (London, 1664).

40. Cynthia Griffin Wolff elaborates on this idea in "Literary Reflections of the Puritan Characters," *JHI*, 29 (1968), 13–32; Bercovitch, 11–14.

41. John Locke, *Essay Concerning Human Understanding*, II, 27.

42. Good recent studies of the "person" include Leo Braudy's "Defoe and the Anxieties of Autobiography," *Genre*, 6 (1973), especially pp. 81–84; Patricia Meyer Spacks, *Imagining a Self* (Cambridge, Mass.: Harvard University Press, 1976).

43. Daniel Defoe, *A Reply to a Pamphlet Entituled the L--d H---sham's Vindication of his Speech* (London, 1706), p. 8.

44. Defoe (London, 1714), pp. 3–4.

45. Defoe, *Crusoe*, I, 2.

46. Swift, "On the Poor Man's Contentment," IX, 195. Proverbs 30:8–9 was a favorite with moralists; Starr, *Autobiography*, 78n.

47. *Badman*, 227.

48. Swift, "Doing Good," IX, 232.

49. Felicity Nussbaum's reading of the poem helps place the poem in the context of Swift's thought. See "Juvenal, Swift, and *The Folly of Love*," *ECS*, 9 (1976), 544–552.

50. Swift, "To Stella, Visiting me in my Sickness" in *The Poems of Jonathan Swift*, ed. Harold Williams, 2nd edition (Oxford: Clarendon Press, 1958), II, 727.

51. Starr argues this point fully, *Casuistry*, pp. v–vi, 166–167 *et passim*.

52. Robert Redfield, *The Little Community. Viewpoints for the Study of the Human Whole* (Chicago: University of Chicago Press, 1955), pp. 30–31.

53. Defoe is generally acknowledged to have been a conservative economist. He called credit a "whore" in *Eleven Opinions about Mr. H[arle]y* (1711), p. 41, and frequently recommended caution. *Cf.* Novak, *Economics*, p. 31; and Peter Earle, pp. 107 *et passim.*

54. Daniel Defoe, *The Pernicious Consequences of the Clergy's Intermedling with Affairs of State* (London, 1714), p. 30.

55. Defoe, *Jack*, I, 44.

56. Daniel Defoe, *The Storm* (London, 1704), p. 82.

57. Daniel Defoe, *Some Considerations on the Danger of the Church from her own Clergy* (London, 1715), p. 10.

58. Some analyses of incidents involving money include Zimmerman, *Defoe*, pp. 28ff.; Richetti, pp. 46–48; Novak, *Economics*, pp. 59–62.

59. Defoe, *Crusoe*, I, 149.

60. Novak, *Economics*, pp. 130–131; Shinagel, pp. 185ff.; Starr, *Casuistry*, p. 51.

61. Richetti, pp. 61–62.

62. Starr notices that Moll's "life becomes even more trying on the Virginia plantation than in London. She must act as vigorously and warily as ever, but does not feel called upon to spend so much ingenuity defending her action, because she is convinced of its justice," *Casuistry*, p. 134. The standards in Virginia are largely her own, and, therefore, less threatening.

63. Swift, *Gulliver's Travels*, XI, 235.

64. Swift, IX, 51.

65. See Swift, IX, 49–50; X, 43; XI, 252–253; XII, 56–57 and 100.

66. Pat Rogers, "Gulliver and the Engineers," *MLR*, 70 (1975), 261. Arthur Case notes the Academy's similarity to the expanding government buildings of Whitehall in *Four Essays on Gulliver's Travels* (Gloucester, Mass.: Peter Smith, 1958), pp. 89–90.

67. Swift, III, 6 and 7, and *Drapier's Letters*, X, 60.

68. For a discussion of the attribution, see Ferguson, p. 70, and Davis, who labels it "probably written by Swift," X.

69. Compare Defoe's treatment of Sir Robert Clayton in *Roxana* and of stock-jobbers in the *Review*, I, 47, 191; III, 139; IV, 197; V, 428; VI, 117–129, 202, 306; VIII, 83 and 226 in A. W. Secord's *Defoe's Review* (New York: Columbia University Press, 1938).

70. Swift, *Drapier's Letters*, X, 61.

71. Swift, "On the Poor Man's Contentment," IX, 193.

72. Swift, *Gulliver's Travels*, XI, 63, 54, 66, 33, and 296.

73. Davis's introduction, VII, xiv–xv.

74. Fred N. Robinson, "Satirists and Enchanters in Early Irish Literature" in *Modern Essays in Criticism: Satire*, ed. Ronald Paulson (New York: Prentice-Hall, 1971), pp. 1–3, 7. See also Robert C. Elliott, *The Power of Satire: Magic, Ritual, Art* (Princeton: Princeton University Press, 1960), pp. 263 *et passim.*

75. Ewald discusses the "mask of humble objectivity" which allows Swift to present a satiric message under the guise of fact, pp. 71–74.
76. Swift, *Examiner,* III, 32.
77. Swift, III, 34 and 37.
78. Swift, III, 137. Swift consistently uses catalogues to associate certain professions with criminals. See, for example, *Gulliver's Travels,* XI, 260–261: "Here were no Gibers, Censurers, Backbiters, Pickpockets, Highwaymen, Housebreakers, Attorneys, Bawds, Buffoons, Gamesters, Politicians. . . ."
79. Swift, III, 96–97.
80. For a detailed study of *Examiner* #14," see Clayton Lein's "Rhetoric and Allegory in Swift's *Examiner* 14," *SEL,* 17 (1977), 407–417.
81. Swift, III, 61–62 and 121–126.
82. Swift, III, 142; see also p. 69. Defoe insisted this was unjust. See *A New Test* (1702), p. 4; *The Dissenters Answer* (1704), pp. 48–49; *The Weakest Go to the Wall* (1714), p. 4, on the commonly held opinion.
83. *Medley* #18, 29 January 1711 and #30, 23 April 1712 are representative reactions to Swift.
84. Martin Price argues that Swift constantly uses "redefinition," *Swift's Rhetorical Art: A Study in Structure and Meaning* (Hamden: Archon, 1963), pp. 24–26.
85. Swift, III, 122; see also III, 92, 111, 166.
86. For a discussion of Bolingbroke's party principles, see H. T. Dickinson, *Bolingbroke* (London: Constable, 1970), pp. 14–15 *et passim;* Sheila Biddle, *Bolingbroke and Harley* (New York: Knopf, 1974), pp. 100 and 112; Pat Rogers, "Swift and Bolingbroke on Faction," *JBS,* 9 (1970), 71–101.
87. Henry St. John, Lord Bolingbroke, "A Dissertation upon Parties" in *Works* (Philadelphia: Carey and Hart, 1841), II, 13.
88. Satires such as *Tatler* #220 and *Spectators* #81 and #125 are familiar to every student of the century. Robert Harley hoped to maintain power without strong party allegiance, and Bolingbroke's "Dissertation upon Parties" laments the results of party prejudice. See also J. G. A. Pocock's *The Machiavellian Moment* (Princeton: Princeton University Press, 1975) for a full discussion of contemporary attitudes toward parties and the shifting political alliances which worked against party strength.
89. Swift, *Examiner,* III, 122.
90. Swift, III, 67.
91. W. A. Speck reminds us that "moneyed interest" was a precise term limited to those involved in public credit. The Bank of England and the East India Company were at the heart of the system, and the factors, jobbers, and brokers who handled or lent money for the government rather than traders or merchants were the "moneyed interest," "Conflict in

Society" in *Britain after the Glorious Revolution,* ed. Geoffrey Holmes (New York: St. Martin's, 1969), pp. 135–136.

92. Swift used the device of having the speaker condemn himself repeatedly. Compare, for example, the Bickerstaff papers. The mock petition is on pages 172–173.

93. Swift, III, 57.

94. John Carswell, *The Old Cause: Three Biographical Studies in Whiggism* (London: Cresset, 1954), pp. 58–59.

95. Davis's introduction, III, xviii–xix.

96. Swift, III, 54.

97. Swift, III, 55 and 142.

98. Swift, III, 95. On 5 March 1711 Steele expands the idea of a smutty man going to a ball into an accusation that Swift's party is trying to mingle with the Whigs until their dirt rubs off, making the Whigs as black as the Tories, *Medley* #23.

99. Compare the prose describing the Tories III, 113–114, 121–126, and 163–164 to descriptions of the Whigs quoted and cited above.

100. Swift, III, 92.

101. *Cf.* Ehrenpreis, *Swift: The Man,* III, 409–412.

CHAPTER IV / The Life of the Mind

1. I use "technique" as Mark Shorer does to cover almost the entire range of the author's choices. See "Technique as Discovery," *Hudson Review,* I (1948), 67–87.

2. The problem of the possible not always seeming probable has been discussed since Aristotle's *Poetics.* Numerous eighteenth-century writers considered it. Fielding, for example, discusses it in the preface to *Joseph Andrews,* the preface to his sister Sarah Fielding's *David Simple,* in "An Essay on the Knowledge of the Characters of Men," and in *Tom Jones,* VIII.i.

3. Leo Braudy, "Penetration and Impenetrability in *Clarissa*" in *New Approaches to Eighteenth-Century Literature,* ed. Phillip Harth (New York: Columbia University Press, 1974), p. 178.

4. See Louis Martz's introduction to *The Pilgrim's Progress* (New York: Holt, Rinehart & Winston, 1949); Starr, *Autobiography,* p. 17; Henri Talon, "Space and the Hero in *The Pilgrim's Progress,*" *Etudes Anglais,* 14 (1961), 127. So much a part of the pious was biblical language that journal entries with anecdotes such as John Pawson's observation that "So true it is, in the midst of life we are in death" when he nearly choked to death on a potato are common, *Lives of the Methodist Preachers,* IV, 48; see also I, 5–6.

5. Mrs. Radcliffe and Dryden ate indigestible foods in the hope of inducing extravagant dreams.

6. Thomas Hobbes, *Leviathan,* Part I, chapter ii.

7. Quoted in Ralph Woods' *The World of Dreams* (New York: Random House, 1947), pp. 152ff.

8. *Works of Sir Thomas Browne,* ed. Geoffrey Keynes (Chicago: University of Chicago Press, 1964), V, iii. Compare Thomas Nashe, "The Terrors of the Night" in *Works,* ed. Ronald B. McKerrow, 5 vols. (Oxford: Blackwell, 1958),

   > A dreame is nothing else but a bubling scum of froath of the fancie, which the day hath left undigested. A Dreame is nothing els but the Eccho of our conceipts in the day, I, 355–356.

9. Browne, III, 231.

10. Browne, III, 230.

11. There are a number of studies of *Pilgrim's Progress* as dream vision. Among the best are Talon, pp. 124–130; Manfred Weidhorn, *Dreams in Seventeenth-Century English Literature* (The Hague: Mouton, 1970), pp. 82–87; Sharrock, "Autobiography," pp. 102–120; J. Wharey, *The Sources of Bunyan's Allegories* (Baltimore: Johns Hopkins University Press, 1904); U. Milo Kaufman, pp. 15 *et passim.*

12. Erich Fromm, *The Forgotten Language: An Introduction to the Understanding of Dreams, Fairy Tales, and Myths* (New York: Rinehart, 1951), pp. 7 and 12.

13. As described in Rev. 9, Apollyon is the king of locusts released from the pit. These locusts cannot harm men with God's seal on their foreheads. In the Dead Sea Hymns (3.19–20), the name is used figuratively to denote the "slough of despond." *IDB.*

14. Talon's appreciation observes this effect, pp. 124–130.

15. Such emphasis was common to the dream allegory. *Cf.* Henry More's "Insomnium Philosophicum" as one example of the obstacles and rewards of the Christian's journey through life.

16. Sharrock, "Autobiography," p. 106.

17. Starr, *Autobiography,* points out a similar phenomenon in *Robinson Crusoe,* p. 83.

18. Stanley E. Fish in *Self-Consuming Artifacts* (Berkeley: University of California Press, 1972) demonstrates how Bunyan subverts the reader's faith in time and space and, thereby, emphasizes human limits, pp. 238ff.

19. Freud explained this as an individual dream-thought being represented by several elements in the dream-content; its converse, "collective and composite personages" he calls "condensation."

20. Fish argues that "And behold it was a dream" relinquishes any claim to content or effect, p. 263.

21. The concept of the initiated reader did not die with the Puritan writers. Fielding considers the idea at length in his works; cf. *Tom Jones,* VII, i, for one example.

22. Cf. Fromm, pp. 27–29.

23. Ignorance has been interpreted as representing the Deists by John W. Draper in "Bunyan's Mr. Ignorance," *MLR,* 22 (1927), 18; the Latitudinarians by Tindall and Talon; the Quakers by Richard F. Hardin, "Bunyan, Mr. Ignorance, and the Quakers," *SP,* 69 (1972), 496–501; and as "carnal confidence" by Maurice Hussey, "Bunyan's 'Mr. Ignorance,' " *MLR,* 44 (1949), 485.

24. For interpretations of the awakening, see J. B. Wharey's notes to his edition of *Pilgrim's Progress* (Oxford: Blackwell, 1956), pp. 313 and 333; Weidhorn, pp. 84–87.

25. Draper offers an interesting psychological interpretation of Ignorance's dropping behind, p. 20.

26. This quotation from Thomas Taylor's *The Practice of Repentance* comes from Hussey's article, p. 483; his discussion influenced my interpretation. See also Draper, p. 17.

27. James Sutherland, *English Satire* (Cambridge: Cambridge University Press, 1958), pp. 15–16, describes the satirist's narrow vision.

28. Morton Kelsey, *Dreams: The Dark Speech of the Spirit* (Garden City: Doubleday, 1968), pp. 201–203.

29. Hunter, *Pilgrim,* pp. 115–117.

30. A number of relevant narrative patterns have been proposed. Among them are Miriam K. Starkman's in *Swift's Satire on Learning in A Tale of a Tub* (Princeton: Princeton University Press, 1950), p. 7; Ronald Paulson's in *Theme and Structure in Swift's Tale of a Tub* (New Haven: Yale University Press, 1960), p. 234; J. A. Levine's in "The Design of *A Tale of a Tub,*" *ELH,* 33 (1966), 206.

31. W. B. Carnochan, *Confinement,* pp. 89–92.

32. Cf. *Tale,* pp. 291 and 369.

33. Carnochan, pp. 104–108.

34. Posterity, "sole Arbiter of the Productions of human Wit," preoccupied Swift throughout his career.

35. The idea is commonplace. See the final plate of Hogarth's *Rake's Progress,* for example.

36. Levine, pp. 214–217.

37. Bailey gives a special definition in law: "An Action is said to be in Personality when it is brought against the right Person." In *Clarissa,* Lovelace is spoken of as having "personalities."

38. R. S. Crane says that the question kept uppermost in *Gulliver's Travels* is "what sort of animal man, as a species, really is," p. 243.

39. Weston La Barre, "The Dream, Charisma, and the Culture-Hero" in *The Dream and Human Societies*, ed. G. E. Von Grunebaum and Roger Caillois (Berkeley: University of California Press, 1966), pp. 231-233.
40. Lukács, *Theory*, p. 71.
41. Kahler, p. 141.
42. Defenses of the single life were not uncommon in the eighteenth-century novel. Lady Bellaston says to Mrs. Western, "I am not married I promise you my dear. You know, Bel, I have try'd the comforts once already, and once I think is enough for any reasonable woman" (*Tom Jones*, XVI, viii). *The Ladies Calling* (1676) includes the observation, "Marriage is so great an adventure, once seems enough for the whole life (II, ii, 244-245), and *The Whole Duty of Woman* goes even further: "Thou art as a galleyslave, who, in the madness of joy for his liberty, runneth himself again into bondage" if the widow remarries, p. 85. Some of the most common reasons for resisting second marriages included "impossible to love again," a "sin against delicacy," and religion (I Corinthians, 7 was much quoted). Roxana, however, argues from ambition, not the desire for retirement and rest.
43. Novak, *Economics*, pp. 130-131; Shinagel, pp. 185ff.; Starr, *Casuistry*, pp. 181ff.
44. *Cf.* Brown who points out that "a strong fear of the menace of other wills" and "the way the self becomes somebody else in conversion" explain the special importance of names in Defoe's works, p. 564. See also Frederick R. Karl, "Moll's Many-Colored Coat: Veil and Disguise in the Fiction of Defoe," *SN*, 5 (1973), 86-97; Leo Braudy, "Daniel Defoe and the Anxieties of Autobiography," pp. 76-97.
45. G. A. Starr's article, "Defoe's Prose Style: 1. The Language of Interpretation," *MP*, 71 (1974), notes that "considerations of utility are often uppermost in Crusoe's mind, and of wealth and social status in Moll's but what is stylistically significant is the process by which these and other values are ascribed to a world of external things by Defoe's narrators." External things are not merely named but presented as they were experienced by or related to the narrator. See especially pp. 289 and 294.
46. Daniel Defoe, *Roxana*, p. 101.
47. On Crusoe's limited abilities see H. F. Robins, "How Smart was Robinson Crusoe?" *PMLA*, 67 (1952), 782-789; Hunter, *Pilgrim*, p. 177.
48. Hunter discusses dreams in *Pilgrim*, p. 161.
49. Robinson Crusoe warns the reader not to ignore premonitions: "Let no Man despise the secret Hints and Notices of Danger which sometimes are given him, when he may think there is no Possibility of its being real" II, 41. *Cf.* Rodney M. Baine, *Daniel Defoe and the Supernatural* (Athens: University of Georgia Press, 1968), 9 *et passim*.

50. Bunyan, *Grace Abounding,* pp. 15–16.

51. *Lives of the Methodist Preachers,* I, 27; I, 181; and IV, 292–293.

52. Brown, p. 566; Ellis, pp. 12–15.

53. Defoe, *Serious Reflections,* pp. 107–109.

54. See the preface to *Serious Reflections,* pp. ix–xiii.

55. Swift parodies this insistence on truth and interpretation, the specious and transparent identity, and the avowed high purpose in his "Letter to Cousin Symond."

56. Zimmerman, *Defoe,* pp. 24–47.

57. Defoe, *An Essay upon Projects* (Gainesville: Scholars Facsimile Reprints, 1969), pp. 284–285. Defoe does include characteristics such as levity which he says are in the nature of women.

58. Zimmerman, *Defoe,* pp. 165–173; Brown, pp. 581–582; Richetti, 203. See my "Personality and Biblical Allusion in Defoe's Letters," *South Atlantic Review,* 47 (1982), 1–20. Matthew Henry, *An Exposition of the Historical Books of the Old Testament* (London, 1715).

59. *Cf.* Zimmerman, pp. 180–187; Higdon, pp. 79–82; Kropf, p. 477.

60. *Roxana,* pp. 83–84. Here Amy compares her behavior to Roxana's, and Roxana extends the parallel to remember that both "had been hansell'd by the same Party."

61. *Roxana,* pp. 188, 197, 206, and 326–327.

62. This discussion is influenced by Lukács, *Theory,* pp. 75–78, and by Kahler, pp. 131–146.

CHAPTER V / Limits and Fulfillment

1. Defoe, *Crusoe,* I, 121.

2. Richetti makes a similar point, pp. 50–60.

3. Brown discusses Defoe's characters' "double compulsion to expose and to conceal themselves," pp. 563–564 and 569–571.

4. Starr, *Casuistry,* pp. vii, 87, 93–94, 100–103, and 109–110.

5. Swift often described the transfer of human passions into political actions. See *Examiner* III, 80–85 and 104; *Four Last Years of the Queen,* VII, 5.

6. Ila D. Traldi discusses the theme of limitations in "Gulliver the 'Educated Fool': Unity in the Voyage to Laputa," *PLL,* 4 (1968), 35–45, as does Kahler, pp. 114–117. *Cf.* Hart, pp. 125–130.

7. Swift, *A Tale of a Tub,* I, 104; *The Conduct of the Allies,* VI, 23; *Gulliver's Travels,* XI, 40 respectively.

8. For a detailed discussion of this point see my article, "The First Blow is

Half the Battle: Swift's *Conduct of the Allies,*" in *Newsletters to Newspapers: Eighteenth-Century Journalism,* ed. D. H. Bond and W. R. McLeod (Morgantown: University of West Virginia Press, 1977), pp. 47–55.

9. Bunyan, *Grace Abounding,* p. 15.

10. Defoe, *Jack,* II, 2.

11. *The Correspondence of Jonathan Swift,* ed. Harold Williams (Oxford: Clarendon Press, 1963), I, 262–263.

12. Defoe also lists "integrity" in *R[ogue]'s on Both Sides* (1711), but this quality is absent in some of his central characters. For a discussion of practical education, see Letter III, "Of the Trading Stile," *The Complete English Tradesman* (1725).

13. Bunyan, *Badman,* pp. 253–257.

14. Spacks says that many novels imply that human identity is fixed, *Imagining a Self,* pp. 8–9.

15. Edward Wasiolek says that Swift uses different forms of reality to expose the real state of society and then as terms of comparison by which society may be judged in "Relativity in *Gulliver's Travels,*" *PQ*, 37 (1958), 111–115.

16. Ehrenpreis traces Swift's fascination with this phenomenon in *Personality,* pp. 65–69.

17. See Brown on the "fear of the menace of other wills," pp. 564–568.

18. Hunter clarifies the relationship of *Crusoe* to travel literature in *Pilgrim,* p. 14.

19. Paul Dottin considers *Serious Reflections* to be Defoe's capitalizing on the charges made by Gildon which brought the parable parallel to the public's attention. Paul Dottin, *Robinson Crusoe Examin'd and Criticis'd* (London: J. M. Dent & Sons, Ltd., 1923), pp. 59–60.

20. Charles Gildon, "A Dialogue betwixt D. . . F. .e, Robinson Crusoe, and his Man Friday" in *The Life and Strange Surprizing Adventures of Mr. D. . . De F. . .., of London, Hosier* (London, 1719), p. viii.

   So that upon the whole, we find that Robinson Crusoe, even when he pretends to repent, is for throwing the Guilt of his Sin upon others, who, as far as we can possibly discover, did not at all deserve the charge; and I dare believe, that he was in reality the only Person among them, who ever liv'd so many Years without saying his Prayers, or acknowledging God and his Providence, and is likely therefore rather to have been the Corrupter, than the Corrupted,"

   "An Epistle to D. . . . D' F. . .., The Reputed Author of Robinson Crusoe," p. 22.

21. Gildon, although he did some political hack writing, may have been unaware of the purpose of Defoe's Scottish trips. His own naiveté led to his conviction for writing a seditious pamphlet in 1707. Dottin, *Crusoe Examin'd,* pp. 25–26.

22. "An Epistle to D... D' F...e," pp. 1-3, 8, 14-16, and 42.

23. Starr discusses Defoe's opinions about the follies of youth in *Autobiography* pp. 74-77; see Richetti, p. 26.

24. Daniel Defoe, *The Memoirs of Major Alexander Ramkins* (London: Gollancz, 1970), p. 272. *Ramkins* was originally published in 1718.

25. Defoe, pp. 326-327.

26. J. W. Johnson, *The Formation of English Neo-Classical Thought* (Princeton: Princeton University Press, 1967), pp. 7-8.

27. Elliott describes Gulliver as "celebrating" England, "the most perfect utopia Gulliver writes of," *Utopia*, pp. 53-54.

28. Hunter, *Pilgrim*, pp. 93-128 *et passim*; Kaufman, pp. 5-15, 156-159; Shenk, p. 91; Golder, "Bunyan's Valley," 59-66; Edwin T. Benjamin, "Symbolic Elements in *Robinson Crusoe*," *PQ*, 30 (1951), 206-211; Kallich, "Archetypes of Hate," 43-58; Robert P. Fitzgerald, "The Allegory of Luggnagg and the Struldbruggs in *Gulliver's Travels*," *SP*, 65 (1968), 657-676.

29. Phillip Harth summarizes the debate and argues that Swift does not intend to portray real events in "The Problem of Political Allegory in *Gulliver's Travels*," *MP*, 73 (1976 supplement), 544-547.

30. Kahler concludes that narrative becomes symbolic, p. 49; Hunter argues that Crusoe is a kind of Everyman, *Pilgrim*, p. 128. Talon sees Everyman in Christian (p. 125) while Hussey disagrees because Christian was a "chosen soul" (p. 483). Edward A. Block demonstrates the pains Swift took in order to make Gulliver an average Englishman in "Lemuel Gulliver: Middle-Class Englishman," *MLN*, 68 (1953), 474-477.

31. Paulson compares the two forms' treatment of actions, *Satire and the Novel*, p. 5.

32. Starr describes the separation of act and actor in *Casuistry; cf.* Richetti, pp. 105-108.

33. Morris Golden, *The Self Observed* (Baltimore: John Hopkins University Press, 1972), pp. 2-5, 33, 44, 52; see also David P. French, "Swift, Temple," *TSLL*, 5 (1963), 53-57.

34. *Cf.* Starr, *Autobiography*, pp. 169-173; *Casuistry*, pp. 181ff.; Maximillian E. Novak, "Crime and Punishment in Defoe's *Roxana*," *JEGP*, 55 (1966), 445; Peterson, pp. 175-191; Richetti, pp. 192-195.

35. Defoe, *Jack*, I, 209.

36. Brown argues that Crusoe comes to see himself as an agent of Providence, even a form of Providence, pp. 576ff. See Paulson, *Satire*, who describes the individual in the novel as trying to "batter his way through to his true destiny," p. 43; Hunter argues that Swift offers an alternative to the artist's being discoverer or creator of order, "one who recalls a former order," *Pilgrim*, p. 210. Swift seems more sceptical to me, however, and I believe

he more often parodies attempts to find order and describes earlier order only to expose its failings later.

Lukács says that the "immanence of meaning" which the novel form offers is "a mere glimpse of meaning," "the highest that life has to offer and that this glimpse is the only thing worth the commitment of an entire life. . . ." *Theory,* p. 80.

37. Sharrock concludes that "the dramatic excitement of the struggle with evil is transferred to the inner life of Christian" in "Autobiography," p. 106.

38. A. Mendilow, *Time and Novel* (London: Nevill, 1952), p. 38, and Georg Lukács, *Soul and Form,* trans. Anna Bostock (Cambridge, Mass.: M.I.T. Press, 1974), pp. 141–144, are among the theorists who interpret fiction as creating a new "reality."

39. Max Weber, *The Protestant Ethic and the Spirit of Capitalism,* trans. Talcott Parsons (New York: Scribner's, 1958), pp. 80–85; Bercovitch, p. 6.

BIBLIOGRAPHY

Alkon, Paul K. "The Odds Against Friday: Defoe, Bayes, and Inverse Probability," in *Probability, Time, and Space in Eighteenth-Century Literature*. Ed. Paula R. Backscheider. New York: AMS Press, 1978, pp. 29–37.

[Allestree, Richard]. *The Ladies Calling,* by the author of *The Whole duty of Man*. London, 1659.

Backscheider, Paula R. "The First Blow is Half the Battle: Swift's *Conduct of the Allies*," in *Newsletters to Newspapers: Eighteenth-Century Journalism*. Ed. D. H. Bond and W. R. McLeod. Morgantown: University of West Virginia Press, 1977, pp. 47–55.

————. "Personality and Biblical Allusion in Defoe's Letters." *South Atlantic Review,* 47 (1982), 1–20.

Baine, Rodney M. *Daniel Defoe and the Supernatural*. Athens: University of Georgia Press, 1968.

Barroll, J. Leeds. "Gulliver and the Struldbruggs." *PMLA,* 73 (1958), 43–50.

Battestin, Martin. *The Moral Basis of Fielding's Art*. Middletown, Conn.: Wesleyan University Press, 1959.

Beaumont, Charles. *Swift's Classical Rhetoric*. Athens: University of Georgia Press, 1961.

Benjamin, Edwin B. "The King of Brobdingnag and *Secrets of State*." *Journal of the History of Ideas,* 18 (1957), 572–577.

————. "Symbolic Elements in *Robinson Crusoe*." *Philological Quarterly,* 30 (1951), 206–211.

Bercovitch, Sacvan. *The Puritan Origins of the American Self*. New Haven: Yale University Press, 1975.

Berger, Morroe. *Real and Imagined Worlds*. Cambridge, Mass.: Harvard University Press, 1977.

Biddle, Sheila. *Bolingbroke and Harley*. New York: Knopf, 1974.

Blackstone, William. *Commentaries on the Laws of England*. 3 vols. Oxford: Clarendon Press, 1770.

Blewett, David. *Defoe's Art of Fiction*. Toronto: University of Toronto Press, 1979.

Block, Edward A. "Lemuel Gulliver: Middle-Class Englishmen." *Modern Language Notes,* 68 (1953), 474–477.

Booth, Wayne C. *The Rhetoric of Fiction*. Chicago: University of Chicago Press, 1961.

Boyce, Benjamin. "The Question of Emotion in Defoe." *Studies in Philology,* 50 (1953), 47–53.

Brady, Frank, ed. *Twentieth-Century Interpretations of Gulliver's Travels*. Englewood Cliffs, N.J.: Prentice-Hall, 1963.

Braudy, Leo. "Defoe and the Anxieties of Autobiography." *Genre,* 6 (1973), 76-97.

Brown, Homer O. "The Displaced Self in the Novels of Daniel Defoe." *Journal of English Literary History,* 38 (1971), 562-590.

Browne, Thomas. *Works of Sir Thomas Browne*. 4 vols. Ed. Geoffrey Keynes. Chicago: University of Chicago Press, 1964.

Bruss, Elizabeth W. *Autobiographical Acts*. Baltimore: Johns Hopkins University Press, 1976.

Bunyan, John. *The Holy War*. Ed. James F. Forrest. New York: New York University Press, 1967.

―――. *The Life and Death of Mr. Badman*. Ed. G. B. Harrison. London: Oxford University Press, 1929.

―――. *The Pilgrim's Progress*. Ed. and Intro. Charles Firth. London: Methuen, 1898.

―――. *The Pilgrim's Progress*. Ed. Roger Sharrock. London: Oxford University Press, 1966.

―――. *The Pilgrim's Progress*. Ed. J. B. Wharey. Oxford: Blackwell, 1956.

―――. *The Works of John Bunyan*. 3 vols. Ed. George Offor. Glasgow: Blackie and Son, 1853.

Carnochan, W. B. "The Complexity of Swift: Gulliver's Fourth Voyage." *Studies in Philology,* 60 (1963), 23-44.

―――. *Confinement and Flight*. Berkeley: University of California Press, 1977.

―――. *Lemuel Gulliver's Mirror for Man*. Berkeley: University of California Press, 1968.

―――. "Some Roles of Lemuel Gulliver." *Texas Studies in Language and Literature,* 5 (1964), 520-529.

Carswell, John. *The Old Cause: Three Biographical Studies in Whiggism*. London: Cresset, 1954.

Case, Arthur E. *Four Essays on Gulliver's Travels*. Princeton: Princeton University Press, 1945; rev. ed. Gloucester, Mass.: Peter Smith, 1958.

Champion, Larry S. "Gulliver's Voyages: The Framing Events as Guide to Interpretation." *Texas Studies in Language and Literature,* 10 (1969), 529-536.

Cohan, Steven. "Gulliver's Fiction." *Studia Neophilologica: A Journal of German and Romance Languages and Literature,* 6 (1974), 7-16.

Cook, R. I. " 'Mr. Examiner' and 'Mr. Review': The Tory Apologetics of Swift and Defoe." *Huntington Library Quarterly,* 29 (1966), 127-146.

Cragg, G. R. *The Church and the Age of Reason*. Grand Rapids: Eerdmans, 1960.

Crane, R. S. "The Houyhnhnms, the Yahoos, and the History of Ideas." in *Reason and the Imagination*. Ed. J. A. Mazzeo. New York: Columbia University Press, 1962, 231-253.

Defoe, Daniel. *An Account of the Late Horrid Conspiracy to Depose their Present Majesties*. London, 1691.

―――. *An Account of the Life of Gow*. London, 1725.

―――. *Advice to the People of Great Britain*. London, 1714.

―――. *An Argument Shewing, that a Standing Army*. London, 1698.

_____._A Brief Reply to the History of Standing Armies in England._ London, 1698.

_____._Caledonia._ Edinburgh, 1706.

_____._Of Captain Misson._ Ed. Maximillian E. Novak. Augustan Reprint Society #87. Los Angeles: Clark Library, 1962.

_____._Captain Singleton._ London, 1720.

_____._The Character of the late Dr. Annesley._ London, 1697.

_____._The Complete English Tradesman._ London, 1725.

_____._Conjugal Lewdness._ London, 1727.

_____._The Consolidator._ London, 1705.

_____._The Dissenters Answer._ London, 1704.

_____._Due Preparations for the Plague._ London, 1722.

_____._The Dyet of Poland._ London, 1705.

_____._Eleven Opinions about Mr. H[arle]y._ London, 1711.

_____._An Essay upon Projects._ Gainesville: Scholars Facsimile Reprints, 1969.

_____._The Family Instructor._ London, 1715.

_____._The Farther Adventures of Robinson Crusoe._ Oxford: Blackwell, 1927.

_____._General History of the Robberies and Murders of the Most Notorious Pirates._ Ed. A. L. Haywood. London: Routledge & Kegan Paul, 1955.

_____._A General History of Discoveries and Improvements._ London, [1726].

_____._Giving Alms No Charity._ London, 1704.

_____._An Historical Account of the Voyages and Adventures of Sir Walter Raleigh._ London, 1719.

_____._The History and Remarkable Life of . . . Col. Jack._ Oxford: Blackwell, 1927.

_____._The History of the Remarkable Life of John Sheppard._ London, 1724.

_____._The History of the Wars, Of his Late Majesty Charles XII._ London, 1720.

_____._The History of the Wars, Of his Present Majesty CharlesXII._ London, 1715.

_____._A Hymn to Peace._ London, 1706.

_____._The Impartial History of the Life of . . . Peter Czar of Russia._ London, 1723.

_____._Impeachment, or No Impeachment._ London, 1714.

_____._A Journal of the Plague Year._ Oxford: Blackwell, 1927.

_____._Jure Divino: A Satyr in Twelve Books._ London, 1706.

_____._The King of Pirates._ London, 1719.

_____._Letter from Mr. Reason,_ London, 1706.

_____._The Life and Strange Surprizing Adventures of Robinson Crusoe._ Oxford: Blackwell, 1927.

_____._The Life of Jonathan Wilde._ London, 1725.

_____._The Livery Man's Reasons, Why he did not give his Vote for a Certain Gentleman._ London, 1701.

_____._Memoirs of a Cavalier._ London: Blackwell, 1927.

_____._Memoirs of an English Officer._ London: Gollancz, 1970.

_____._The Memoirs of Major Alexander Ramkins._ London: Gollancz, 1970.

_____._Mist's Weekly Journal._

_____._Moll Flanders._ Oxford: Blackwell, 1927.

_____._More Reformation._ London, 1703.

————.*A New Family Instructor.* London, 1727.

————.*A New Test of the Church of England's Loyalty.* London, 1702.

————.*The Pacificator.* London, 1700.

————.*Peace, or Poverty.* London, 1712.

————.*The Pernicious Consequences of the Clergy's Intermedling.* London, [1714].

————.*Reasons against a War with France.* London, 1701.

————.*Religious Courtship.* London, 1722.

————.*A Reply to a Pamphlet Entitled the L[ord] H[aversham]'s Vindication.* London, 1706.

————.*Review.*

————.*Robert Drury's Journal.* London, 1729.

————.*R[ogue]'s on Both Sides.* London, 1711.

————.*Roxana: The Fortunate Mistress.* Ed. Jane Jack. London: Oxford University Press, 1964.

————.*The Secret History of the October Club.* London, 1711.

————.*A Secret History of One Year.* London, 1714.

————.*Serious Reflections . . . of Robinson Crusoe.* Ed. G. H. Maynadier. New York: Crowell, 1903.

————.*A Short Narrative of the Life of Marlborough.* London, 1711.

————.*The Shortest Way with the Dissenters.* Oxford: Blackwell, 1927.

————.*Some Account of the Life of Sir Charles Sedley.* London, 1722.

————.*Some Considerations on the Danger of the Church from her own Clergy.* London, 1715.

————.*Some Reflections on a Pamphlet.* London, 1697.

————.*The Storm.* London, 1704.

————.*Tories and Tory Principles Ruinous.* London, 1714.

————.*The True and Genuine Account . . . of the late Jonathan Wild.* London, 1725.

————.*The True-born Englishman.* London, 1700.

————.*The True State of the Case between the Government and the Creditors of the Navy.* London, 1711.

————.*The Two Great Questions Consider'd.* London, 1707.

———— *The Validity of the Renunciation Of Former Powers, Enquired into, And The Present Renunciation Of The Duke of Anjou, Impartially Considered.* London, 1712.

———— *The Weakest Go to the Wall.* London, 1714.

———— *The Shakespeare Head Edition of the Novels and Selected Writings of Daniel Defoe.* 14 vols. Oxford: Blackwell, 1927-28.

Dickinson, H.T. *Bolingbroke.* London: Constable, 1970.

Dottin, Paul. *Daniel Defoe et ses Romans.* Paris: Les presses universitaires de France, 1924.

————. *Robinson Crusoe Examin'd and Criticis'd.* London: J. M. Dent & Sons, 1923.

Draper, John W. "Bunyan's Mr. Ignorance." *Modern Language Review,* 22 (1927), 15-21.

Earle, Peter. *The World of Defoe.* New York: Atheneum, 1977.

Egan, James. "Crusoe's Monarchy and the Puritan Concept of the Self." *Studies in English Literature, 1500-1900,* 13 (1973), 451-460.

Ehrenpreis, Irvin. *The Personality of Jonathan Swift.* Cambridge, Mass.: Harvard University Press, 1958.

————. *Swift: The Man, His Works, and the Age.* 2 vols. Cambridge, Mass.: Harvard University Press, 1962 and 1967.

Elliott, Robert C. *The Power of Satire: Magic, Ritual, Art.* Princeton: Princeton University Press, 1960.

———. *The Shape of Utopia.* Chicago: University of Chicago Press, 1970.

———. "Swift's Satire: Rules of the Game." *Journal of English Literary History,* 41 (1974), 413–428.

———. "Swift's *Tale of a Tub:* An Essay in Problems of Structure." *PMLA,* 66 (1951), 441–455.

Ellis, Frank H., ed. *Twentieth-Century Interpretations of Robinson Crusoe.* Englewood Cliffs, N. J.: Prentice-Hall, 1969.

Ewald, William B. *The Masks of Jonathan Swift.* Cambridge, Mass.: Harvard University Press, 1954.

Falle, George. "Divinity and Wit: Swift's Attempted Reconciliation." *University of Toronto Quarterly,* 46 (1976), 14–30.

Ferguson, Oliver. *Jonathan Swift and the Irish.* Urbana, Ill.: University of Illinois Press, 1962.

Fielding, Henry. *Tom Thumb.* Ed. L. J. Morrissey. Berkeley: University of California Press, 1970.

Fink, Z. S. "Political Theory in *Gulliver's Travels.*" *Journal of English Literary History,* 14 (1947), 151–161.

Firth, Charles. *Essays, Historical and Literary.* Oxford: Clarendon Press, 1938.

Fish, Stanley E. *Self-Consuming Artifacts.* Berkeley: University of California Press, 1972.

Fitzgerald, Robert P. "The Allegory of Luggnagg and the Struldbruggs in *Gulliver's Travels.*" *Studies in Philology,* 65 (1968), 657–676.

French, David P. "Swift and Hobbes—A Neglected Parallel." *Boston University Studies in English,* 3 (1957), 243–255.

———. "Swift, Temple, and A Digression on Madness." *Texas Studies in Language and Literature,* 5 (1963), 42–57.

Fromm, Erich. *The Forgotten Language: An Introduction to the Understanding of Dreams, Fairy Tales, and Myths.* New York: Rinehart, 1951.

Frye, Roland M. "Swift's Yahoo and the Christian Symbols for Sin." *Journal of the History of Ideas,* 15 (1954), 201–217.

Furlong, Monica. *Puritan's Progress.* New York: Coward, McCann, and Geoghegan, 1975.

Gildon, Charles. *The Life and Strange Surprizing Adventures of Mr. D. . . . De F. . . , of London, Hosier.* London, 1719.

———. *The Life of Mr. Thomas Betterton.* London, 1710.

Gill, James E. "Beast Over Man: Theriophilic Paradox in Gulliver's 'Voyage to the Country of the Houyhnhnms'." *Studies in Philology,* 67 (1970), 532–549.

Golden, Morris. *The Self Observed.* Baltimore: John Hopkins University Press, 1972.

Golder, Harold. "Bunyan's Giant Despaire." *Journal of English and Germanic Philology,* 30 (1931), 361–378.

———. "Bunyan's Valley of the Shadow." *Modern Philology,* 27 (1929), 55–72.

Green, Herbert E. "The Allegory as employed by Spenser, Bunyan, and Swift." *PMLA,* 4 (1888–1889), 145–193.

Greif, Martin J. "The Conversion of Robinson Crusoe." *Studies in English Literature, 1500–1900,* 6 (1966), 551–574.

Hardin, Richard F. "Bunyan, Mr. Ignorance, and the Quakers." *Studies in Philology*, 69 (1972), 496–508.

Hart, Jeffrey. "The Ideologue as Artist: Some Notes on *Gulliver's Travels*." *Criticism*, 2 (1960), 125–133.

Harth, Phillip, ed. *New Approaches to Eighteenth-Century Literature. Selected Papers from the English Institute.* New York: Columbia University Press, 1977.

———. "The Problem of Political Allegory in *Gulliver's Travels*." *Modern Philology*, 73 (1976 supplement), 544–547.

———. *Swift and Anglican Rationalism.* Chicago: University of Chicago Press, 1961.

Hausermann, Hans W. "Aspects of Life and Thought in *Robinson Crusoe*." *Review of English Studies*, 2 (1935), 447–450.

Hay, Douglas. *Albion's Fatal Tree: Crime and Society in Eighteenth-Century England.* New York: Pantheon, 1975.

Henry, Matthew. *An Exposition of the Historical Books of the Old Testament.* London, 1712.

Higdon, David L. "The Critical Fortunes and Misfortunes of Defoe's *Roxana*." *Bucknell Review*, 20 (1972), 67–82.

Holmes, Geoffrey, ed. *Britain after the Glorious Revolution.* New York: St. Martin's, 1969.

Hopkins, Robert H. "The Personation of Hobbism in Swift's *Tale of a Tub* and Mechanical Operation of the Spirit." *Philological Quarterly*, 45 (1966), 372–378.

Hunter, J. Paul. "The Loneliness of the Long-Distance Reader." *Genre*, 10 (1977), 455–484.

———. *The Reluctant Pilgrim.* Baltimore: Johns Hopkins University Press, 1966.

Hussey, Maurice. "Bunyan's 'Mr. Ignorance'." *Modern Language Review*, 44 (1949), 485–489.

Iser, Wolfgang. *The Implied Reader.* Baltimore: Johns Hopkins University Press, 1974.

Jackson, Thomas, ed. *The Lives of the Early Methodist Ministers.* Third Edition (with additional lives), 6 vols. London: Wesleyan Conference Office, 1865–66.

Jeffares, A. Norman, ed. *Swift: Modern Judgements.* New York: Macmillan, 1968.

Johnson, J. W. *The Formation of English Neo-Classical Thought.* Princeton: Princeton University Press, 1967.

———. "Swift's Historical Outlook." *Journal of British Studies*, 4 (1965), 52–77.

Kahler, Erich. *The Inward Turn of Narrative.* Trans. Richard and Clara Winston. Princeton: Princeton University Press, 1973.

Kallich, Martin. "Swift and the Archetypes of Hate: *A Tale of a Tub*," in *Studies in Eighteenth-Century Culture.* Ed. Harold E. Pagliaro IV. Madison: University of Wisconsin Press, 1975, pp. 47–52.

Karl, Frederick R. "Moll's Many-Colored Coat: Veil and Disguise in the Fiction of Defoe." *Studia Neophilologica*, 5 (1973), 86–97.

Kaufman, U. Milo. *The Pilgrim's Progress and Traditions in Puritan Meditation.* New Haven: Yale University Press, 1966.

Kelly, Anne Cline. "Swift's Explorations of Slavery in Houyhnhnmland and Ireland." *PMLA*, 91 (1976), 846–855.

Kelsey, Morton. *Dreams: The Dark Speech of the Spirit.* Garden City, N. Y.: Doubleday, 1968.

Kettle, Arnold. "In Defence of Moll Flanders," in *Of Books and Humankind*. Ed. John Butt. London: Routledge & Kegan Paul, 1964, pp. 55–67.

Kirk, Rudolf and C. F. Main, eds. *Essays in Literary History*. New Brunswick, N. J.: Rutgers University Press, 1960.

Kropf, C. R. "Theme and Structure in Defoe's *Roxana*." *Studies in English Literature, 1500–1900*, 12 (1972), 467–480.

Labaree, Leonard E. *Royal Government in America*. New Haven: Yale University Press, 1930.

La Barre, Weston. "The Dream, Charisma, and the Culture-Hero," in *The Dream and Human Societies*. Ed. G. E. Von Grunebaum and Roger Caillois. Berkeley: University of California Press, 1966, pp. 229–235.

Lawry, Jon S. "Dr. Lemuel Gulliver and 'The Thing Which Was Not.' " *Journal of English and Germanic Philology*, 67 (1968), 212–234.

Lein, Clayton. "Rhetoric and Allegory in Swift's *Examiner* 14." *Studies in English Literature, 1500–1900*, 17 (1977), 407–417.

Leith, John H., ed. *Creeds of the Churches*. Garden City, N. Y.: Doubleday, 1963.

Levine, Jay A. "The Design of *A Tale of a Tub* (With a Digression on a Mad Modern Critic)." *Journal of English History*, 33 (1966), 198–227.

Lovejoy, A. O. *The Great Chain of Being*. New York: Harper & Row, 1936; rpt. 1965.

Lowes, John L. *Essays in Appreciation*. Boston: Houghton Mifflin Co., 1936.

Lukács, Georg. *Soul and Form*. Trans. Anna Bostock. Cambridge, Mass.: M. I. T. Press, 1974.

———. *The Theory of the Novel*. Trans. Anna Bostock. Cambridge, Mass.: M. I. T. Press, 1971.

Lyles, Albert M. *Methodism Mocked*. London: Epworth, 1960.

McBurney, William H. "Colonel Jacque: Defoe's Definition of the Complete Gentleman." *Studies in English Literature, 1500–1900*, 2 (1962), 321–336.

McKillop, Alan D. *The Early Masters of English Fiction*. Lawrence: University of Kansas Press, 1956.

Manlove, C. N. "The Image of the Journey in *Pilgrim's Progress*: Narrative versus Allegory." *Journal of Narrative Technique*, 10 (1980), 16–38.

Martz, Louis. Introduction, *The Pilgrim's Progress*. New York: Holt, Rinehart & Winston, 1949.

Maxfield, Ezra K. "Daniel Defoe and the Quakers." *PMLA*, 47 (1932), 179–190.

Mendilow, A. *Time and Novel*. London: Nevill, 1952.

Miller, Perry, ed. *The American Puritans: Their Prose and Poetry*. Garden City, N. Y.: Doubleday, 1956.

Miner, Earl, ed. *Literary Uses of Typology*. Princeton: Princeton University Press, 1977.

Moore, John Robert. *A Checklist of the Writings of Daniel Defoe*. 2nd ed. Hamden, Conn.: Archon Books, 1971.

———. *Daniel Defoe: Citizen of the Modern World*. Chicago: University of Chicago Press, 1958.

———. "Swift as Historian." *Studies in Philology*, 49 (1952), 583–606.

Mylne, Vivienne. *The Eighteenth-Century French Novel*. New York: Barnes and Noble, 1965.

Nashe, Thomas. *Works*. 5 vols. Ed. Ronald B. McKerrow. Oxford: Blackwell, 1958.

Novak, Maximillian E. "Crime and Punishment in Defoe's *Roxana*." *Journal of English and Germanic Philology*, 55 (1966), 445–465.

———. *Defoe and the Nature of Man*. London: Oxford University Press, 1963.

———. *Economics and the Fiction of Daniel Defoe*. Berkeley: University of California Press, 1962.

———. "Robinson Crusoe's Fear and the Search for Natural Man." *Modern Philology*, 58 (1961), 238–245.

Nussbaum, Felicity. "Juvenal, Swift, and *The Folly of Love*." *Eighteenth-Century Studies*, 9 (1976), 540–552.

Paulson, Ronald. *The Fictions of Satire*. Baltimore: John Hopkins University Press, 1967.

———. ed. *Modern Essays in Criticism: Satire*. Englewood Cliffs, N.J.: Prentice-Hall, 1971.

———. *Satire and the Novel in Eighteenth-Century England*. New Haven: Yale University Press, 1967.

———. *Theme and Structure in Swift's Tale of a Tub*. New Haven: Yale University Press, 1960.

Peterson, Leland D. "Swift's *Project*: A Religious and Political Satire." *PMLA*, 82 (1967), 54–63.

Peterson, Spiro T. "The Matrimonial Theme of Defoe's *Roxana*." *PMLA*, 70 (1955), 166–191.

Pinkus, Philip. *Swift's Vision of Evil*. 2 vols. Victoria: *English Literary Studies*, University of Victoria, 1975.

Pocock, J. G. A. *The Machiavellian Moment*. Princeton: Princeton University Press, 1975.

Price, Martin. *Swift's Rhetorical Art: A Study in Structure and Meaning*. Hamden: Archon, 1963.

Quintana, Ricardo. *The Mind and Art of Jonathan Swift*. London: Methuen, 1936; rpt. 1953.

———. "Situational Satire: A Commentary on the Method of Swift." *University of Toronto Quarterly*, 17 (1947), 130–136.

Radner, John B. "The Struldbruggs, the Houyhnhnms, and the Good Life." *Studies in English Literature, 1500–1900*, 17 (1977), 419–433.

Rawson, C. J. *Gulliver and the Gentle Reader*. London: Routledge & Kegan Paul, 1973.

Redfield, Robert. *The Little Community. Viewpoints for the Study of the Human Whole*. Chicago: University of Chicago Press, 1955.

Reichard, Hugo. "Gulliver the Pretender." *Papers on English Language and Literature*, 1 (1965), 316–326.

Richetti, John J. *Defoe's Narratives: Situation and Structure*. Oxford: Clarendon Press, 1975.

Robins, H. F. "How Smart was Robinson Crusoe?" *PMLA*, 67 (1952), 782–789.

Rogers, Pat. "Gulliver and the Engineers." *Modern Language Review*, 70 (1975), 260–270.

———. "Swift and Bolingbroke on Faction." *Journal of British Studies*, 9 (1970), 71–101.

Ross, John F. *Swift and Defoe: A Study in Relationship*. Berkeley: University of California Press, 1941.

Sacks, Sheldon. *Fiction and the Shape of Belief*. Berkeley: University of California Press, 1964.

St. John, Henry, Viscount Bolingbroke. *Works*. 4 vols. Philadelphia: Carey and Hart, 1841.

Sams, Henry W. "Swift's Satire of the Second Person." *Journal of English Literary History*, 26 (1959), 36–44.

Secord, A. W. *Defoe's Review*. New York: Columbia University Press, 1938.

_____. *Studies in the Narrative Method of Defoe*. New York: Russell and Russell, 1963.

Sharrock, Roger. "Bunyan and the English Emblem Writers." *Review of English Studies*, 21 (1945), 105–116.

_____. *Bunyan: The Pilgrim's Progress*. London: Arnold, 1966.

_____. *John Bunyan*. London: Macmillan, 1968.

_____. "Personal Vision and Puritan Tradition in Bunyan." *The Hibbert Journal*, 56 (1957), 47–60.

_____. "Spiritual Autobiography in *The Pilgrim's Progress*." *Review of English Studies*, 24 (1948), 102–120.

Shenk, Robert. "John Bunyan: Puritan or Pilgrim?" *Cithara*, 14 (1974), 77–93.

Shinagel, Michael. *Daniel Defoe and Middle-Class Gentility*. Cambridge, Mass.: Harvard University Press, 1967.

Shorer, Mark. "Technique as Discovery." *Hudson Review*, I (1948), 67–87.

Smith, Shelton H., R. T. Handy, and L. A. Loetscher. *American Christianity*. New York: Scribner's, 1960.

Sorel, Charles. *The anti-romance or, The History of the Shepherd Lysis in XIV Books*. Trans. J. Davies. London, 1660.

_____. *The Extravagant Shepherd*. Trans. J. Davies. London: Thomas Heath, 1653.

Spacks, Patricia Meyer. *Imagining a Self*. Cambridge, Mass.: Harvard University Press, 1976.

Spilka, Mark, ed. "Character as a Lost Cause." *Novel*, 11 (1978), 197–217.

Starkman, Miriam K. *Swift's Satire on Learning in A Tale of a Tub*. Princeton: Princeton University Press, 1950.

Starr, G. A. *Defoe and Casuistry*. Princeton: Princeton University Press, 1971.

_____. *Defoe and Spiritual Autobiography*. Princeton: Princeton University Press, 1965.

_____. "Defoe's Prose Style: 1. The Language of Interpretation." *Modern Philology*, 71 (1974), 277–294.

Sutherland, James. *Defoe*. London: Longmans, Green & Co., 1954.

_____. *English Satire*. Cambridge, Cambridge University Press, 1958.

Swift, Jonathan. *The Correspondence of Jonathan Swift*. Ed. Harold Williams. Oxford: Clarendon Press, 1963.

_____. *The Poems of Jonathan Swift*. 3 vols. Ed. Harold Williams. 2nd ed. Oxford: Clarendon Press, 1958.

_____. *The Prose Works of Jonathan Swift*. 12 vols. Ed. Herbert Davis. Oxford: Blackwell, 1948.

Talon, Henri. "Space and the Hero in the *Pilgrim's Progress*: A Study of the Meaning of the Allegorical Universe." *Études Anglais*, 14 (1961), 124–130.

Tillyard, E. M. W. *The Epic Strain in the English Novel*. London: Chatto and Windus, 1954.

Tindall, William York. *John Bunyan: Mechanick Preacher*. New York: Columbia University Press, 1934.

Torchiana, Donald T. "Jonathan Swift, the Irish and the Yahoos: The Case Reconsidered." *Philological Quarterly*, 54 (1975), 195–212.

212 A Being More Intense

Traldi, Ila D. "Gulliver the 'Educated Fool': Unity in the Voyage to Laputa." *Papers in Language and Literature,* 4 (1968), 34–45.

Trevelyan, George M. *England Under Queen Anne: The Peace and the Protestant Succession.* London: Longsmans, Green, 1934.

Du Vair, Guillaume. *The Morall Philosophy of the Stoicks.* Trans. Charles Cotton. London, 1664.

Vickers, Brian, ed. *The World of Swift.* Cambridge, Mass.: Harvard University Press, 1968.

Wasioleck, Edward. "Relativity in *Gulliver's Travels.*" *Philological Quarterly,* 37 (1958), 111–115.

Watt, Ian. *The Rise of the Novel.* London: Chatto and Windus, 1957.

Weber, Max. *The Protestant Ethic and the Spirit of Capitalism.* Trans. Talcott Parsons. New York: Scribner's, 1958.

Webster, C. M. "The Satiric Background on the Attack on the Puritans in Swift's *A Tale of a Tub.*" *PMLA,* 50 (1935), 210–223.

―――. "Swift's *Tale of a Tub* Compared with Earlier Satires of the Puritans." *PMLA,* 47 (1932), 171–178.

Wedel, T. O. "On the Philosophical Background of *Gulliver's Travels.*" *Studies in Philology,* 23 (1926), 434–450.

Weidhorn, Manfred. *Dreams in Seventeenth-Century English Literature.* The Hague: Mouton, 1970.

Wharey, J. *The Sources of Bunyan's Allegories.* Baltimore: John Hopkins University Press, 1904.

Williams, Kathleen. *Jonathan Swift and the Age of Compromise.* Lawrence: University of Kansas Press, 1958.

Winton, Calhoun. "Conversion on the Road to Houyhnhnmland." *Sewanee Review,* 68 (1960), 20–30.

Wolff, Cynthia Griffin. "Literary Reflections Of the Puritan Characters." *Journal of the History of Ideas,* 29 (1968), 13–32.

Woods, Ralph. *The World of Dreams.* New York: Random House, 1947.

Zimmerman, Everett. "Defoe and Crusoe." *Journal of English Literary History,* 38 (1971), 377–396.

―――. *Defoe and the Novel.* Berkeley: University of California Press, 1975.

INDEX